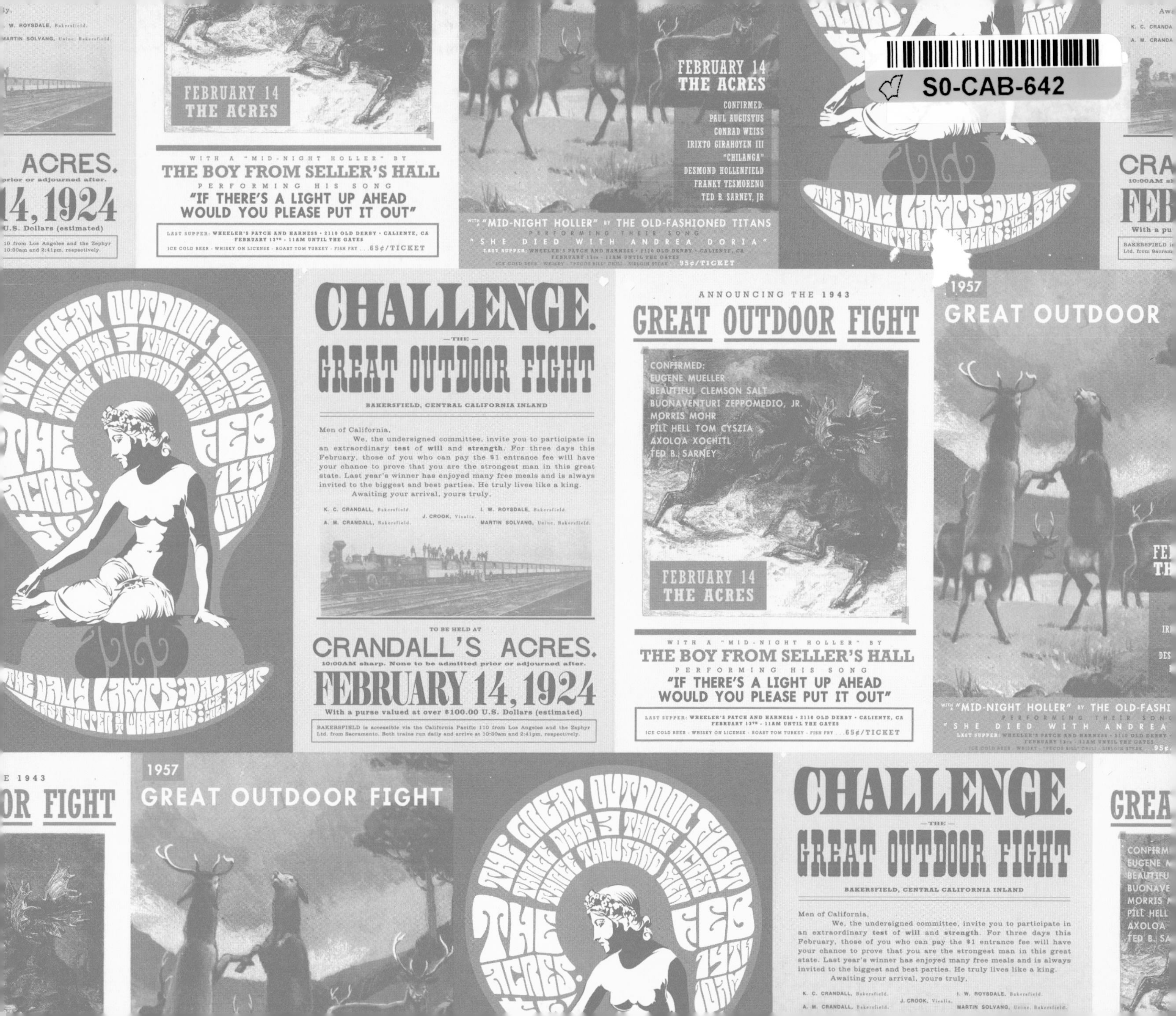

CHALLENGE.
THE
GREAT OUTDOOR FIGHT
BAKERSFIELD, CENTRAL CALIFORNIA INLAND
Men of California,
We, the undersigned committee, invite you to participate in an extraordinary test of will and strength. For three days this February, those of you who can pay the $1 entrance fee will have your chance to prove that you are the strongest man in this great state. Last year's winner has enjoyed many free meals and is always invited to the biggest and best parties. He truly lives like a king.
Awaiting your arrival, yours truly,
K. C. CRANDALL, Bakersfield.
I. W. ROYSDALE, Bakersfield.
J. CROOK, Visalia.
A. M. CRANDALL, Bakersfield.
MARTIN SOLVANG, Union, Bakersfield.
TO BE HELD AT
CRANDALL'S ACRES.
10:00AM sharp. None to be admitted prior or adjourned after.
FEBRUARY 14, 1924
With a purse valued at over $100.00 U.S. Dollars (estimated)
BAKERSFIELD is accessible via the California Pacific 110 from Los Angeles and the Zephyr Ltd. from Sacramento. Both trains run daily and arrive at 10:30am and 2:41pm, respectively.
ANNOUNCING THE 1943
GREAT OUTDOOR FIGHT
CONFIRMED:
EUGENE MUELLER
BEAUTIFUL CLEMSON SALT
BUONAVENTURI ZEPPOMEDIO, JR.
MORRIS MOHR
PILL HELL TOM CYSZIA
AXOLOA XOCHITL
TED B. SARNEY
FEBRUARY 14
THE ACRES
WITH A "MID-NIGHT HOLLER" BY
THE BOY FROM SELLER'S HALL
PERFORMING HIS SONG
"IF THERE'S A LIGHT UP AHEAD
WOULD YOU PLEASE PUT IT OUT"
LAST SUPPER: WHEELER'S PATCH AND HARNESS • 2110 OLD DERBY • CALIENTE, CA
FEBRUARY 13TH • 11AM UNTIL THE GATES
ICE COLD BEER • WHISKY ON LICENSE • ROAST TOM TURKEY • FISH FRY . . . 65¢/TICKET
1957
GREAT OUTDOOR FIGHT
FEBRUARY 14
THE ACRES
CONFIRMED:
PAUL AUGUSTUS
CONRAD WEISS
IRIXTO GIRAHOYEN III
"CHILANGA"
DESMOND HOLLENFIELD
FRANKY TESMORENO
TED B. SARNEY, JR
WITH A "MID-NIGHT HOLLER" BY THE OLD-FASHIONED TITANS
PERFORMING THEIR SONG
"SHE DIED WITH ANDREA DORIA"
LAST SUPPER: WHEELER'S PATCH AND HARNESS • 2110 OLD DERBY • CALIENTE, CA
FEBRUARY 13TH • 11AM UNTIL THE GATES
95¢/TICKET
S0-CAB-642

THE GREAT OUTDOOR FIGHT

—

by

CHRIS ONSTAD

—

DARK HORSE BOOKS®
PUBLISHERS

MILWAUKIE

Publisher - Mike Richardson

Art Director - Lia Ribacchi

Designers - Amy Arendts and Chris Onstad

Associate Editor - Katie Moody

Editorial Assistant - Patrick Thorpe

G.O.F. Historian - Joel Steinmetz

Editor - Dave Land

Published by
Dark Horse Books
A division of Dark Horse Comics, Inc.
10956 SE Main Street
Milwaukie, OR 97222

———

darkhorse.com

achewood.com

———

First edition: September 2008
ISBN 978-1-59307-997-0

1 3 5 7 9 10 8 6 4 2

Printed in China

ACHEWOOD: THE GREAT OUTDOOR FIGHT™

Contents

Introduction

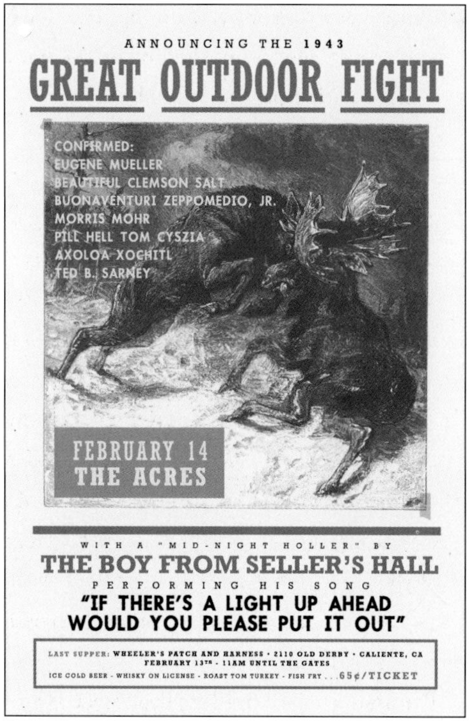
ANNOUNCING THE 1943
GREAT OUTDOOR FIGHT
CONFIRMED:
EUGENE MUELLER
BEAUTIFUL CLEMSON SALT
BUONAVENTURI ZEPPOMEDIO, JR.
MORRIS MOHR
PILL HELL TOM CYSZIA
AXOLOA XOCHITL
TED B. SARNEY
FEBRUARY 14
THE ACRES
WITH A "MID-NIGHT HOLLER" BY
THE BOY FROM SELLER'S HALL
PERFORMING HIS SONG
"IF THERE'S A LIGHT UP AHEAD
WOULD YOU PLEASE PUT IT OUT"
LAST SUPPER: WHEELER'S PATCH AND HARNESS · 2110 OLD DERBY · CALIENTE, CA
FEBRUARY 13TH · 11AM UNTIL THE GATES
ICE COLD BEER - WHISKY ON LICENSE - ROAST TOM TURKEY - FISH FRY . . . 65¢/TICKET

In the history of the modern world, there has scarcely been a contest as celebrated—and as uncompromised—as California's Great Outdoor Fight. Drawing entrants from around the globe, the G.O.F. has been the international proving ground for masculine strength and resilience for eighty-five years. To compare the rigorously structured, highly commercialized Olympics, or televised "Ultimate Fighting" championships, to the G.O.F. is to miss the philosophy of the event entirely: the Fight has no trainers, no commercial sponsors, no official endorsements. There is no sure way to know how to win. It is a highly private and unregulated body whose rules are largely understood and unspoken, and whose goal is singular—to open up a spot on the earth each year where men go to pit fist against fist until they can do so no longer. It is ultimately democratic, in that a man with nothing can rise from his bedroll and, with only his god-given qualities, work his way to day three without so much as a shave or a five-dollar bill.

There is no awards ceremony, there is no supermarket magazine coverage. Winners of the G.O.F. do not go on to date Hollywood starlets. They return to obscurity, to their toil. To be sure, they enjoy the benefits of notoriety in the low orbits they inhabit, and can relate rough stories over comped roadhouse meals as often as the desire to hold court takes them, but they are not "real" celebrities. Or are they? Do the fawn-and-forget fans of A-list Hollywooders hold loyal the way that followers of the G.O.F. do? Decidedly not. An actor has proven nothing more than the ability to perform a certain specialized task. A champion of the Great Outdoor Fight has proven that he can perform a far more difficult task—survival against the world's worst odds. It is not reality television. It is reality.

The Great Outdoor Fight is a lifestyle to its legions, the highest stratum to which they might ever aspire, a stratum which they typically lack the education, economic gravity, or social ability to supersede. It is the arena in which those who have nothing compete. Its appeal is of the highest importance and lowest common denominator. It is the Great Outdoor Fight, and those who follow it need no other worldly benchmark.

Joel Steinmetz
Boston, MA
2006

The Beginning 1923, KEN CRANDALL'S FARM (THE "FIRST FEW YEARS")

Early lore of the Fight is largely oral tradition, with but a few surviving photographs of the period 1923-1928. According to legend, in January of '23, Bakersfield-area artichoke farmer Kenneth C. Crandall, during a long gentlemen's evening with his fellow land owners, proposed a "fool-proof contest" to determine the strongest among them. He collected a dollar from every soul interested, promising the whole sum would go to the winner (those without a dollar to wager were made to promise a day's work on Crandall's farm, or were staked by local gamblers). The next morning, he cleared his barn of livestock, chained shut all but one entrance, and placed gallon buckets of water at each of the four interior corners, accompanied by a few dozen rags. By noon, the competitors, drawn by the thirty-three-dollar purse that had been collected, began to arrive. Crandall sagely asked his wife to begin baking turkeys, and also to procure several bottles of the "cheapest, meanest" purple wine from their stores.

Not having thought much beyond the basic premise of the contest, Crandall set fairly few rules forth for the competitors. His gifted first son, Ashley Margaret, suggested that no outside weapons be allowed, and also laid the groundwork for disqualification rules in stating that any man so beaten that he could not "walk, or speak English, or name the Lord by any deed, for the period of ten minutes," was declared out (Ashley later attended Columbia University and began a

---

Crandall noted with pleasure that the water buckets and rags were properly used to sop at eyes that had become saturated with blood.

---

small seafood brokerage in Baltimore). His father saw the basic logic in this and, standing on a crate, made these official proclamations. He then announced that he was going into his house to fetch his shotgun, and that when the first barrel fired, the fight was understood to be on, and that any man attempting to escape the brawl under his own power would be treated to the contents of the second barrel. This whipped the men into a demonstrative frenzy, and by the time Crandall returned from the house, the barn was filled with whoops and hollers.

Crandall, quickly adapting to the role of showman and ringleader, extemporaneously shouldered his Winchester and shot the chain that suspended the barn's 12-lamp oil chandelier from the center joists. It burst into flames as it hit the ground, and the men went into a melee around the resulting pyre. The weakest were quickly dispatched by the brawniest, and the strongest inculcated a smart system of regular periods of inactivity and regrouping. Crandall noted with pleasure that the water buckets and rags were properly used to sop at eyes that had become saturated with blood.

The shotgun had fired its first blast at two in the afternoon, and Crandall considered it only polite to give the men a break for supper. He fired again at eight and, having gathered their attention, called a halt to the proceedings. Owing to a curious social dynamic, the remaining fifteen fighters* fell

* His estimate, based on later remarks about the amount of turkey consumed.

in with one another like brothers, at the handsomely outfitted victuals table that sat just outside the barn, under a pair of quickly hung charity lights. Mrs. Crandall, that night, set forth a feast of roast Tom Turkey, chickpea salad with onion, trout, split spuds, ammonia bread, stewed driver's lash (a local savory nettle), and the aforementioned raw purple wine. The men, roughed up as they were, sated themselves on the feast so heartily that Crandall was moved to break out his personal bottle of Los Angeles–made brandy, from which he gave each man one measured jigger.

Another round from the Winchester got them going again around eleven in the evening, and the fighting, by all accounts, was as good and steady as the meal. Fist met face with a pleasing, meaty soundness. A boot upside the head left an adversary sprawled in the sweat- and blood-soaked dust. The new elbow-on-kidney jut that the men had recently seen in the moving picture *Palermo by Day* was tried with varying degrees of success. It looked like the fighting would be over by morning.

As the number of fighters grew smaller, however, things became increasingly complicated. A team of two men conspired to work together, claim a split victory, and share the purse. This didn't sit well with Crandall, who saw it as a mockery of his contest and an act of cowardice. Thinking quickly, he roused Ashley from his slumber and laid the circumstances out before him. Ashley's sleepy proclamation—one that has stood through the present day—was that if two men remained, they had one hour before

---

. . . if two men remained, they had one hour before Crandall would drive his car into the barn and run over them.

Crandall would drive his car into the barn and run over them. Minutes later, Crandall fired his gun and made this addendum to the rules. To punctuate his statement, he allegedly pulled out his pocket watch and yelled to his wife, "Honey, go start the car!"

The added dimension of a suddenly cruel, armed captor gave the fight the sense of fear and unpredictability it may have been lacking. The half-dozen remaining competitors apparently forgot that the two-man rule had not yet been broken, and the fight ended within the hour, with hardware-store owner Szudor Pwalycsza defeating Ezekiel Samuels, a local mechanic. Crandall fired off another round to signal the end of the fight, and those who had recovered sufficiently from their wounds chaired Pwalycsza around the barn.

As word of the event trickled throughout the county, then the state, and then the nation, a few key details were, of course, amplified, omitted, or added. Some had Crandall shooting the victor dead and burning down the barn with all the bodies in it before killing himself; some merely substituted flank steak for the turkey. The power of the basic premise, though—of determining one man's superiority over all other men—was the juggernaut mill at the center of the rumor machine.

By the time the gossip got back to Crandall in the coming months, the public had even given the event a name: The Great Outdoor Fight (a rumor originating in the Northeast had the fight occuring in a snow-blanketed corral). Penny paperbacks, utter pulp fan-fiction accounts of the event, were widely circulated. There was an illustrated Great

Outdoor Fight training manual for children, a weekly radio program recapping the latest rumors, and even a book of Great Outdoor Fight recipes targeted at women (*Recipes of the Great Outdoor Fight: Hearty Food for Your Strong-Hearted Man*). The Catholic Church decried the event, using it to outline how the country had sunk even lower into a moral depravity that only their ways could cure.

Figuring that where there was noise, there must surely be money, Crandall decided to make the G.O.F. an annual event and become wealthy by selling sandwiches to the crowds who came to compete. He cleared an acre of his land, put up a high chainlink fence around it, and distributed hastily printed fliers throughout central California. An excited public quickly phoned, mailed, or telegrammed the information not only throughout the nation, but throughout the world. Newspapers in Italy ran sensational articles about the "Festival of Beasts," while papers in China advertised trips to California so that one might "Defeat Over Long-Time Dudes."

Crandall's remarkable inability to gauge the public interest in his second contest led to severe logistical problems in the area. He had casually guessed that a field of "probably a hundred" men would come to fight. Ashley's extensive research and analysis showed that closer to two hundred thousand arrived by car, train, steamer, and even aeroplane. The Bakersfield area was quickly depleted of all food, drink, lodging, fuel, prostitutes, textiles, and musical entertainment. Scores of men, frustrated with the

---

The Catholic Church decried the event, using it to outline how the country had sunk even lower into a moral depravity that only their ways could cure.

---

unlivable conditions, departed for home. Some, more serious about their craft, held impromptu fights in gymnasiums or fields, around which small communities of bettors arose. But none had the cachet of the vaunted Crandall farm.

Thinking quickly, Ashley had the grounds expanded overnight and set up a series of qualifying rounds on "The Acres," which now numbered three (he had estimated that twenty were needed, but there was not enough chainlink to be had). Between his qualifying rounds and the sloughing off of less-serious competitors, the field was quickly reduced to a more manageable three thousand, and an official start date was announced. The three thousand confirmed men had two days to buck up and gather strength (which was hard to do, although food supplies had begun to trickle in from Los Angeles and San Francisco). They also had time to internalize Ashley's carefully revised sheet of rules, which was distributed throughout the area.

After Crandall's now-traditional opening salvo, the second Great Outdoor Fight was underway. Energy ran high for the first twenty-four hours, at which point he sensed that the men needed nourishment. Unfortunately, in the depleted landscape, he had been able to source only one turkey, so Ashley, who had been carefully monitoring the movements and ad-hoc alliances taking shape on the field, suggested that the men put two leaders forth for a summit. Remarkably, this was quickly accomplished, and on the afternoon of the second day Crandall's son supped on turkey and Jack

Dandy cake with Ed Grommell, Jr., of Orange County, and Maximilliano Tempestua, of Padua, Italy. He later recounted carefully probing for the psychological trends the leading men noticed among their fellow competitors, with the intent of designing an even better Great Outdoor Fight. As with the previous year, the elder Crandall dispensed a generous glass of his brandy to each of the men before escorting them back to the gates of The Acres.

The second Fight was eventually won by a turncoat member of Tempestua's army, "Red Rice" Laloux, of Louisiana. News of a victory, along with literally thousands of incorrect rumors, allegations, and unfounded drama, left the grounds within minutes, and soon the wires of the world were once again ablaze with the news of this infamous carnival of destruction. Laloux was treated to food and drink wherever he went, and signed lucrative endorsement deals. Among others, there were: Morton's Place (a gym for troubled boys), Levy's Fine Cake Soaps, Fleischer's Grain Cereal For Young Kings, and a chain of fried-fish restaurants named Ganty's.

Crandall's sandwich proceeds had been non-trivial, and with this endowment he made twelve-year-old Ashley the Fight's first employee, charging him with the planning of the third Fight and all that came with it, including far-flung regional qualifying matches (so that the local authorities wouldn't continue to breathe down his neck about the ruin to which his contest had subjected their city).

By the time Ashley headed off to Columbia five years later, he had become the architect

---

The second Fight was eventually won by a turncoat member of Tempestua's army, "Red Rice" Laloux, of Louisiana.

---

of a grand and relatively unbreakable contest. In his personal journals of the time, however, he revealed the truth of his sensitive nature:

I was glad to have the opportunity, but now I am glad to be rid of it. The constant violence, or the impending threat of it, and the toll of seeing so many casualties, over time, has enveloped me in an environment that weighs as heavily as a wool shroud even on pleasant days. To be the tiller at the wheel of man's hatred for man should be a tour of duty, not a career.

Ashley checked in on the Fight from time to time, presumably to observe the continuing validity of the framework he had put in place, but he rarely saw a whole Fight out, let alone allowed himself to become embroiled in the always-heated discussions taking place on the sidelines.

With that, the Fight was off and running for the next eighty years. It was eventually relocated to a nearby property owned by a shadowy shell corporation that could not be held responsible for the goings-on, and Crandall himself eventually retired from the sandwich concession, passing away in 1966. As of this printing, his son Ashley is in his late nineties, still very much alive and alert. He declined to comment for this project, citing an urgent need to ". . . visit a friend on down the way, seems I have fewer and fewer each day."

. . .

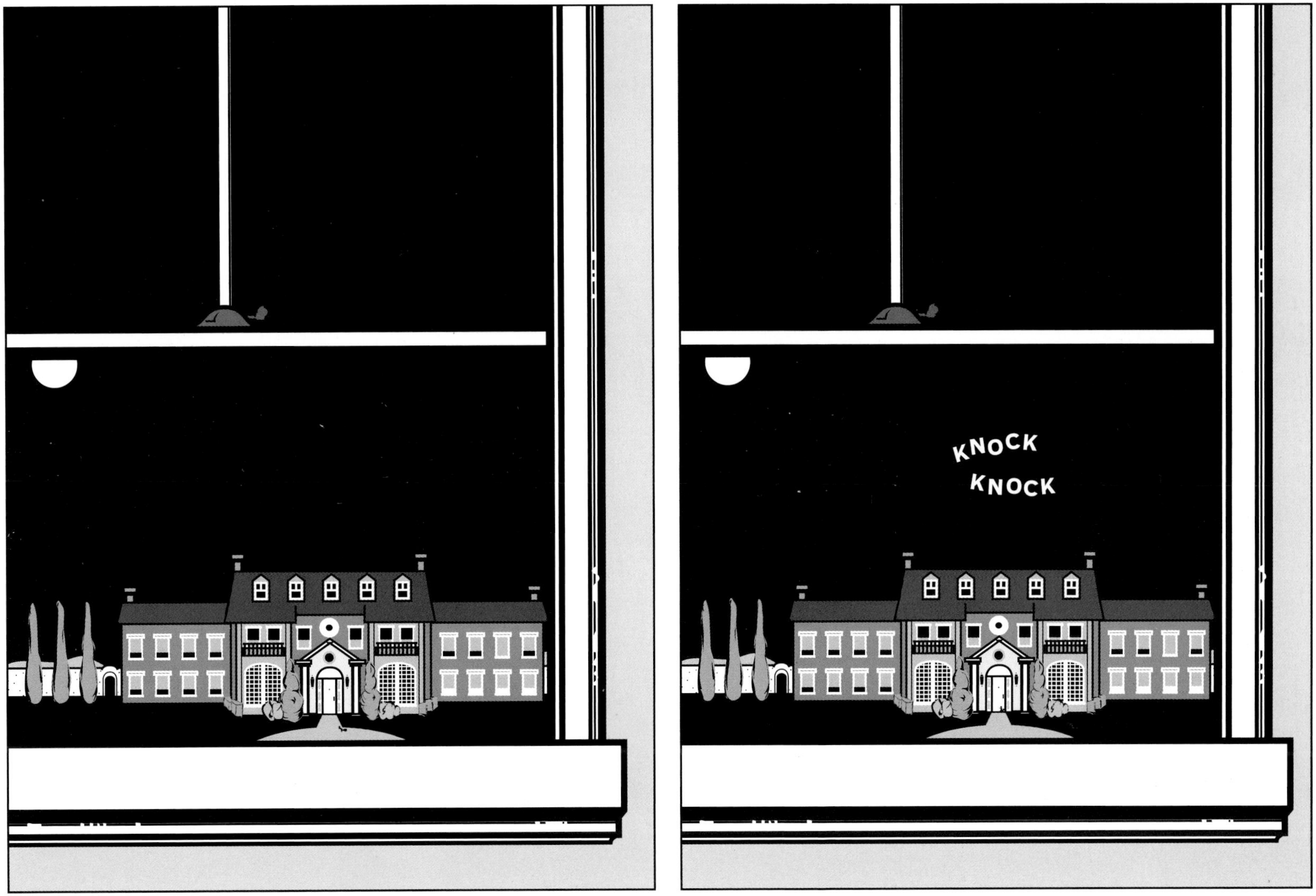
KNOCK
KNOCK

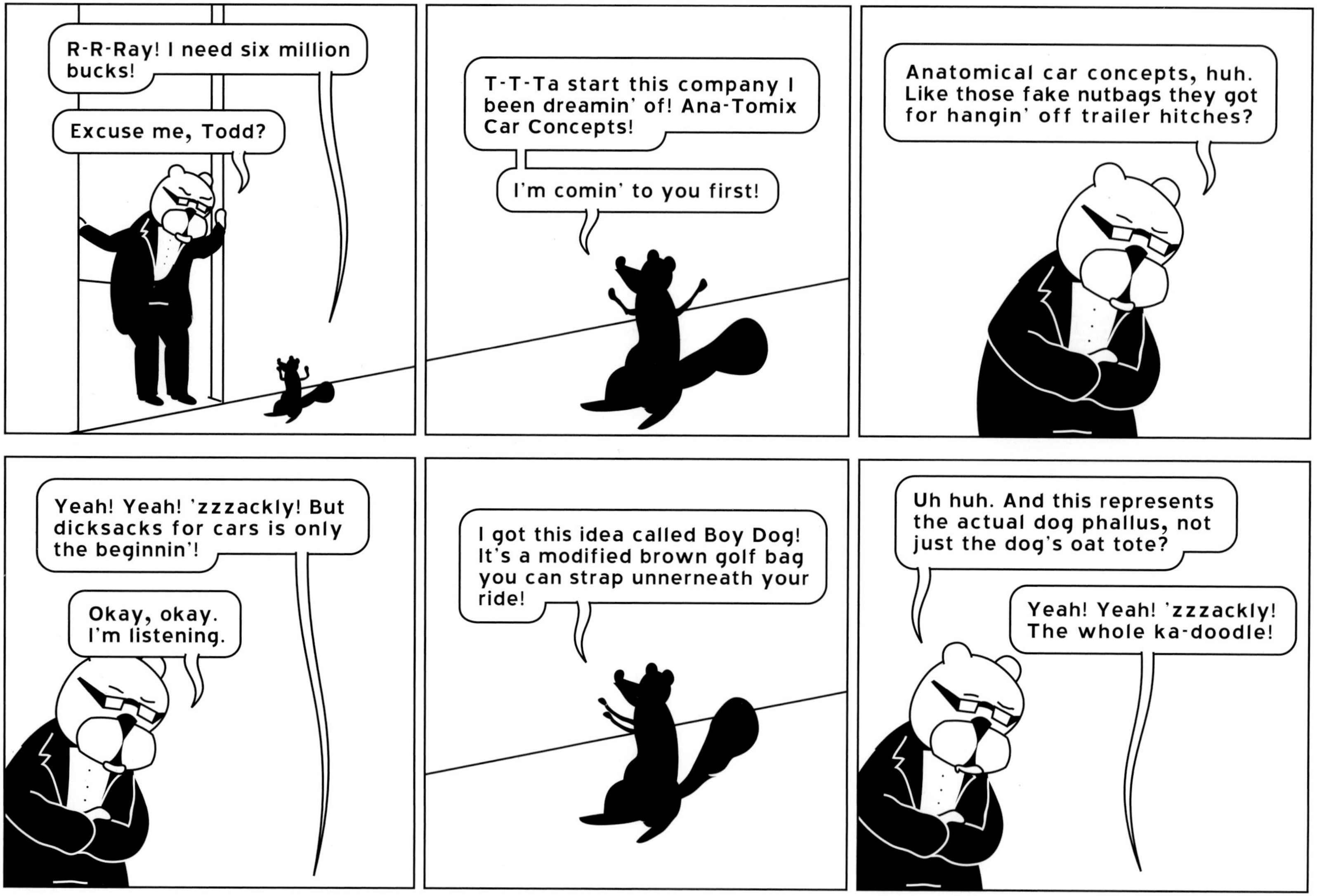
R-R-Ray! I need six million bucks!
Excuse me, Todd?
T-T-Ta start this company I been dreamin' of! Ana-Tomix Car Concepts!
I'm comin' to you first!
Anatomical car concepts, huh. Like those fake nutbags they got for hangin' off trailer hitches?
Yeah! Yeah! 'zzzackly! But dicksacks for cars is only the beginnin'!
Okay, okay. I'm listening.
I got this idea called Boy Dog! It's a modified brown golf bag you can strap unnerneath your ride!
Uh huh. And this represents the actual dog phallus, not just the dog's oat tote?
Yeah! Yeah! 'zzzackly! The whole ka-doodle!

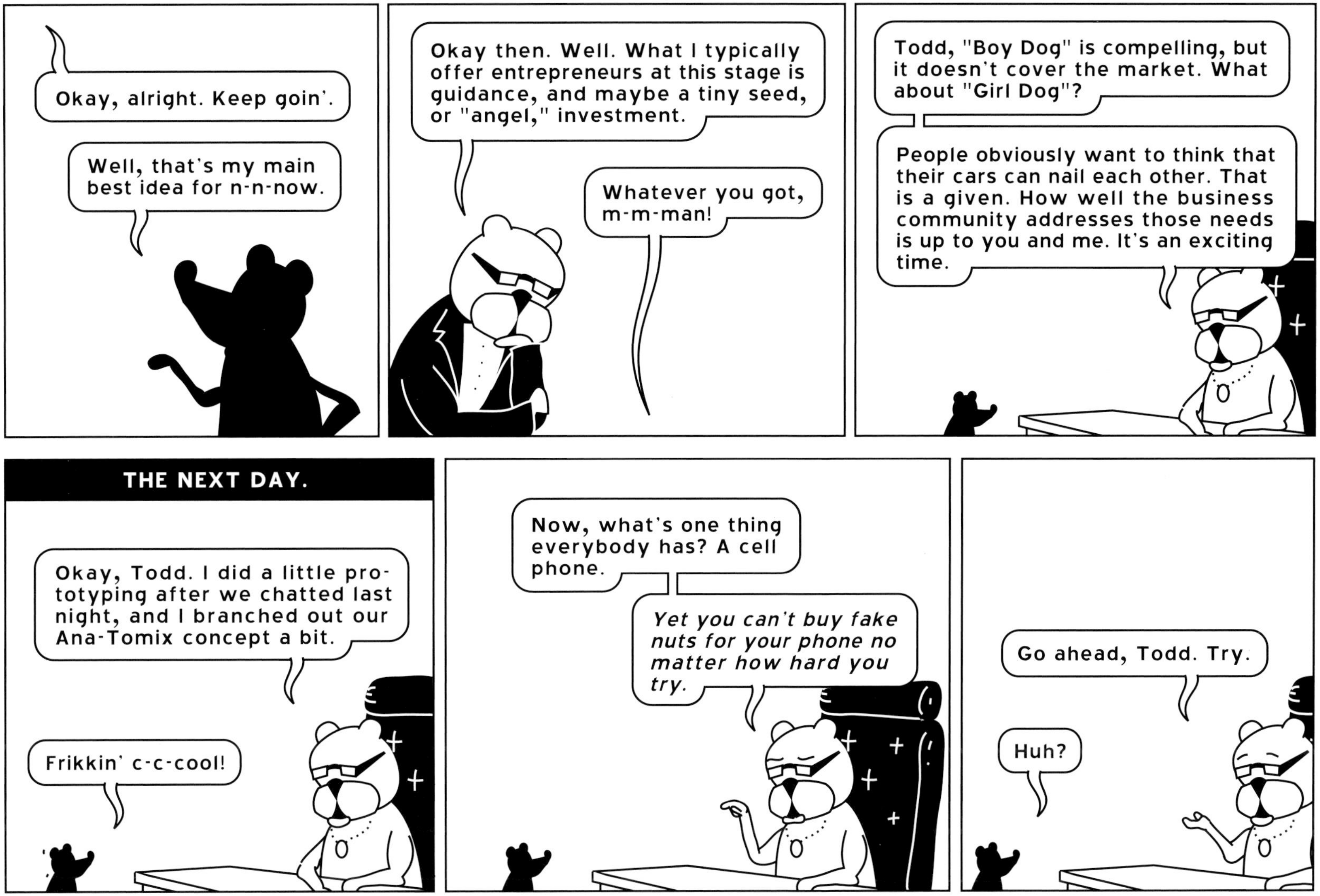
Okay, alright. Keep goin'.
Well, that's my main best idea for n-n-now.
Okay then. Well. What I typically offer entrepreneurs at this stage is guidance, and maybe a tiny seed, or "angel," investment.
Whatever you got, m-m-man!
Todd, "Boy Dog" is compelling, but it doesn't cover the market. What about "Girl Dog"?
People obviously want to think that their cars can nail each other. That is a given. How well the business community addresses those needs is up to you and me. It's an exciting time.
THE NEXT DAY.
Okay, Todd. I did a little prototyping after we chatted last night, and I branched out our Ana-Tomix concept a bit.
Frikkin' c-c-cool!
Now, what's one thing everybody has? A cell phone.
Yet you can't buy fake nuts for your phone no matter how hard you try.
Go ahead, Todd. Try.
Huh?

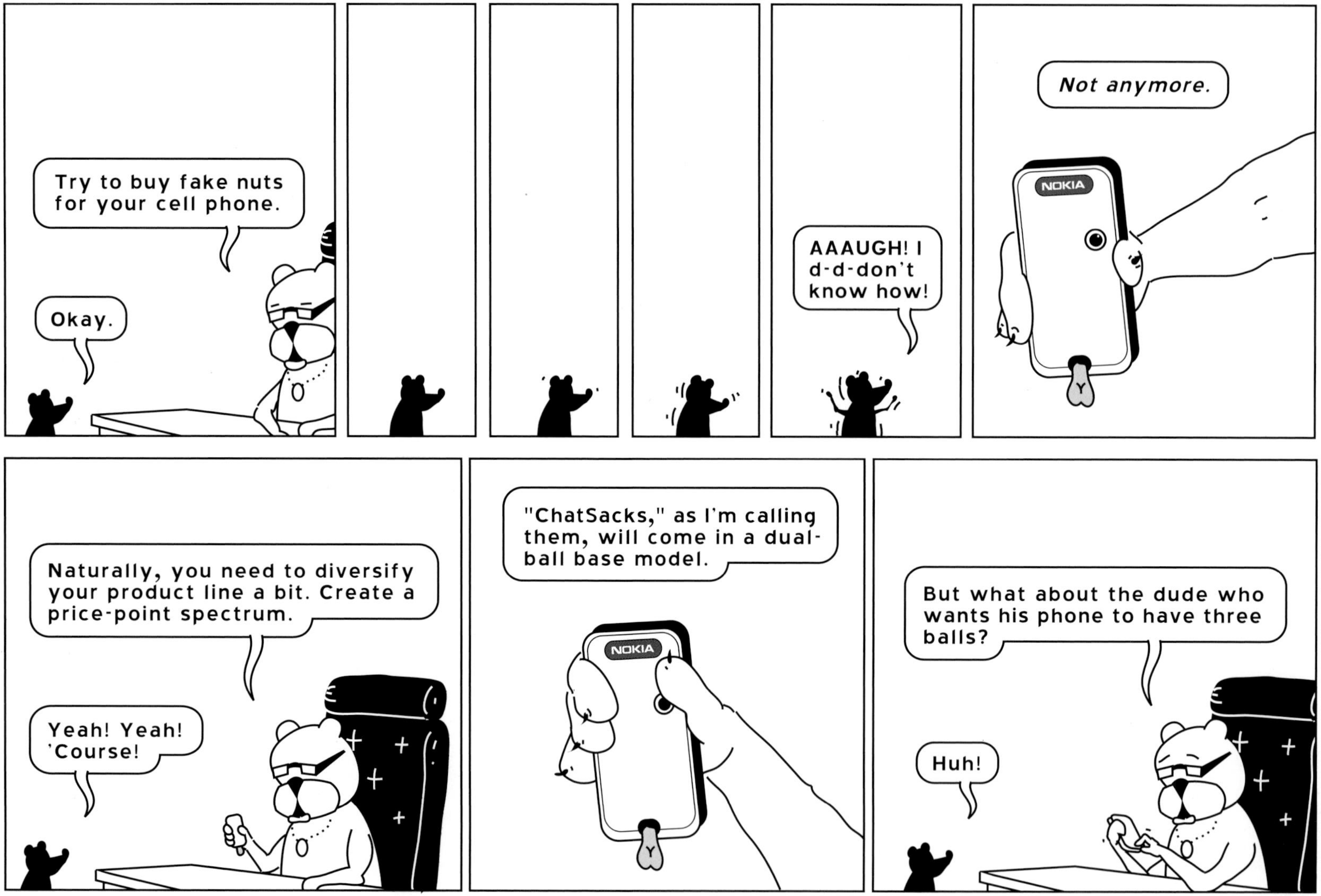
Try to buy fake nuts for your cell phone.
Okay.
AAAUGH! I d-d-don't know how!
Not anymore.
NOKIA
Naturally, you need to diversify your product line a bit. Create a price-point spectrum.
Yeah! Yeah! 'Course!
"ChatSacks," as I'm calling them, will come in a dual-ball base model.
NOKIA
But what about the dude who wants his phone to have three balls?
Huh!

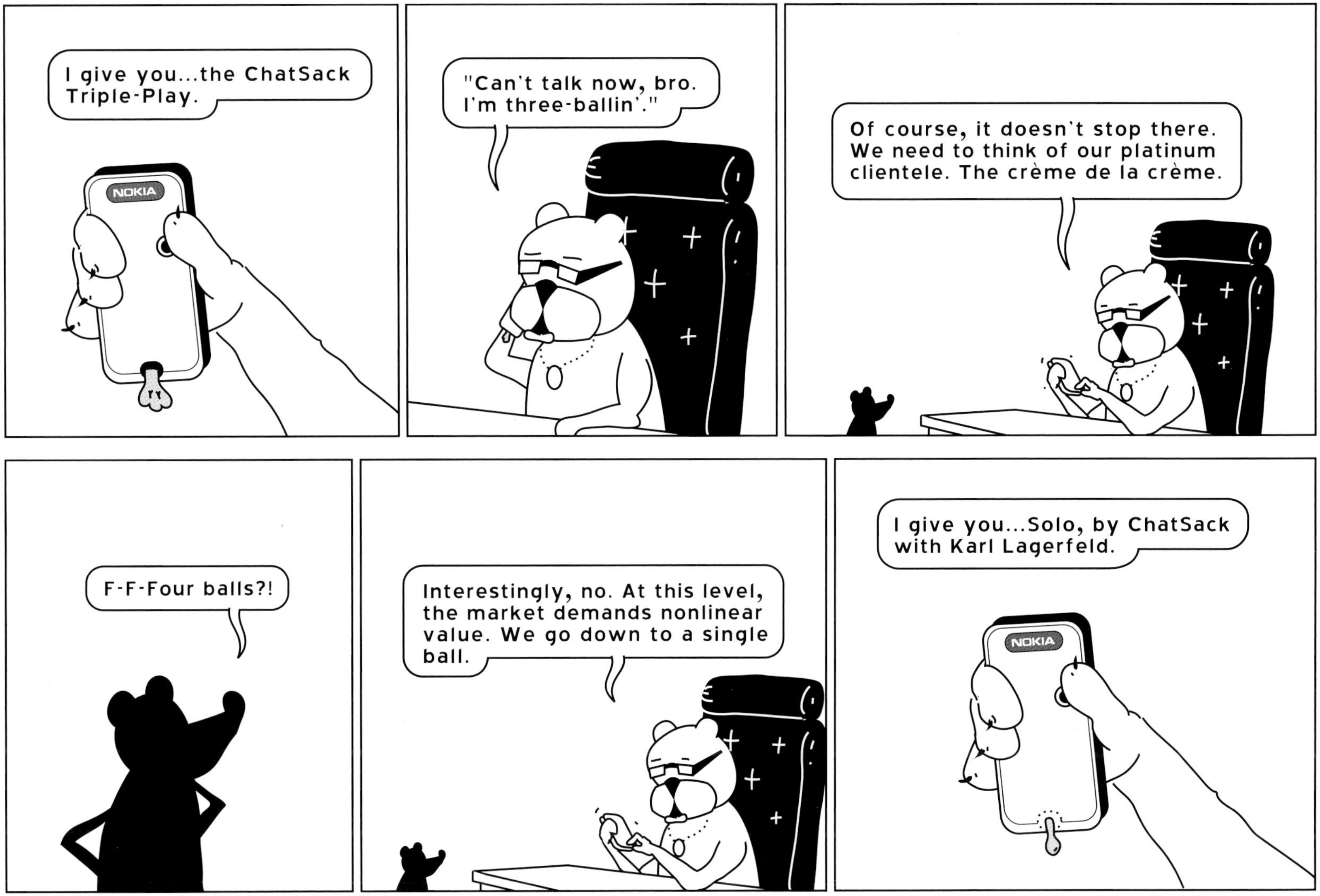
I give you...the ChatSack Triple-Play.
NOKIA
"Can't talk now, bro. I'm three-ballin'."
Of course, it doesn't stop there. We need to think of our platinum clientele. The crème de la crème.
F-F-Four balls?!
Interestingly, no. At this level, the market demands nonlinear value. We go down to a single ball.
I give you...Solo, by ChatSack with Karl Lagerfeld.
NOKIA

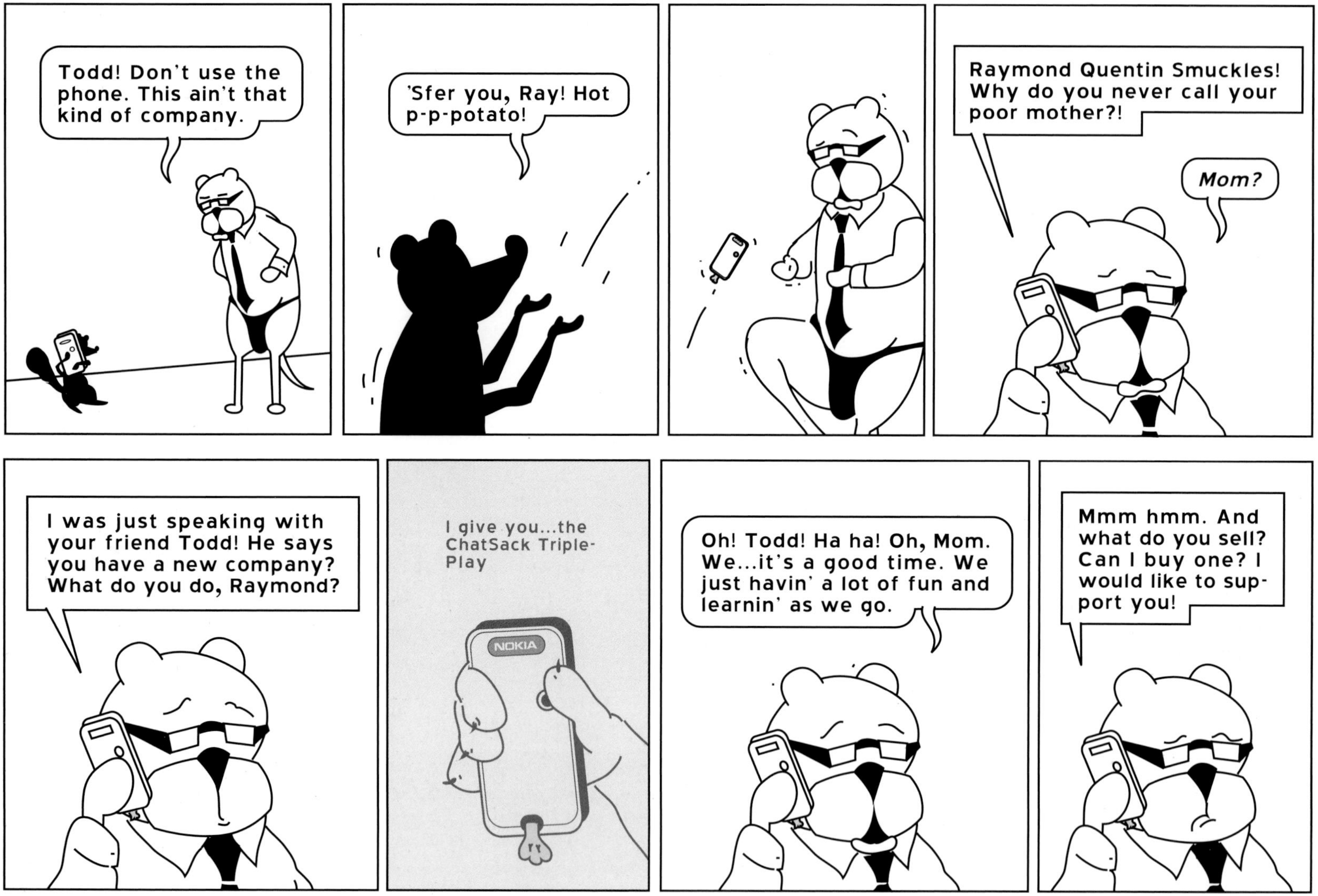
Todd! Don't use the phone. This ain't that kind of company.
'Sfer you, Ray! Hot p-p-potato!
Raymond Quentin Smuckles! Why do you never call your poor mother?!
Mom?
I was just speaking with your friend Todd! He says you have a new company? What do you do, Raymond?
I give you...the ChatSack Triple-Play
NOKIA
Oh! Todd! Ha ha! Oh, Mom. We...it's a good time. We just havin' a lot of fun and learnin' as we go.
Mmm hmm. And what do you sell? Can I buy one? I would like to support you!

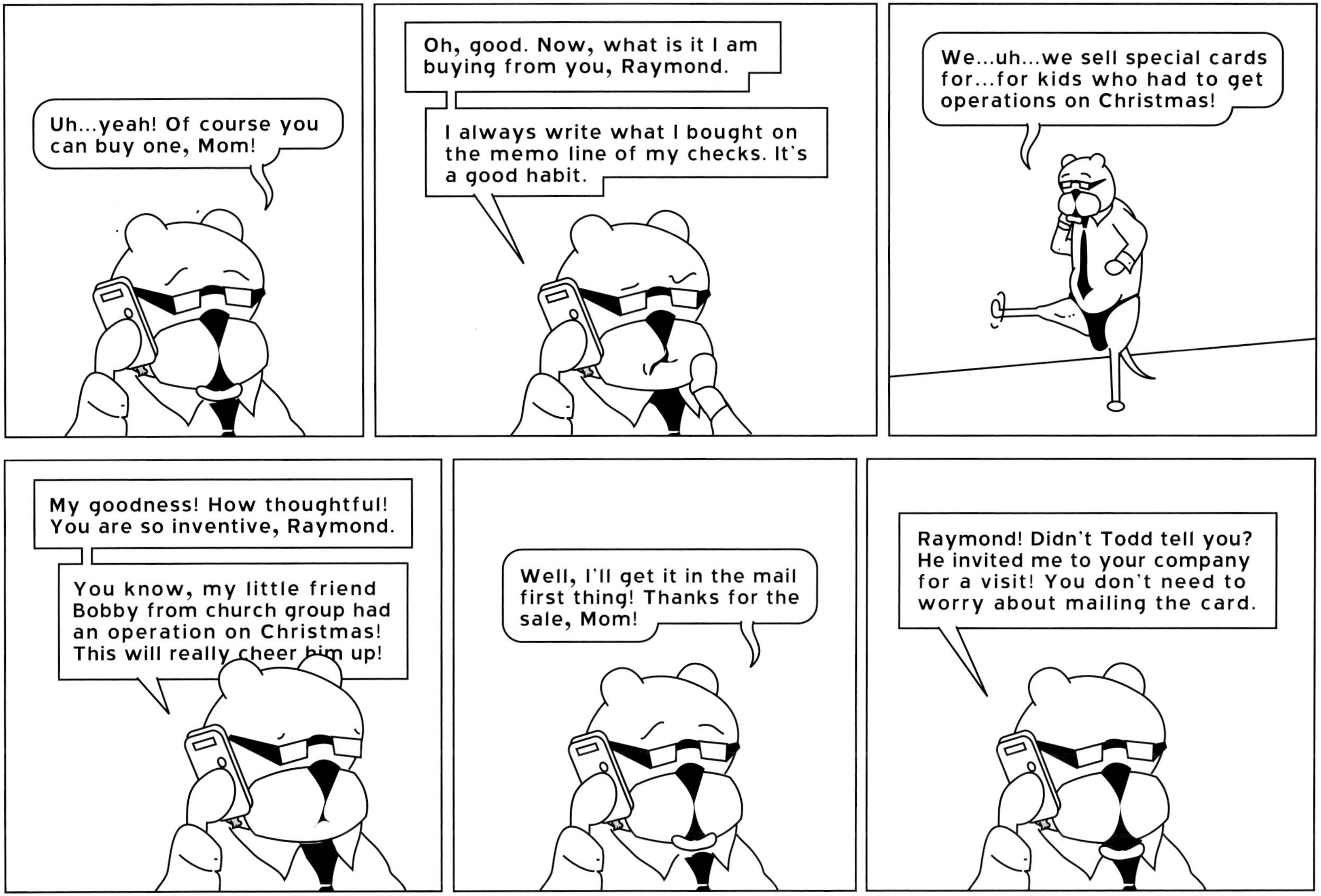
Uh...yeah! Of course you can buy one, Mom!
Oh, good. Now, what is it I am buying from you, Raymond.
I always write what I bought on the memo line of my checks. It's a good habit.
We...uh...we sell special cards for...for kids who had to get operations on Christmas!
My goodness! How thoughtful! You are so inventive, Raymond.
You know, my little friend Bobby from church group had an operation on Christmas! This will really cheer him up!
Well, I'll get it in the mail first thing! Thanks for the sale, Mom!
Raymond! Didn't Todd tell you? He invited me to your company for a visit! You don't need to worry about mailing the card.

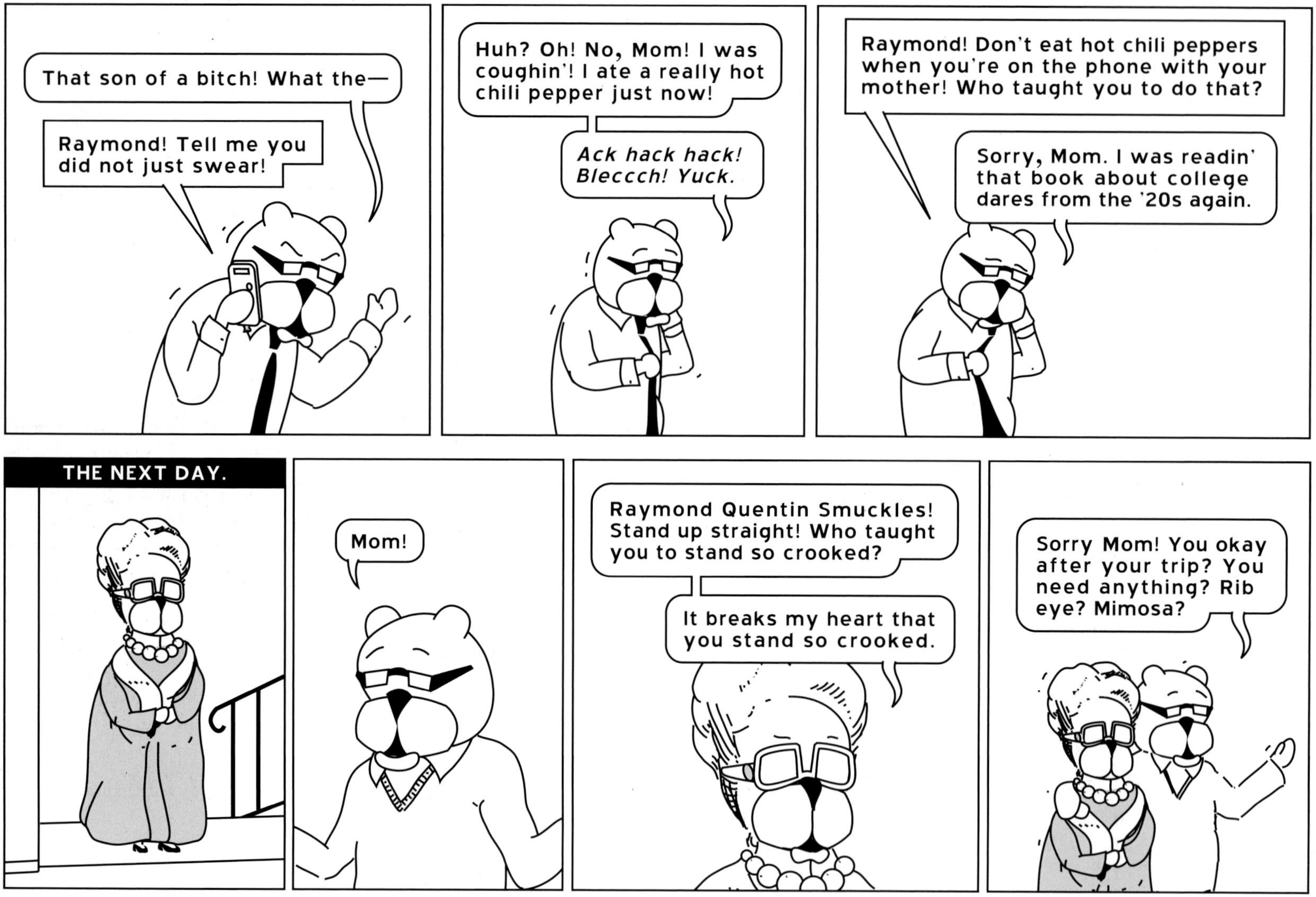
That son of a bitch! What the—
Raymond! Tell me you did not just swear!
Huh? Oh! No, Mom! I was coughin'! I ate a really hot chili pepper just now!
Ack hack hack! Bleccch! Yuck.
Raymond! Don't eat hot chili peppers when you're on the phone with your mother! Who taught you to do that?
Sorry, Mom. I was readin' that book about college dares from the '20s again.
THE NEXT DAY.
Mom!
Raymond Quentin Smuckles! Stand up straight! Who taught you to stand so crooked?
It breaks my heart that you stand so crooked.
Sorry Mom! You okay after your trip? You need anything? Rib eye? Mimosa?

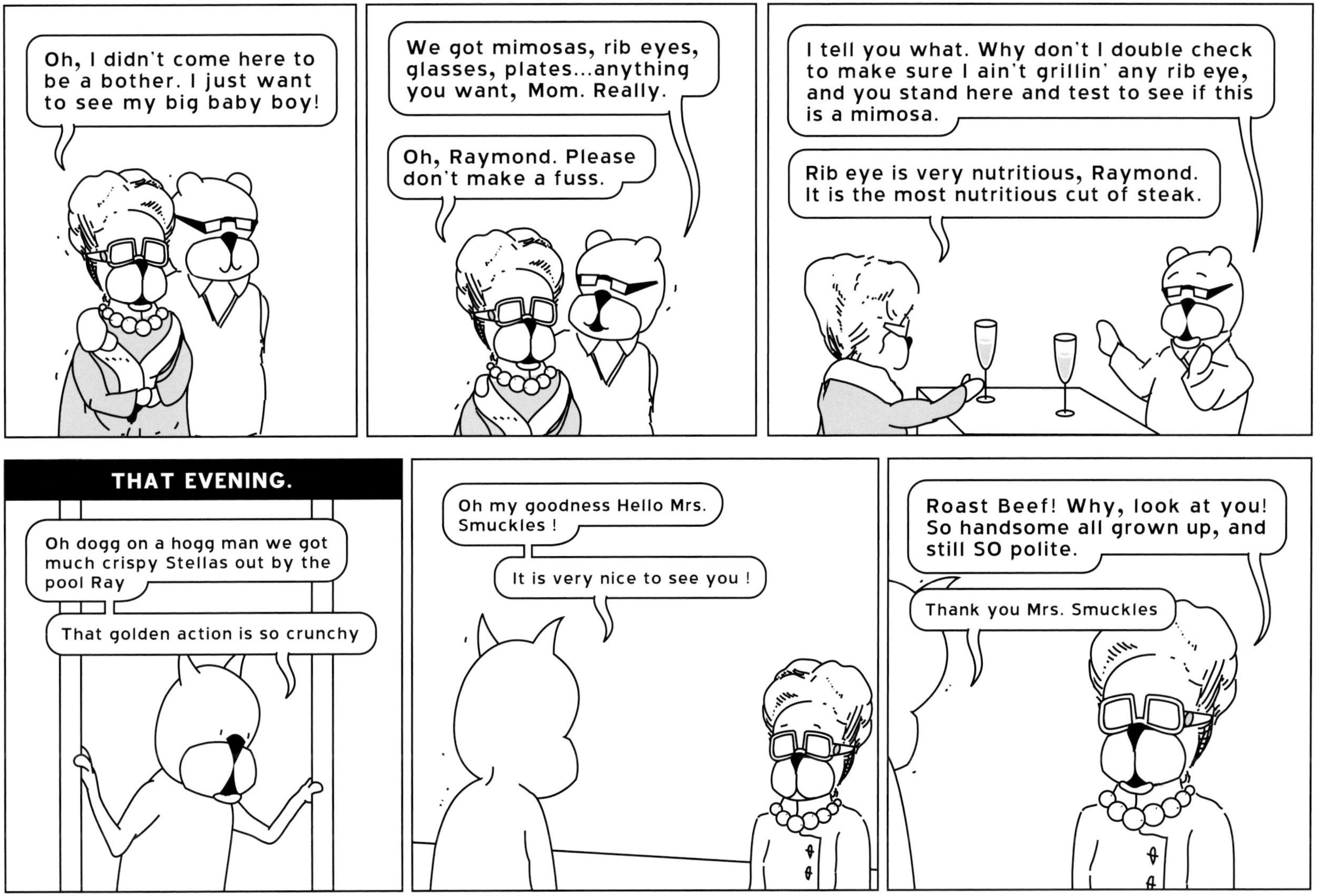
Oh, I didn't come here to be a bother. I just want to see my big baby boy!
We got mimosas, rib eyes, glasses, plates...anything you want, Mom. Really.
Oh, Raymond. Please don't make a fuss.
I tell you what. Why don't I double check to make sure I ain't grillin' any rib eye, and you stand here and test to see if this is a mimosa.
Rib eye is very nutritious, Raymond. It is the most nutritious cut of steak.
THAT EVENING.
Oh dogg on a hogg man we got much crispy Stellas out by the pool Ray
That golden action is so crunchy
Oh my goodness Hello Mrs. Smuckles !
It is very nice to see you !
Roast Beef! Why, look at you! So handsome all grown up, and still SO polite.
Thank you Mrs. Smuckles

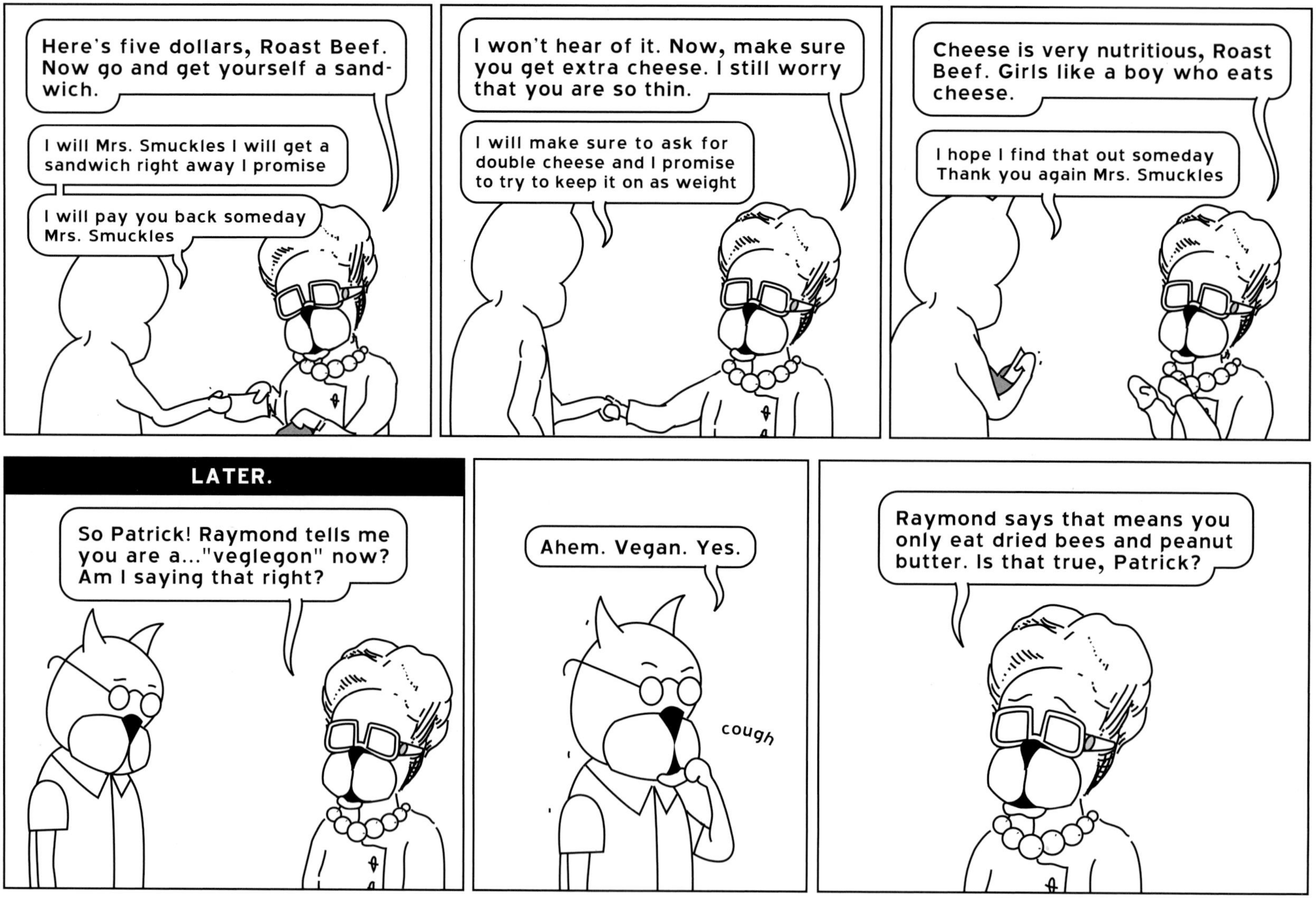
Here's five dollars, Roast Beef. Now go and get yourself a sandwich.
I will Mrs. Smuckles I will get a sandwich right away I promise
I will pay you back someday Mrs. Smuckles
I won't hear of it. Now, make sure you get extra cheese. I still worry that you are so thin.
I will make sure to ask for double cheese and I promise to try to keep it on as weight
Cheese is very nutritious, Roast Beef. Girls like a boy who eats cheese.
I hope I find that out someday Thank you again Mrs. Smuckles
LATER.
So Patrick! Raymond tells me you are a..."veglegon" now? Am I saying that right?
Ahem. Vegan. Yes.
cough
Raymond says that means you only eat dried bees and peanut butter. Is that true, Patrick?

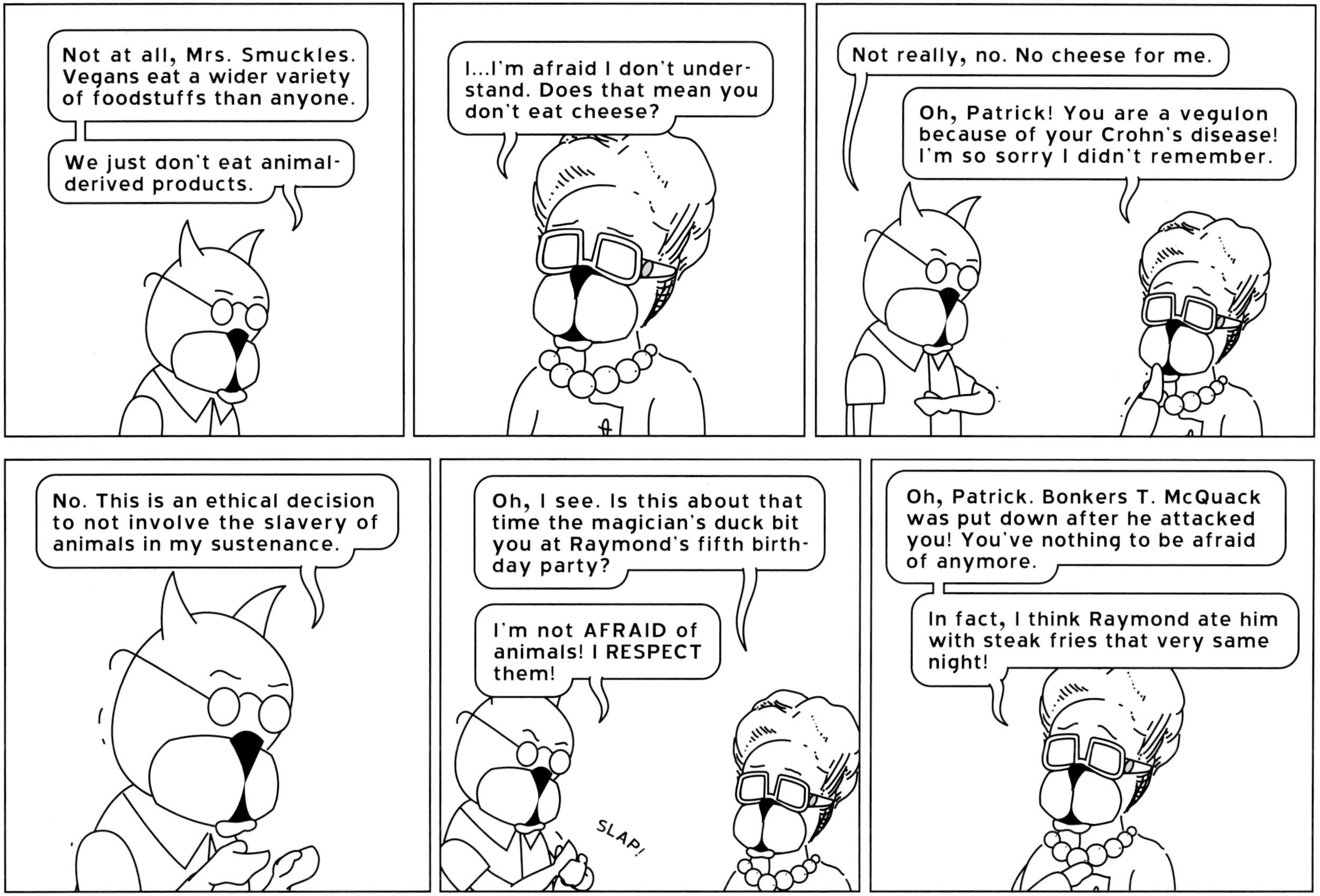
Not at all, Mrs. Smuckles. Vegans eat a wider variety of foodstuffs than anyone.
We just don't eat animal-derived products.
I...I'm afraid I don't understand. Does that mean you don't eat cheese?
Not really, no. No cheese for me.
Oh, Patrick! You are a vegulon because of your Crohn's disease! I'm so sorry I didn't remember.
No. This is an ethical decision to not involve the slavery of animals in my sustenance.
Oh, I see. Is this about that time the magician's duck bit you at Raymond's fifth birthday party?
I'm not AFRAID of animals! I RESPECT them!
SLAP!
Oh, Patrick. Bonkers T. McQuack was put down after he attacked you! You've nothing to be afraid of anymore.
In fact, I think Raymond ate him with steak fries that very same night!

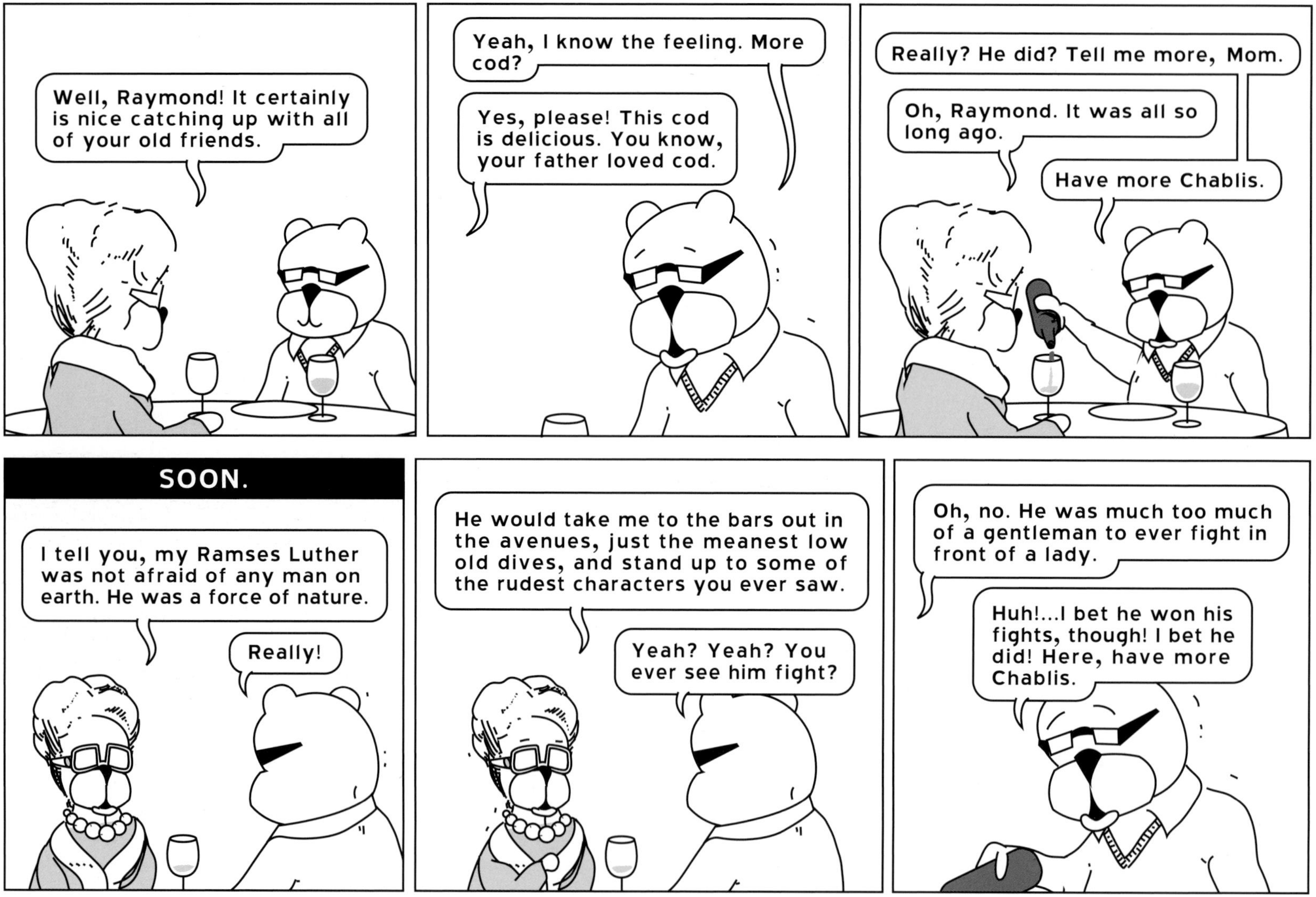
Well, Raymond! It certainly is nice catching up with all of your old friends.
Yeah, I know the feeling. More cod?
Yes, please! This cod is delicious. You know, your father loved cod.
Really? He did? Tell me more, Mom.
Oh, Raymond. It was all so long ago.
Have more Chablis.
SOON.
I tell you, my Ramses Luther was not afraid of any man on earth. He was a force of nature.
Really!
He would take me to the bars out in the avenues, just the meanest low old dives, and stand up to some of the rudest characters you ever saw.
Yeah? Yeah? You ever see him fight?
Oh, no. He was much too much of a gentleman to ever fight in front of a lady.
Huh!...I bet he won his fights, though! I bet he did! Here, have more Chablis.

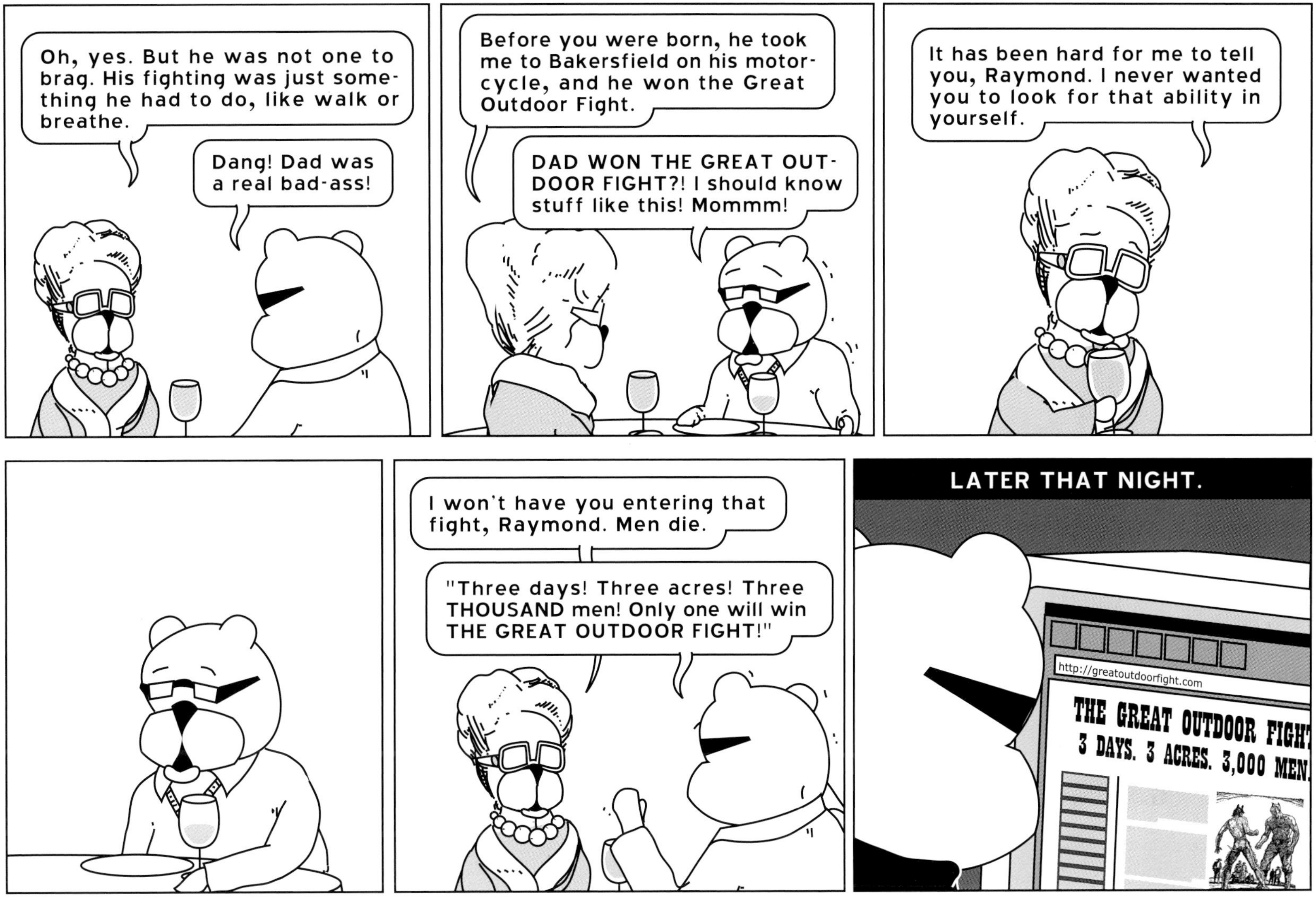
Oh, yes. But he was not one to brag. His fighting was just something he had to do, like walk or breathe.
Dang! Dad was a real bad-ass!
Before you were born, he took me to Bakersfield on his motorcycle, and he won the Great Outdoor Fight.
DAD WON THE GREAT OUTDOOR FIGHT?! I should know stuff like this! Mommm!
It has been hard for me to tell you, Raymond. I never wanted you to look for that ability in yourself.
I won't have you entering that fight, Raymond. Men die.
"Three days! Three acres! Three THOUSAND men! Only one will win THE GREAT OUTDOOR FIGHT!"
LATER THAT NIGHT.
http://greatoutdoorfight.com
THE GREAT OUTDOOR FIGH
3 DAYS. 3 ACRES. 3,000 MEN

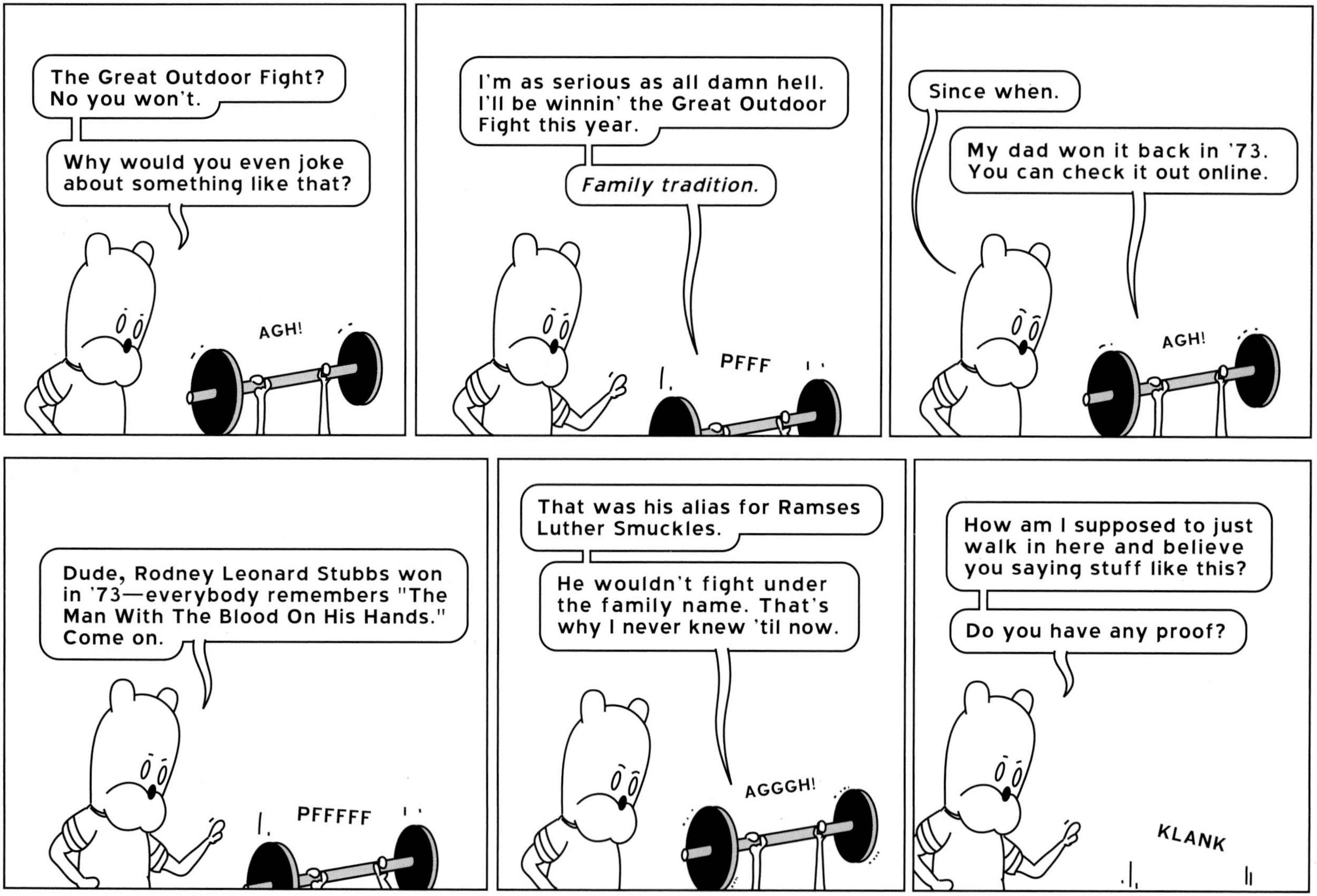

The Great Outdoor Fight? No you won't.
Why would you even joke about something like that?
AGH!
I'm as serious as all damn hell. I'll be winnin' the Great Outdoor Fight this year.
Family tradition.
PFFF
Since when.
My dad won it back in '73. You can check it out online.
AGH!
Dude, Rodney Leonard Stubbs won in '73—everybody remembers "The Man With The Blood On His Hands." Come on.
PFFFFF
That was his alias for Ramses Luther Smuckles.
He wouldn't fight under the family name. That's why I never knew 'til now.
AGGGH!
How am I supposed to just walk in here and believe you saying stuff like this?
Do you have any proof?
KLANK

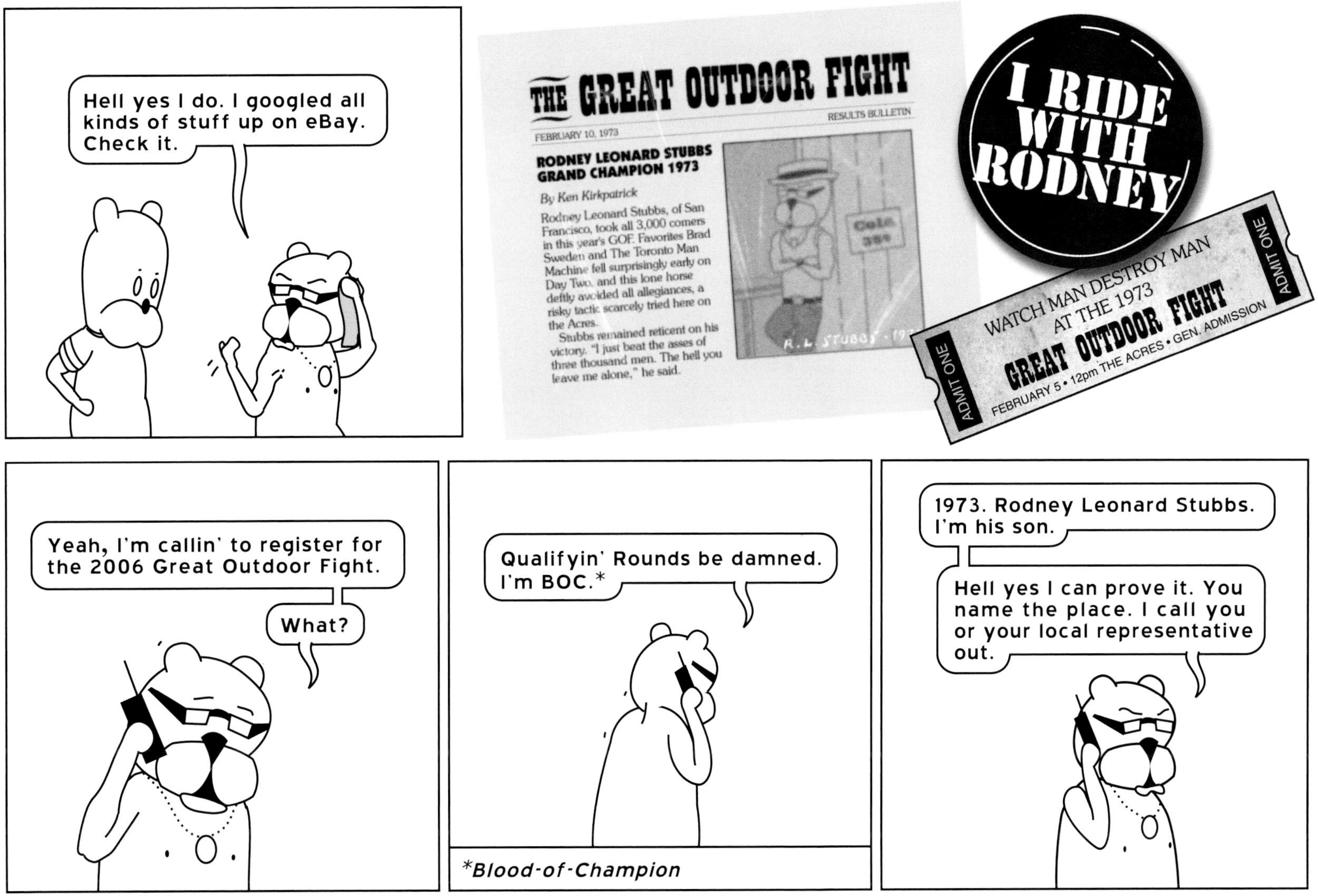
Hell yes I do. I googled all kinds of stuff up on eBay. Check it.
THE GREAT OUTDOOR FIGHT
RESULTS BULLETIN
FEBRUARY 10, 1973
RODNEY LEONARD STUBBS GRAND CHAMPION 1973
By Ken Kirkpatrick
Rodney Leonard Stubbs, of San Francisco, took all 3,000 comers in this year's GOF. Favorites Brad Sweden and The Toronto Man Machine fell surprisingly early on Day Two, and this lone horse deftly avoided all allegiances, a risky tactic scarcely tried here on the Acres.
Stubbs remained reticent on his victory. "I just beat the asses of three thousand men. The hell you leave me alone," he said.
Cola 35¢
R. L. STUBBS
I RIDE WITH RODNEY
ADMIT ONE
WATCH MAN DESTROY MAN AT THE 1973
GREAT OUTDOOR FIGHT
FEBRUARY 5 • 12pm THE ACRES • GEN. ADMISSION
ADMIT ONE
Yeah, I'm callin' to register for the 2006 Great Outdoor Fight.
What?
Qualifyin' Rounds be damned. I'm BOC.*
*Blood-of-Champion
1973. Rodney Leonard Stubbs. I'm his son.
Hell yes I can prove it. You name the place. I call you or your local representative out.

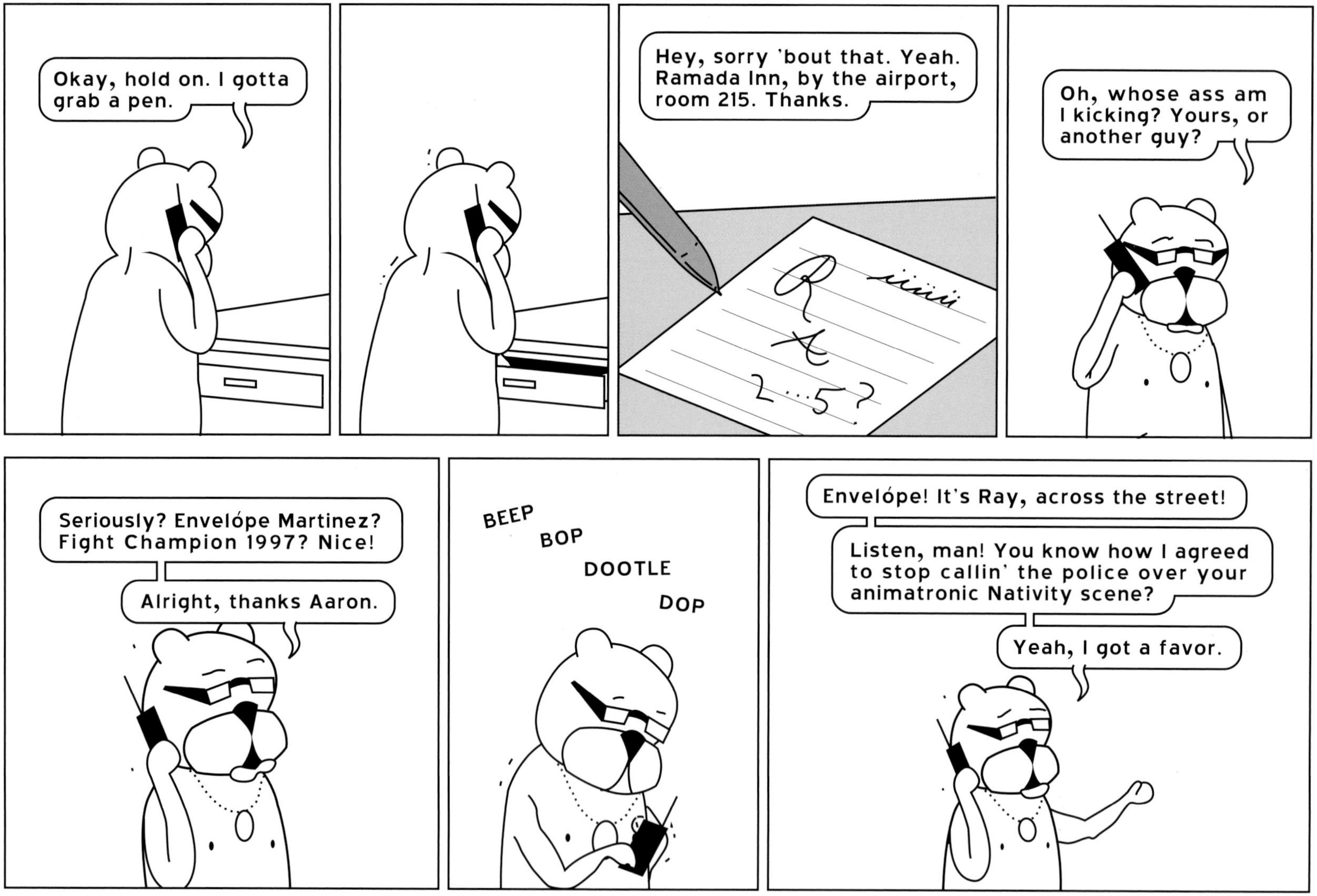

Okay, hold on. I gotta grab a pen.
Hey, sorry 'bout that. Yeah. Ramada Inn, by the airport, room 215. Thanks.
Oh, whose ass am I kicking? Yours, or another guy?
Seriously? Envelópe Martinez? Fight Champion 1997? Nice!
Alright, thanks Aaron.
BEEP
BOP
DOOTLE
DOP
Envelópe! It's Ray, across the street!
Listen, man! You know how I agreed to stop callin' the police over your animatronic Nativity scene?
Yeah, I got a favor.

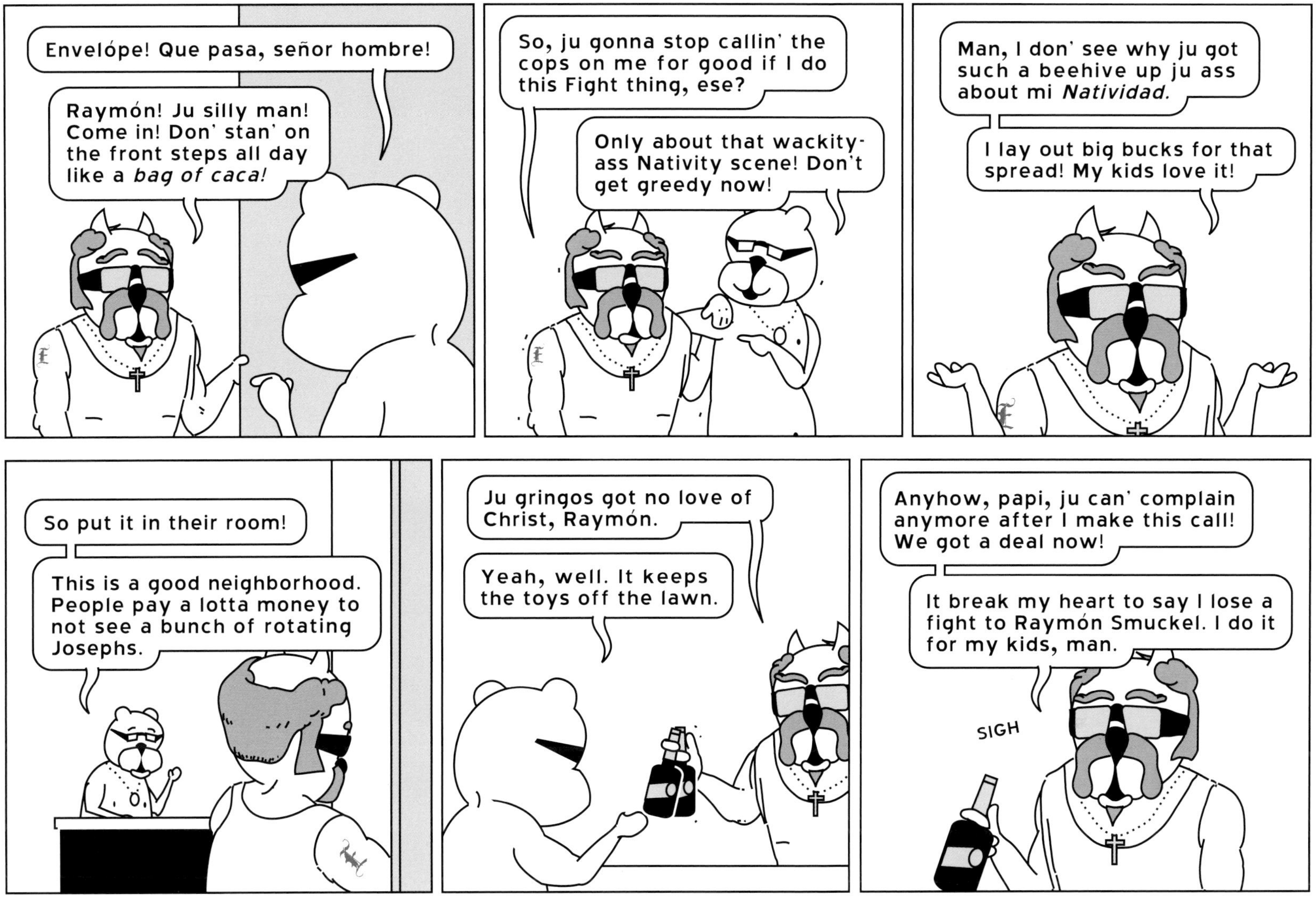
Envelópe! Que pasa, señor hombre!
Raymón! Ju silly man! Come in! Don' stan' on the front steps all day like a *bag of caca!*
So, ju gonna stop callin' the cops on me for good if I do this Fight thing, ese?
Only about that wackity-ass Nativity scene! Don't get greedy now!
Man, I don' see why ju got such a beehive up ju ass about mi *Natividad.*
I lay out big bucks for that spread! My kids love it!
So put it in their room!
This is a good neighborhood. People pay a lotta money to not see a bunch of rotating Josephs.
Ju gringos got no love of Christ, Raymón.
Yeah, well. It keeps the toys off the lawn.
Anyhow, papi, ju can' complain anymore after I make this call! We got a deal now!
It break my heart to say I lose a fight to Raymón Smuckel. I do it for my kids, man.
SIGH

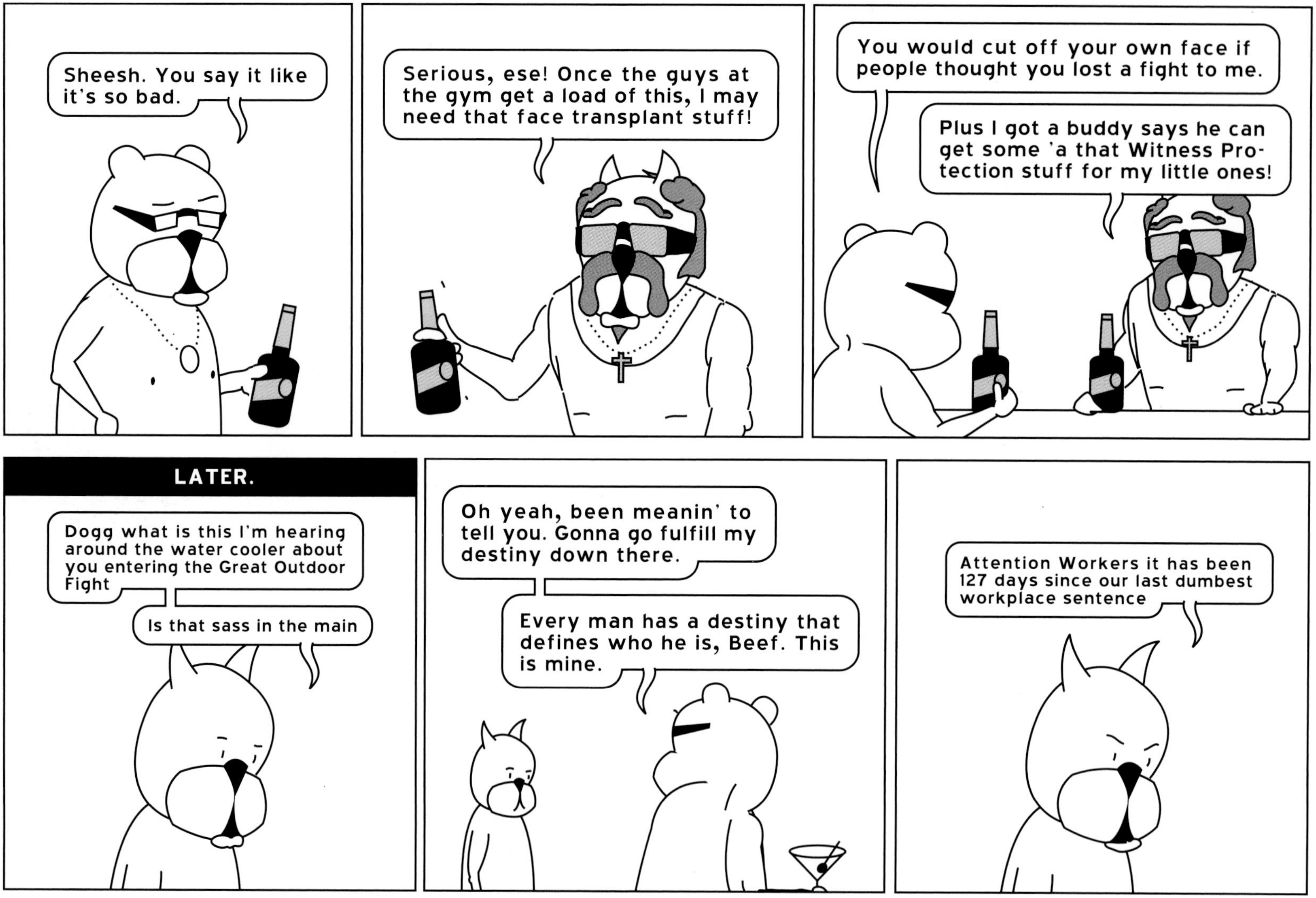
Sheesh. You say it like it's so bad.
Serious, ese! Once the guys at the gym get a load of this, I may need that face transplant stuff!
You would cut off your own face if people thought you lost a fight to me.
Plus I got a buddy says he can get some 'a that Witness Protection stuff for my little ones!
LATER.
Dogg what is this I'm hearing around the water cooler about you entering the Great Outdoor Fight
Is that sass in the main
Oh yeah, been meanin' to tell you. Gonna go fulfill my destiny down there.
Every man has a destiny that defines who he is, Beef. This is mine.
Attention Workers it has been 127 days since our last dumbest workplace sentence

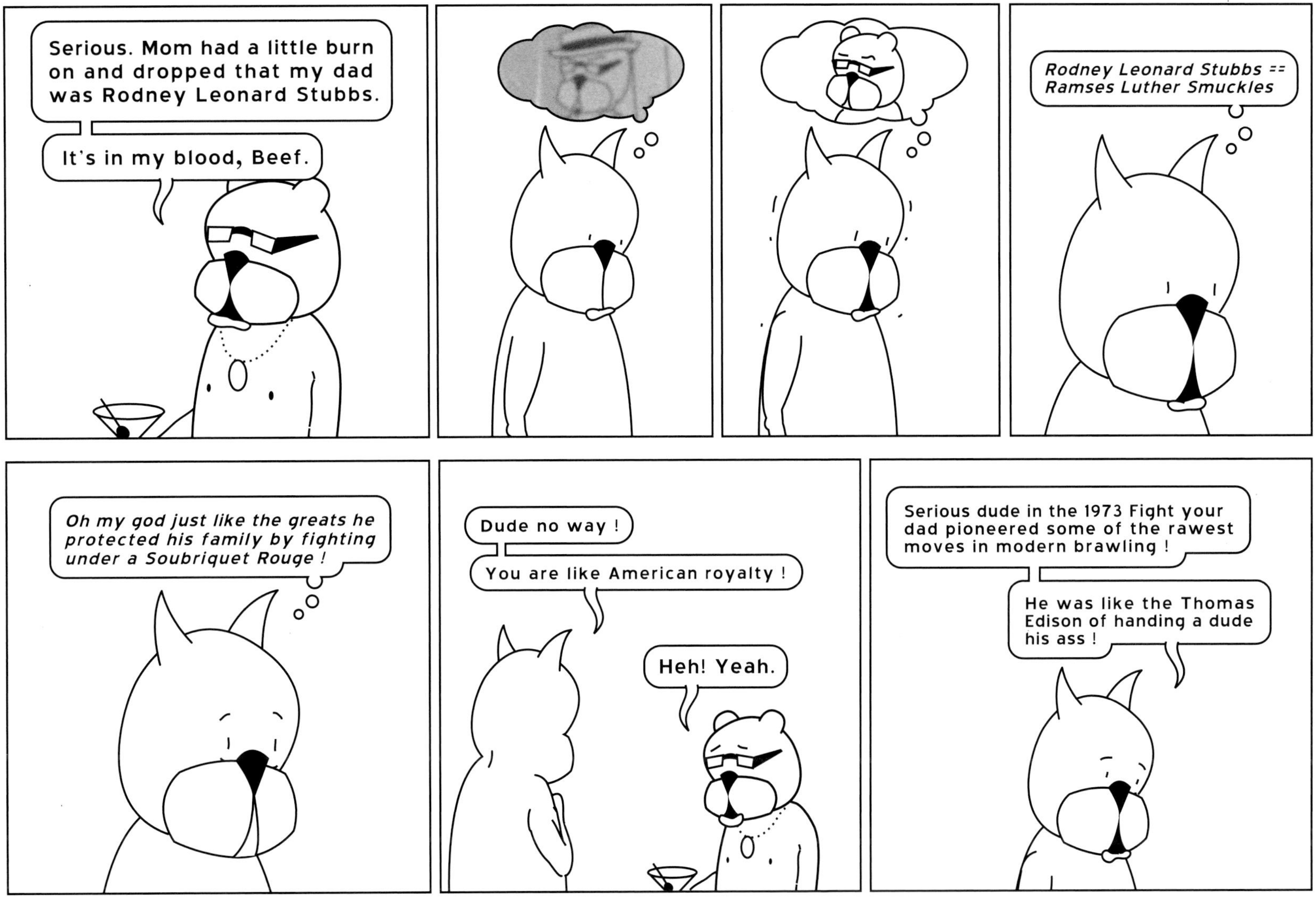

Serious. Mom had a little burn on and dropped that my dad was Rodney Leonard Stubbs.
It's in my blood, Beef.
Rodney Leonard Stubbs == Ramses Luther Smuckles
Oh my god just like the greats he protected his family by fighting under a Soubriquet Rouge !
Dude no way !
You are like American royalty !
Heh! Yeah.
Serious dude in the 1973 Fight your dad pioneered some of the rawest moves in modern brawling !
He was like the Thomas Edison of handing a dude his ass !

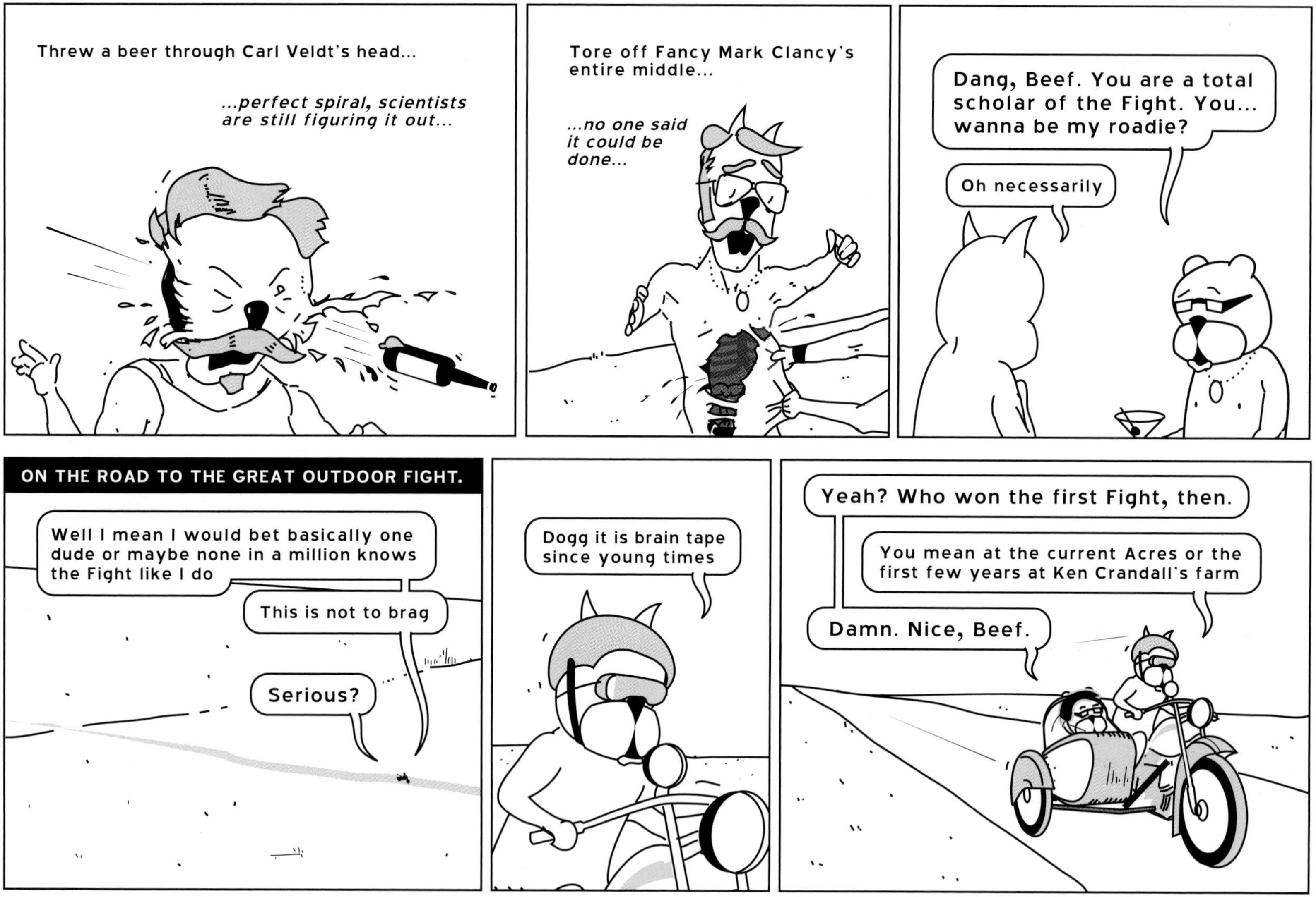

Threw a beer through Carl Veldt's head...
...perfect spiral, scientists are still figuring it out...
Tore off Fancy Mark Clancy's entire middle...
...no one said it could be done...
Dang, Beef. You are a total scholar of the Fight. You... wanna be my roadie?
Oh necessarily
ON THE ROAD TO THE GREAT OUTDOOR FIGHT.
Well I mean I would bet basically one dude or maybe none in a million knows the Fight like I do
This is not to brag
Serious?
Dogg it is brain tape since young times
Yeah? Who won the first Fight, then.
You mean at the current Acres or the first few years at Ken Crandall's farm
Damn. Nice, Beef.

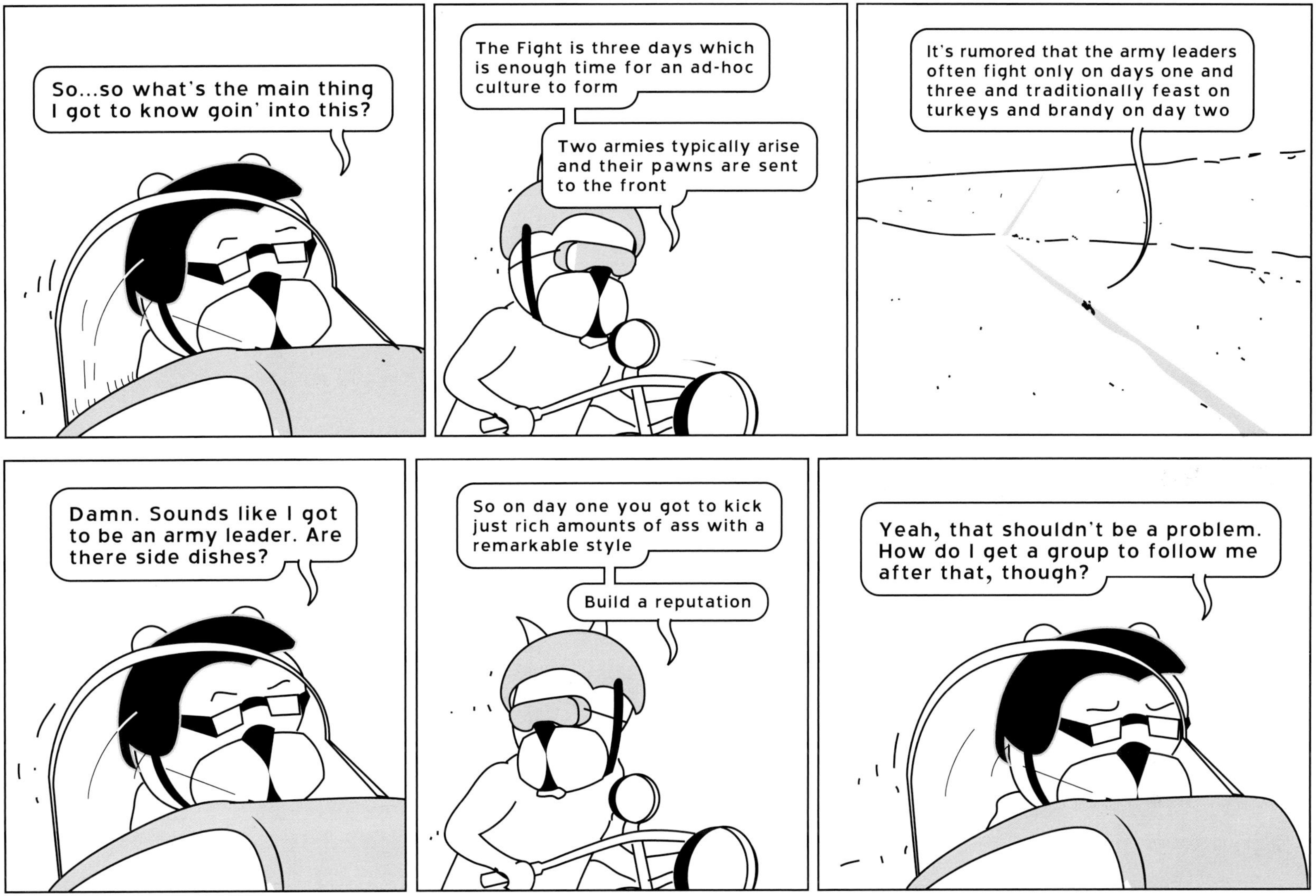
So...so what's the main thing I got to know goin' into this?
The Fight is three days which is enough time for an ad-hoc culture to form
Two armies typically arise and their pawns are sent to the front
It's rumored that the army leaders often fight only on days one and three and traditionally feast on turkeys and brandy on day two
Damn. Sounds like I got to be an army leader. Are there side dishes?
So on day one you got to kick just rich amounts of ass with a remarkable style
Build a reputation
Yeah, that shouldn't be a problem. How do I get a group to follow me after that, though?

Men are of two kinds

When contained...

They either want to be a hero or be with a hero

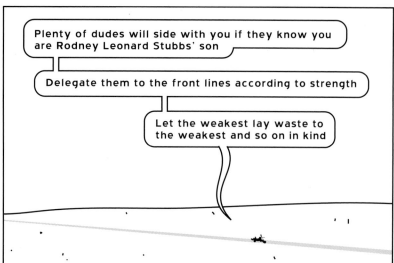

Plenty of dudes will side with you if they know you are Rodney Leonard Stubbs' son

Delegate them to the front lines according to strength

Let the weakest lay waste to the weakest and so on in kind

And when it's day three, what do I do?

We'll figure that out then

Dude, we'll be cut off from communicating during the...wait.

Beef, are you in the Fight?

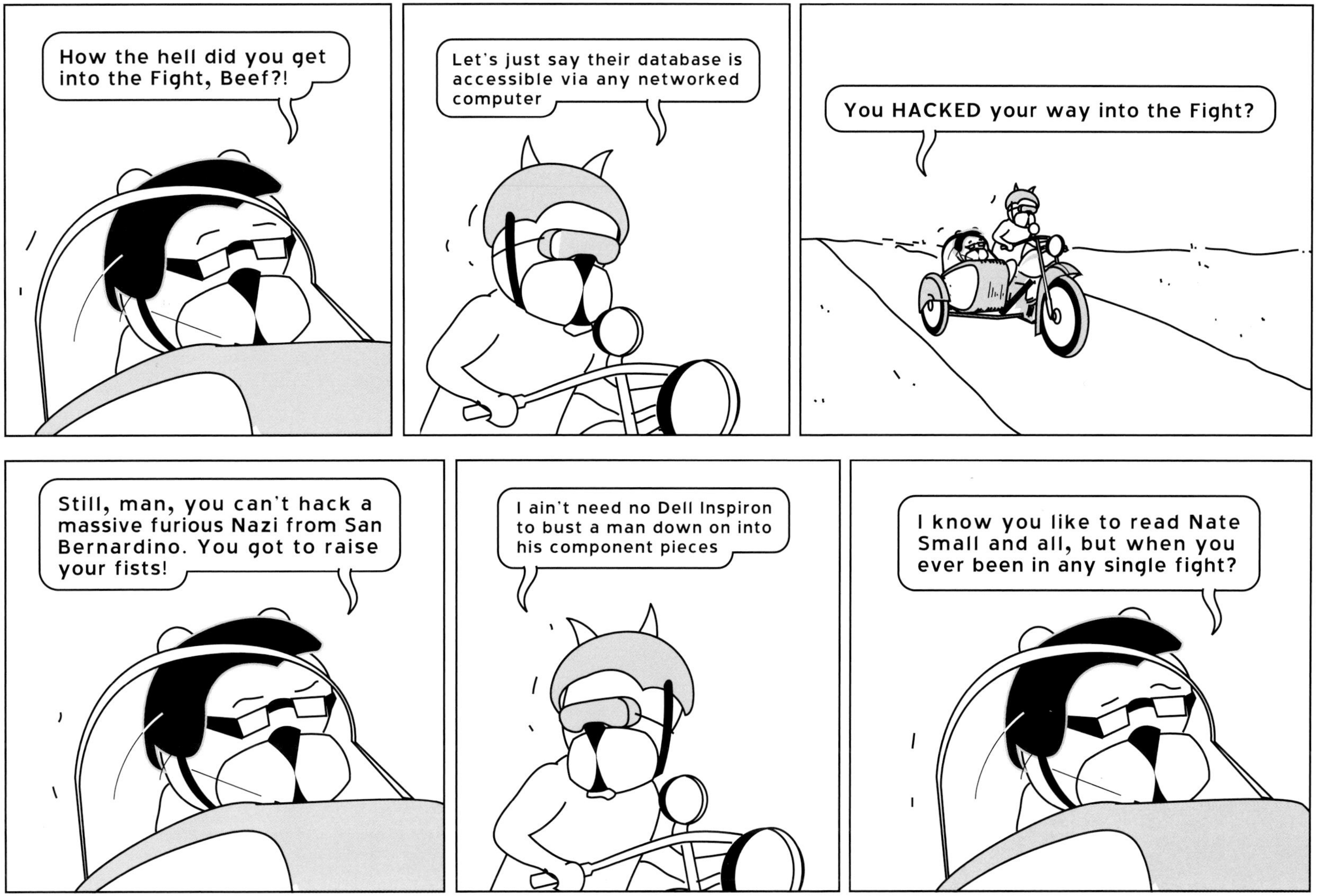
How the hell did you get into the Fight, Beef?!
Let's just say their database is accessible via any networked computer
You HACKED your way into the Fight?
Still, man, you can't hack a massive furious Nazi from San Bernardino. You got to raise your fists!
I ain't need no Dell Inspiron to bust a man down on into his component pieces
I know you like to read Nate Small and all, but when you ever been in any single fight?

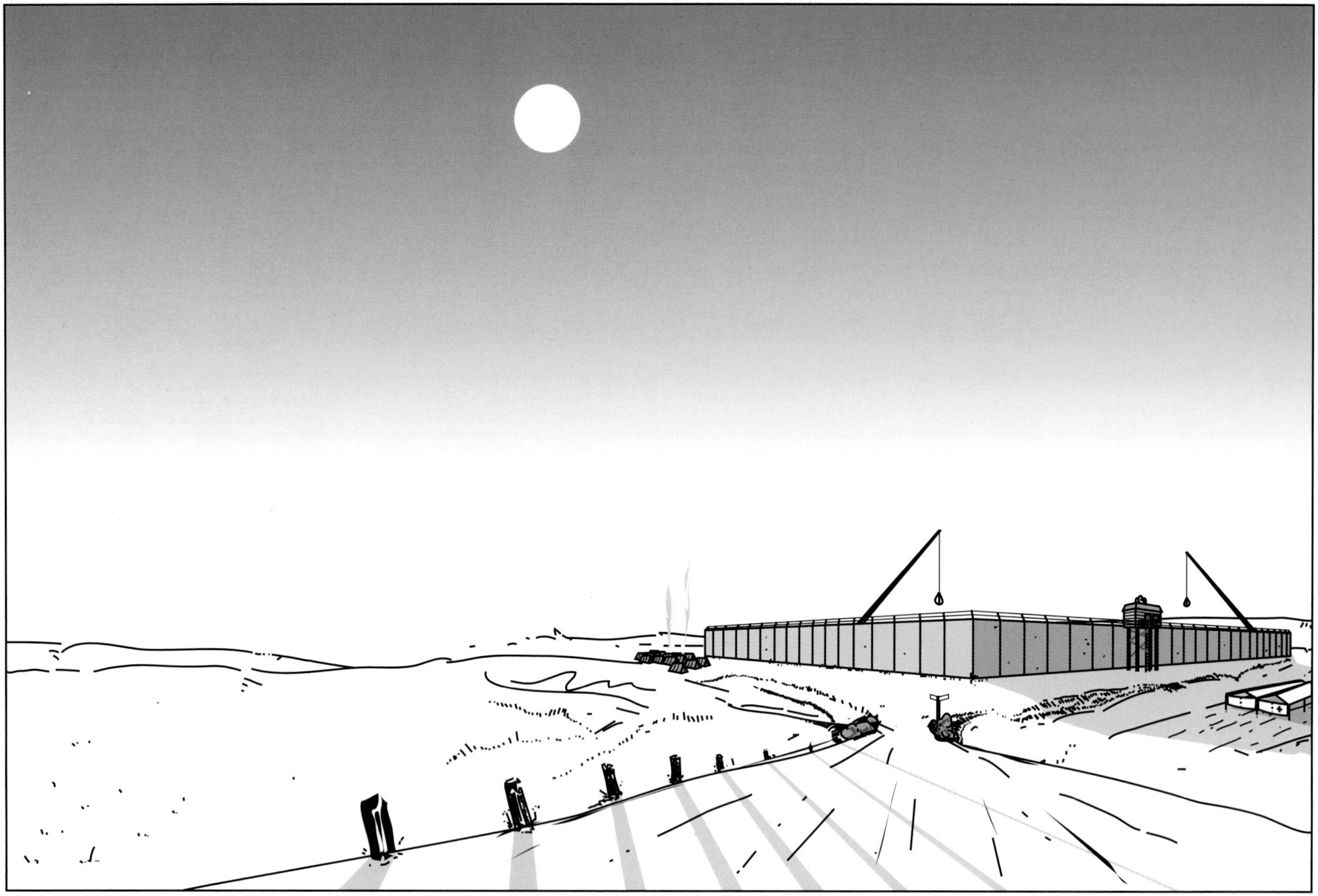

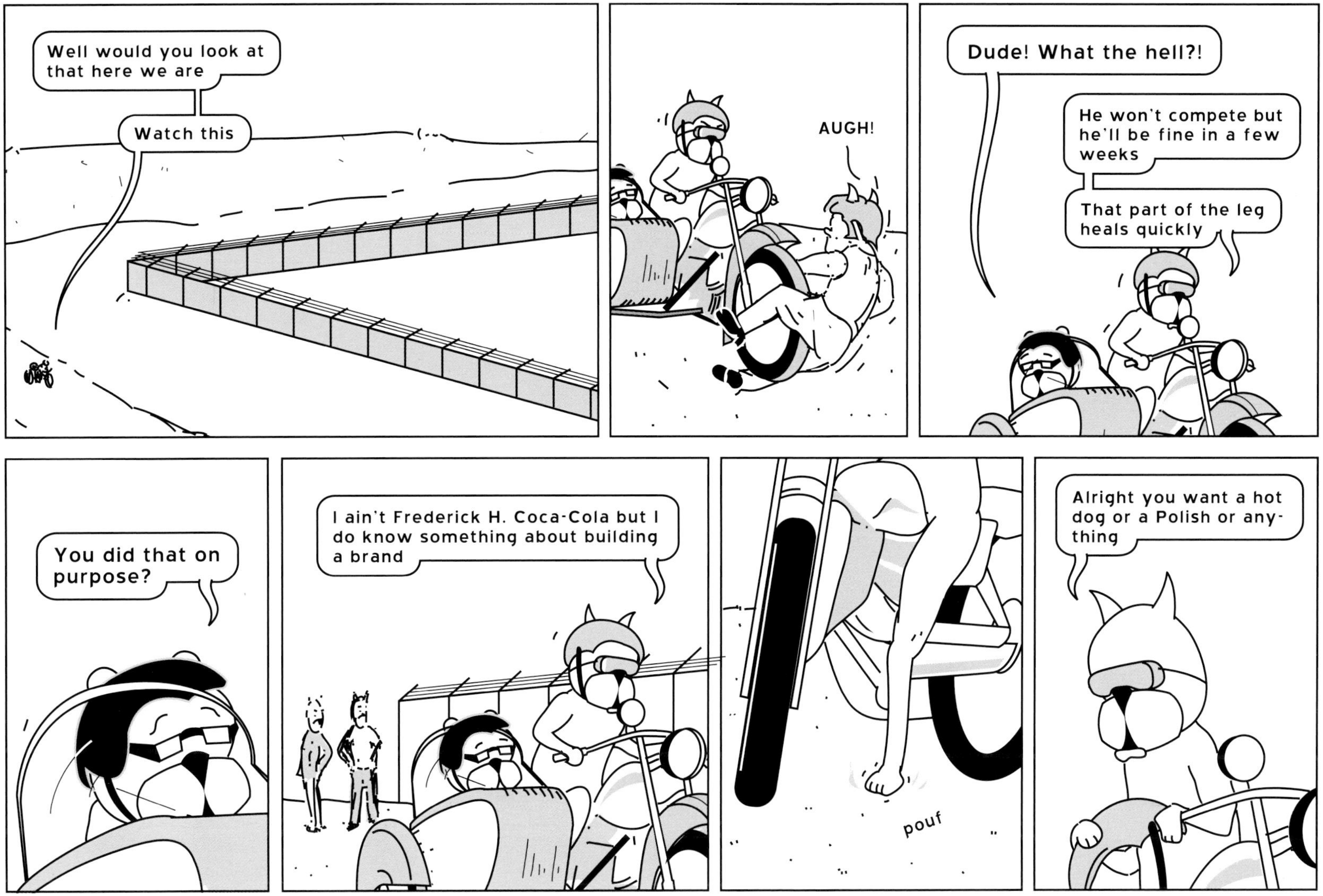
Well would you look at that here we are
Watch this
AUGH!
Dude! What the hell?!
He won't compete but he'll be fine in a few weeks
That part of the leg heals quickly
You did that on purpose?
I ain't Frederick H. Coca-Cola but I do know something about building a brand
pouf
Alright you want a hot dog or a Polish or any-thing

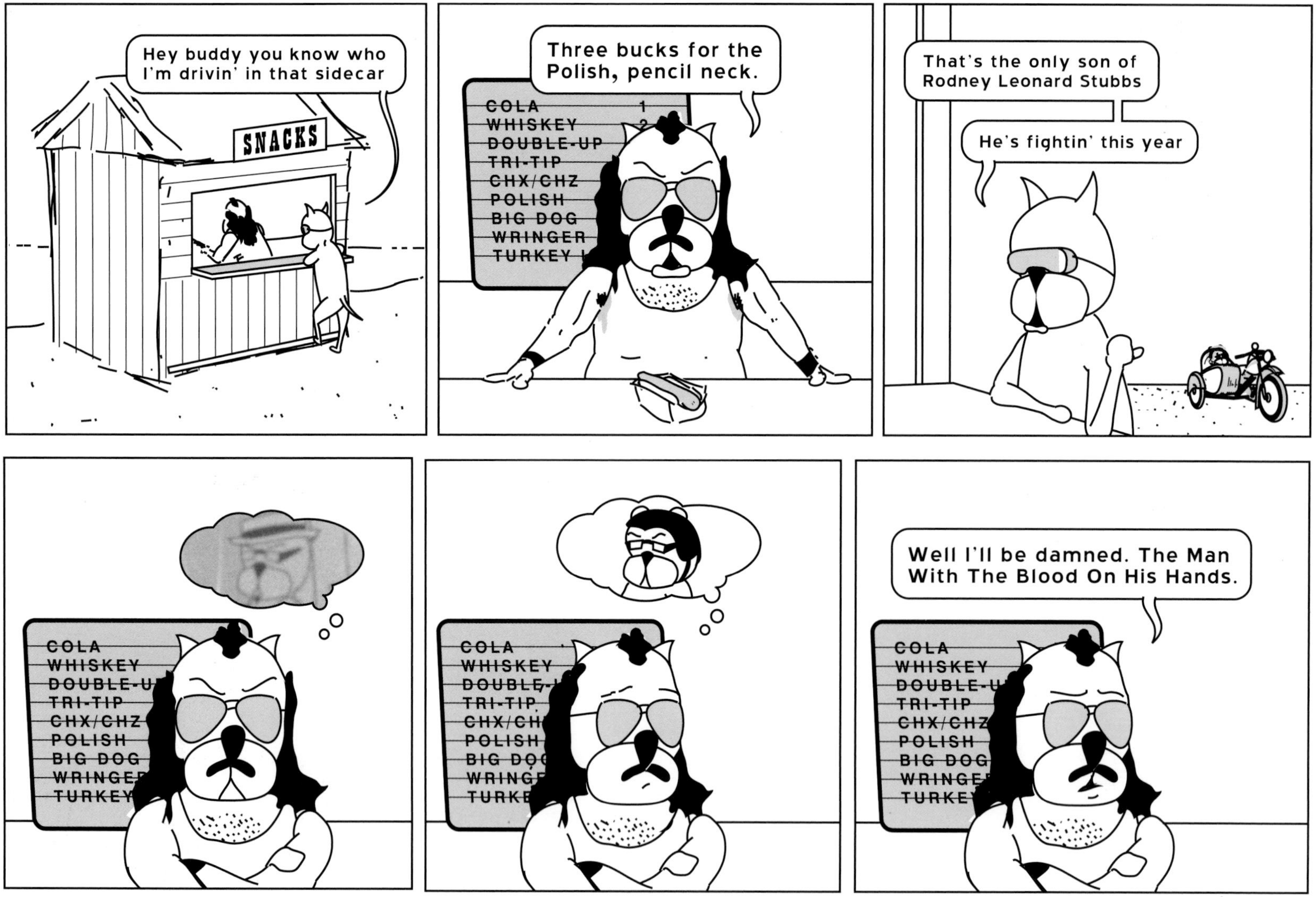
SNACKS
Hey buddy you know who I'm drivin' in that sidecar
Three bucks for the Polish, pencil neck.
COLA
WHISKEY
DOUBLE-UP
TRI-TIP
CHX/CHZ
POLISH
BIG DOG
WRINGER
That's the only son of Rodney Leonard Stubbs
He's fightin' this year
Well I'll be damned. The Man With The Blood On His Hands.

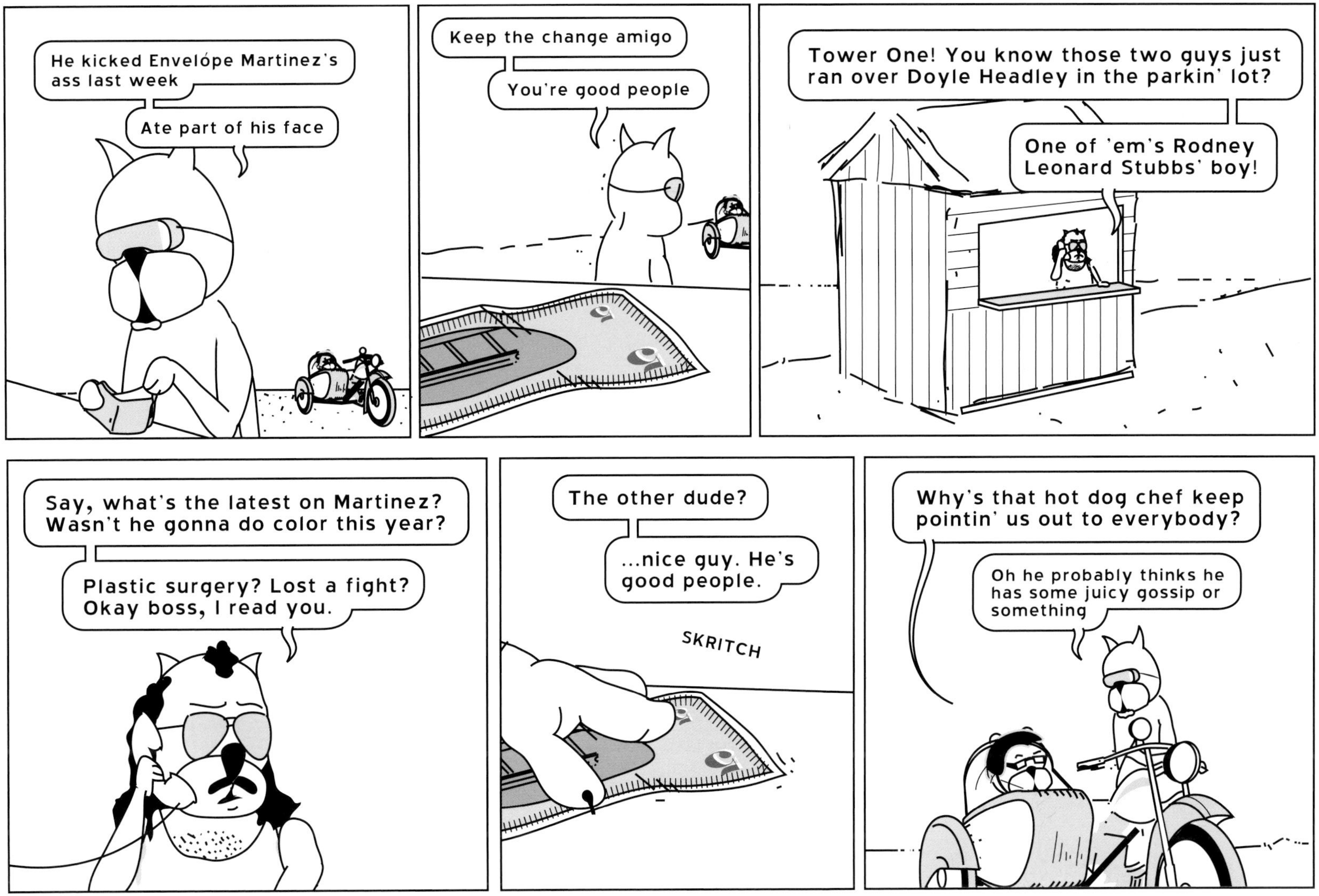
He kicked Envelópe Martinez's ass last week
Ate part of his face
Keep the change amigo
You're good people
Tower One! You know those two guys just ran over Doyle Headley in the parkin' lot?
One of 'em's Rodney Leonard Stubbs' boy!
Say, what's the latest on Martinez? Wasn't he gonna do color this year?
Plastic surgery? Lost a fight? Okay boss, I read you.
The other dude?
...nice guy. He's good people.
SKRITCH
Why's that hot dog chef keep pointin' us out to everybody?
Oh he probably thinks he has some juicy gossip or something

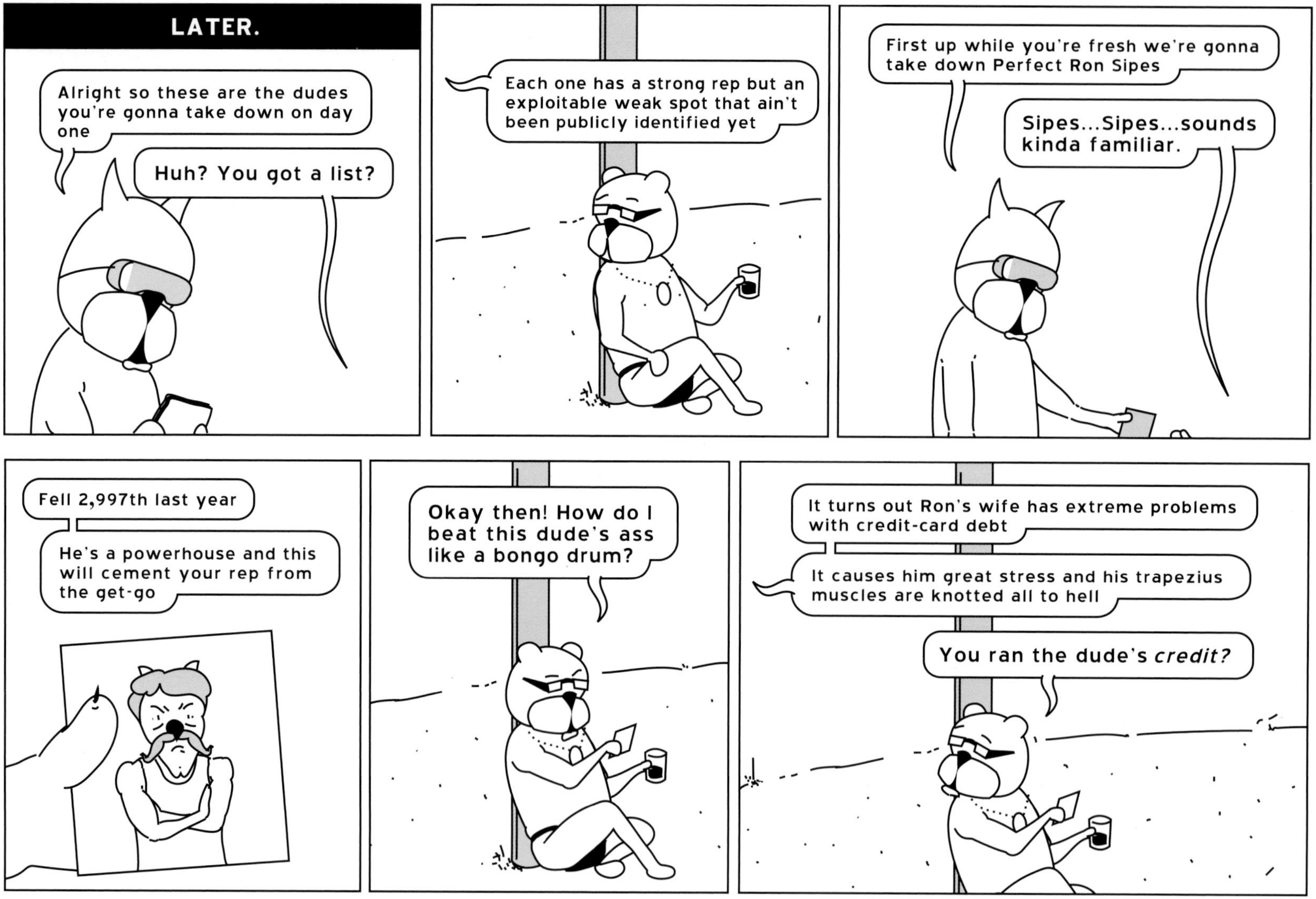
LATER.
Alright so these are the dudes you're gonna take down on day one
Huh? You got a list?
Each one has a strong rep but an exploitable weak spot that ain't been publicly identified yet
First up while you're fresh we're gonna take down Perfect Ron Sipes
Sipes...Sipes...sounds kinda familiar.
Fell 2,997th last year
He's a powerhouse and this will cement your rep from the get-go
Okay then! How do I beat this dude's ass like a bongo drum?
It turns out Ron's wife has extreme problems with credit-card debt
It causes him great stress and his trapezius muscles are knotted all to hell
You ran the dude's *credit?*

You can see it in last year's tapes once you know what to look for

OK. So I start to give him a backrub, but then I surprise him by kicking his ass. Right.

No you give him one stiff jab at the nerve center here and his whole back will freeze up like iron

Dude will plead and cry for the medics to take him away

Instant D/Q

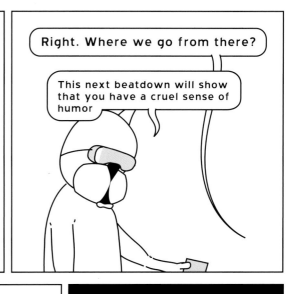

Right. Where we go from there?

This next beatdown will show that you have a cruel sense of humor

Sound and Motion is one of those new-age experimental-technique guys from Santa Cruz

They always get in 'cause no one else in their region tries to qualify

Sound and Motion

So what's his whole thing?

Recumbent tai chi

You'll know what to do

...AND SO ON INTO THE NIGHT DID THE TWO FRIENDS CONTEMPLATE THE DAY THAT LAY BEFORE THEM...THE FIRST DAY OF...

THE GREAT OUTDOOR FIGHT!

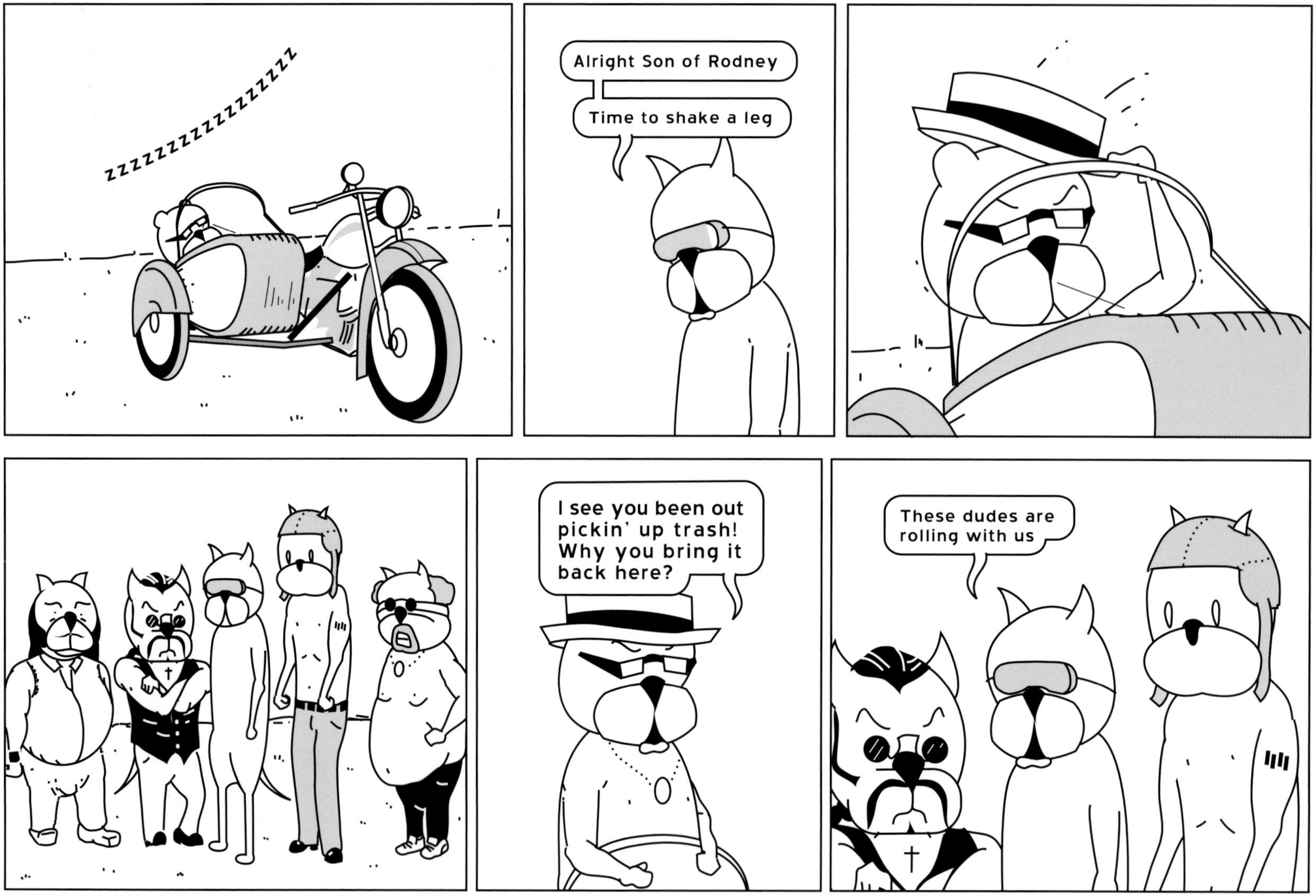
ZZZZZZZZZZZZZZZZZZZ
Alright Son of Rodney
Time to shake a leg
I see you been out pickin' up trash! Why you bring it back here?
These dudes are rolling with us

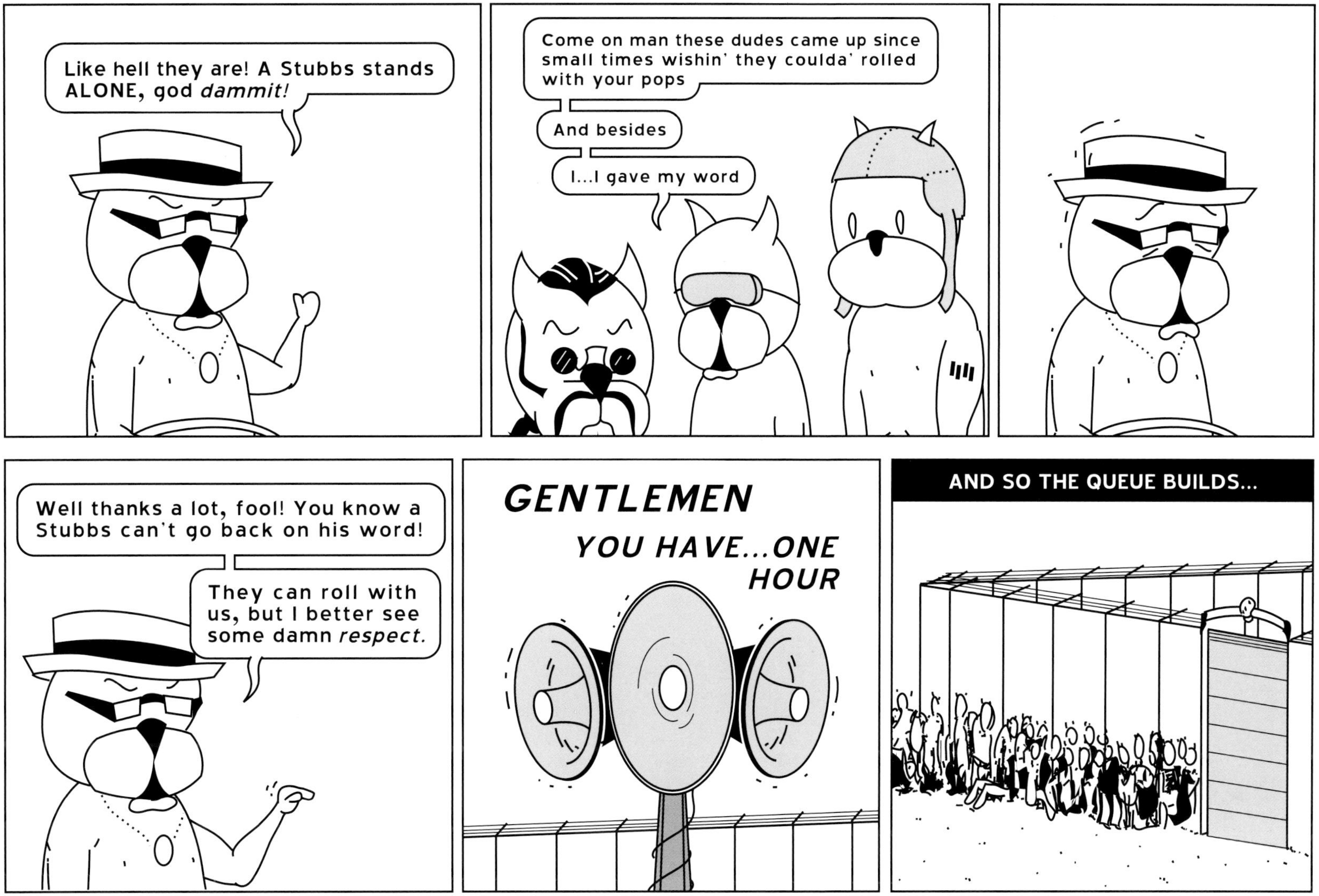
Like hell they are! A Stubbs stands ALONE, god *dammit!*
Come on man these dudes came up since small times wishin' they coulda' rolled with your pops
And besides
I...I gave my word
Well thanks a lot, fool! You know a Stubbs can't go back on his word!
They can roll with us, but I better see some damn *respect.*
GENTLEMEN
YOU HAVE...ONE HOUR
AND SO THE QUEUE BUILDS...

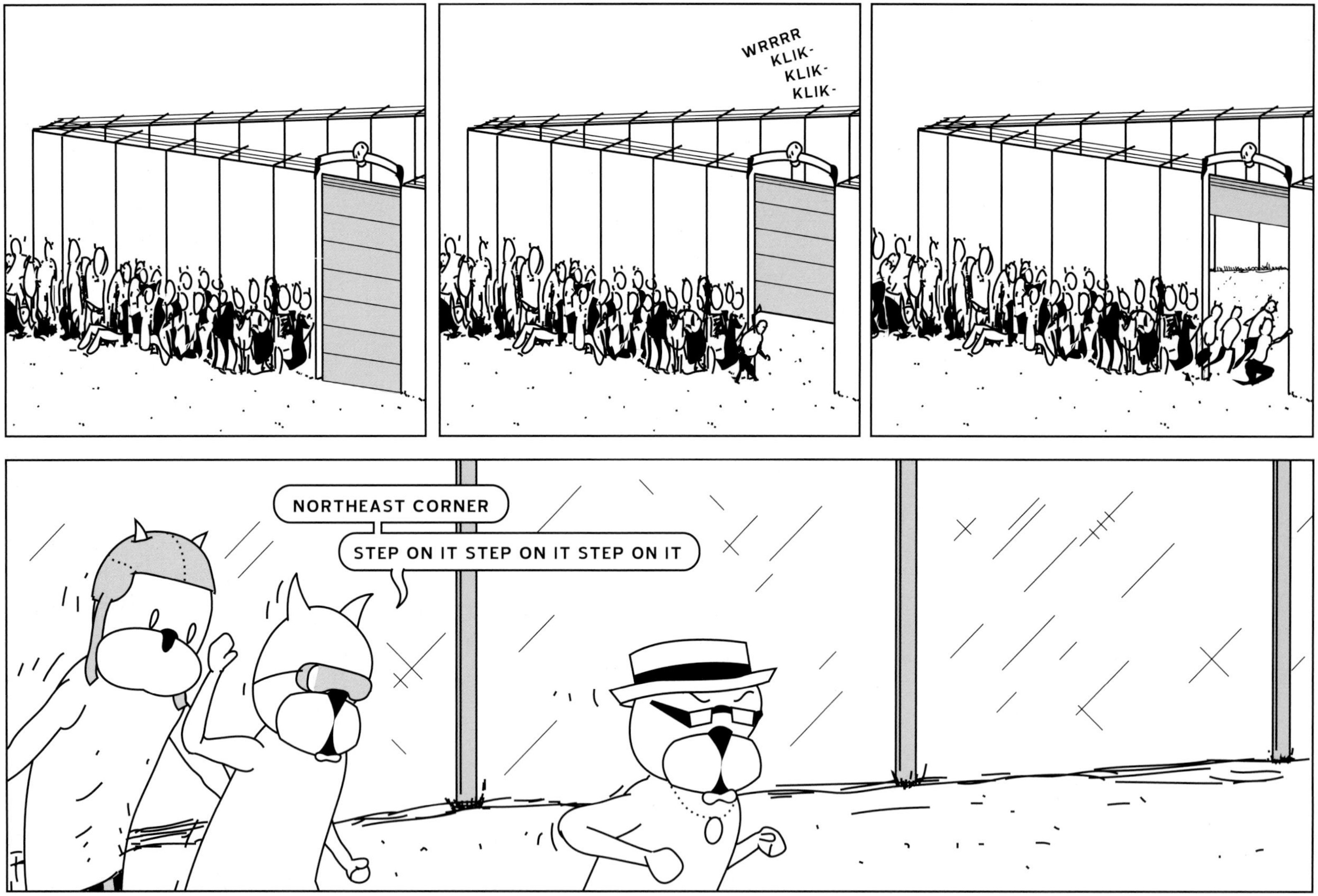
WRRRR
KLIK-
KLIK-
KLIK-
NORTHEAST CORNER
STEP ON IT STEP ON IT STEP ON IT

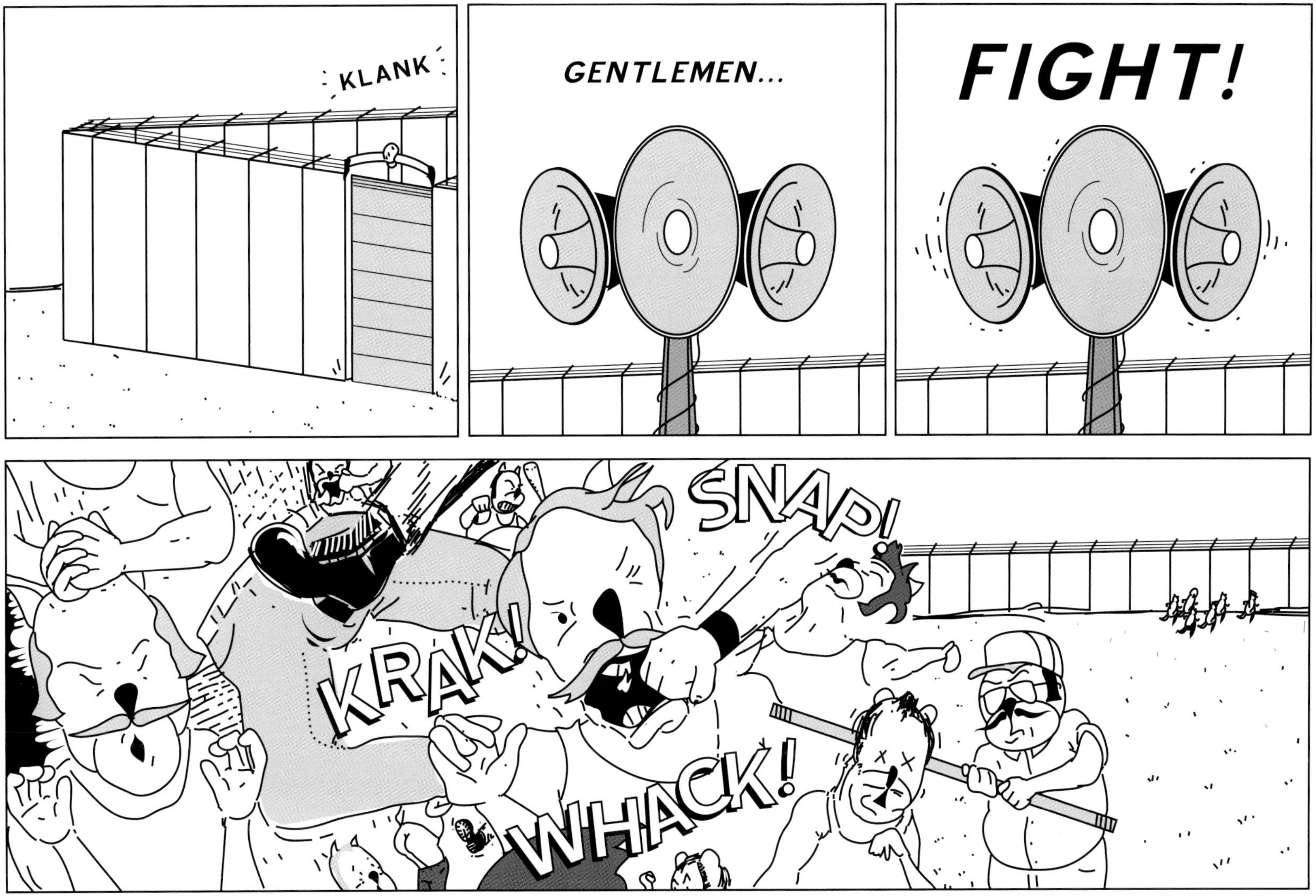
KLANK
GENTLEMEN...
FIGHT!
SNAP!
KRAK!
WHACK!

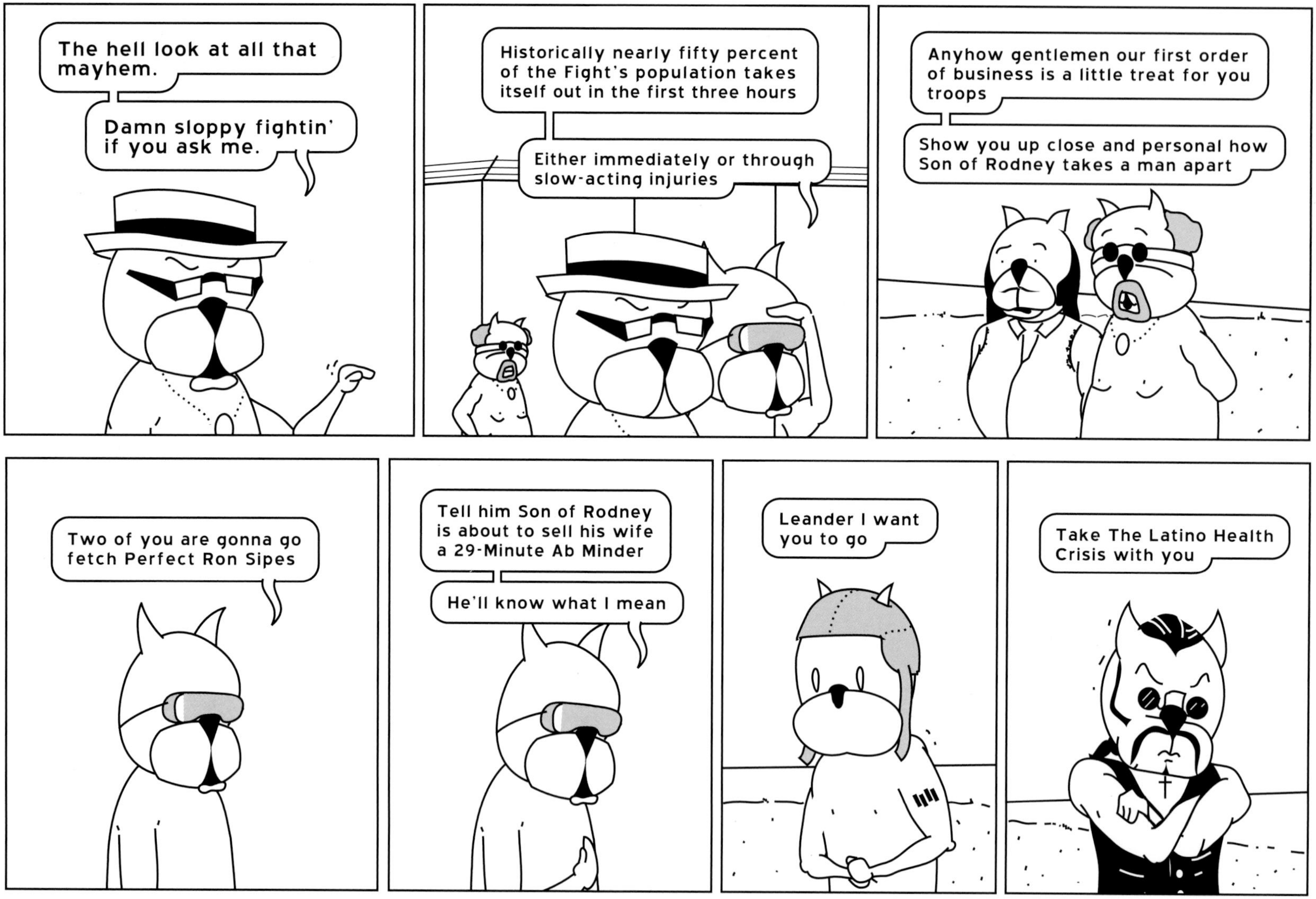
The hell look at all that mayhem.
Damn sloppy fightin' if you ask me.
Historically nearly fifty percent of the Fight's population takes itself out in the first three hours
Either immediately or through slow-acting injuries
Anyhow gentlemen our first order of business is a little treat for you troops
Show you up close and personal how Son of Rodney takes a man apart
Two of you are gonna go fetch Perfect Ron Sipes
Tell him Son of Rodney is about to sell his wife a 29-Minute Ab Minder
He'll know what I mean
Leander I want you to go
Take The Latino Health Crisis with you

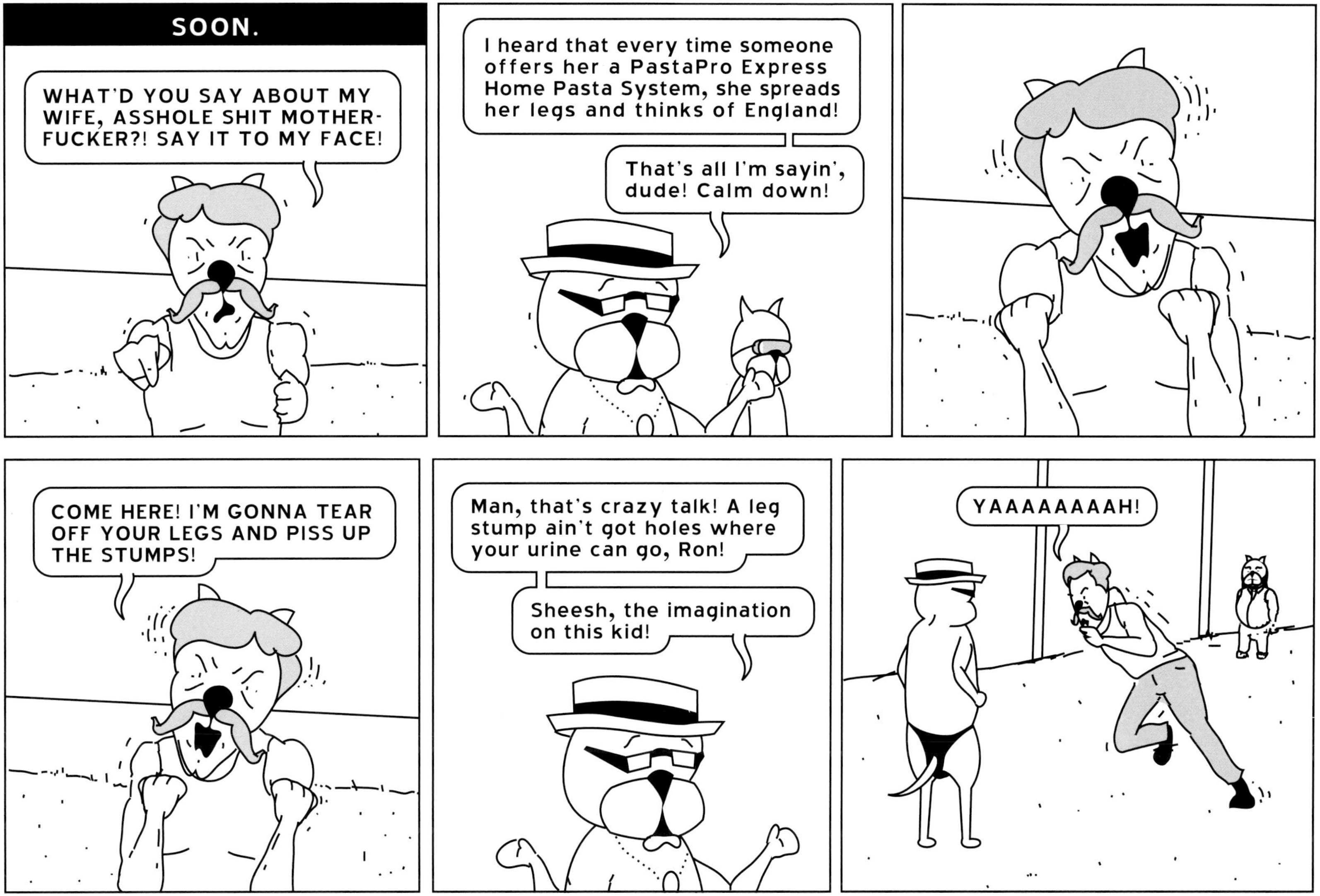
SOON.
WHAT'D YOU SAY ABOUT MY WIFE, ASSHOLE SHIT MOTHER-FUCKER?! SAY IT TO MY FACE!
I heard that every time someone offers her a PastaPro Express Home Pasta System, she spreads her legs and thinks of England!
That's all I'm sayin', dude! Calm down!
COME HERE! I'M GONNA TEAR OFF YOUR LEGS AND PISS UP THE STUMPS!
Man, that's crazy talk! A leg stump ain't got holes where your urine can go, Ron!
Sheesh, the imagination on this kid!
YAAAAAAAAH!

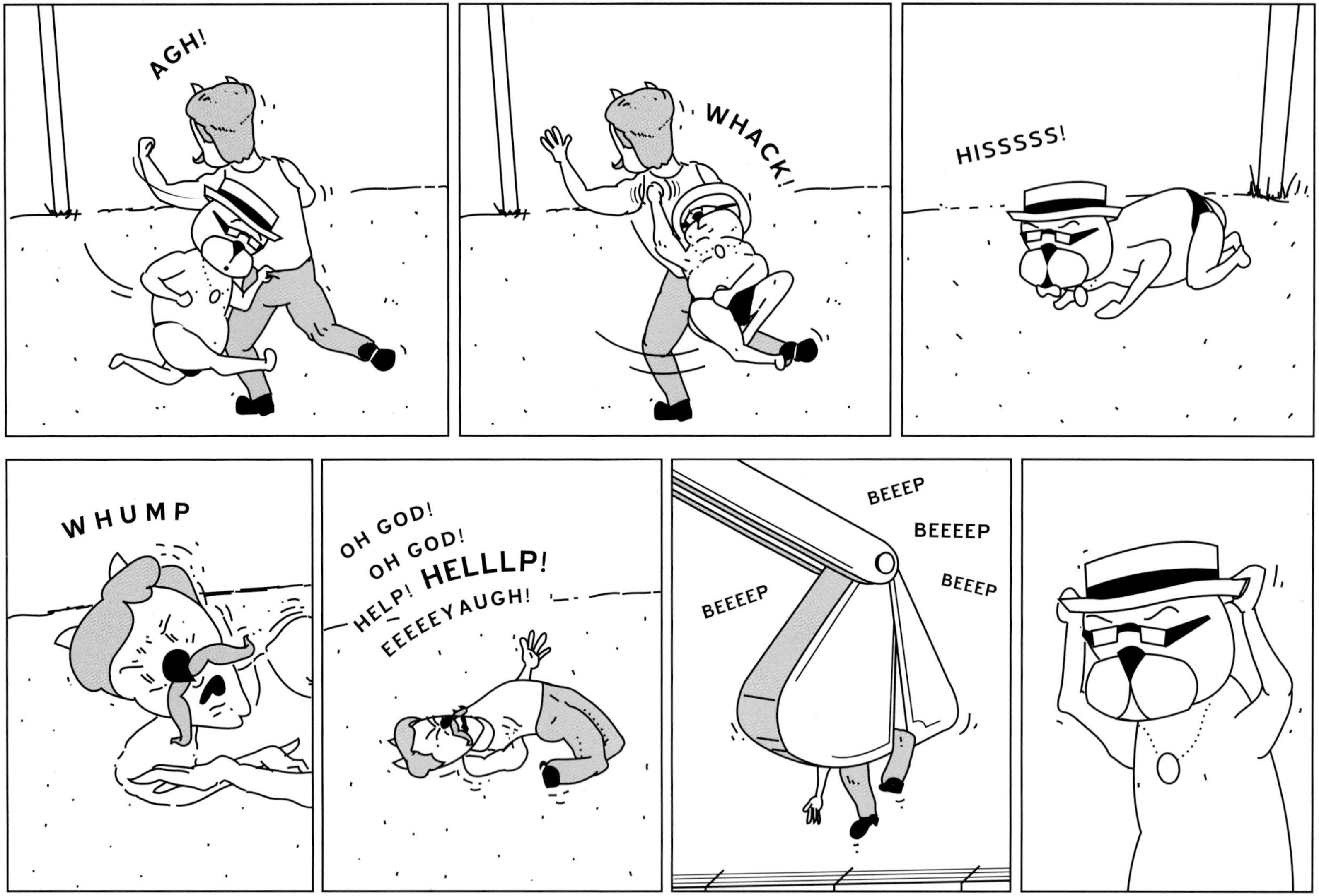
AGH!
WHACK!
HISSSSS!
WHUMP
OH GOD!
OH GOD!
HELP! HELLLP!
EEEEEYAUGH!
BEEEP
BEEEEP
BEEEP
BEEEEP

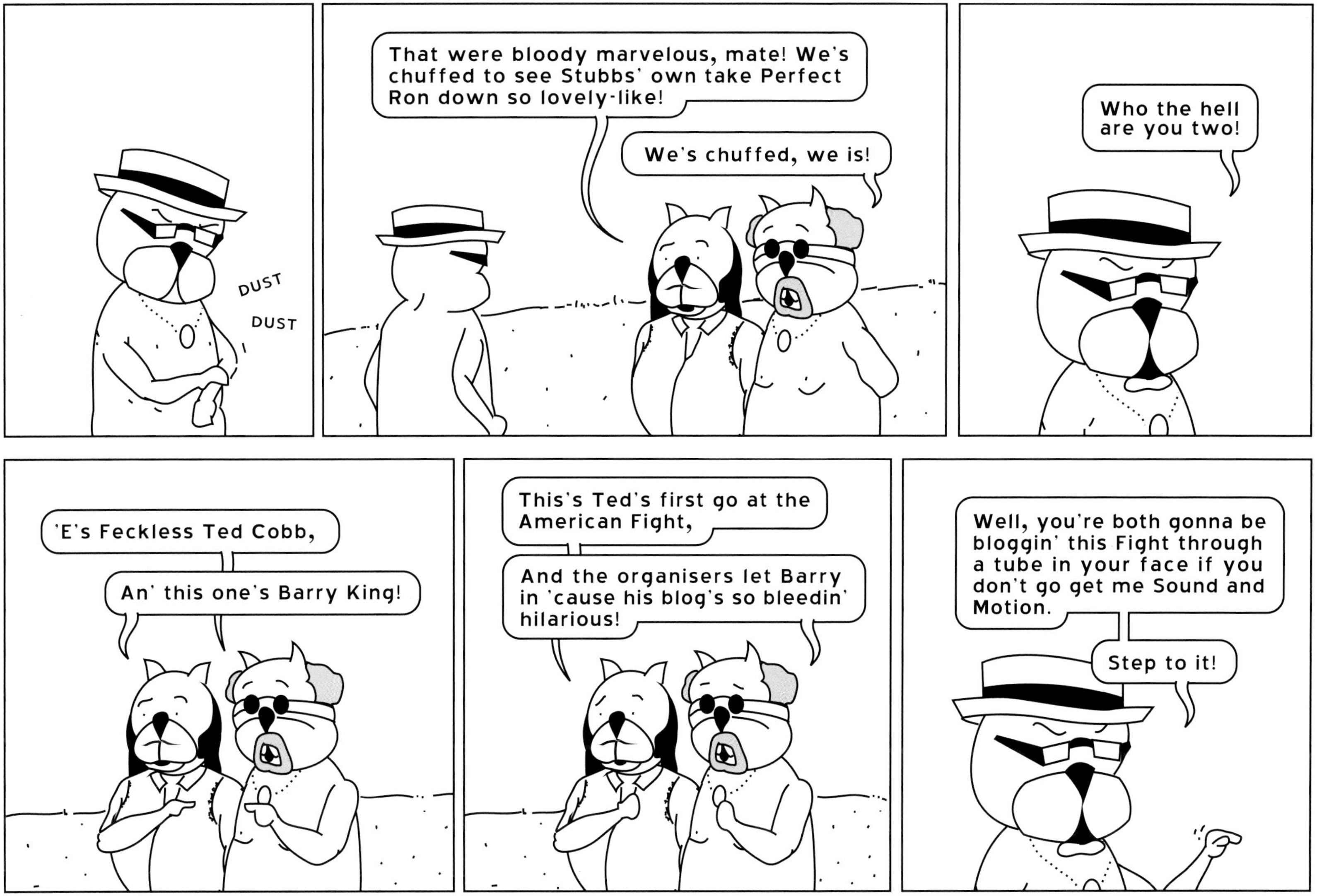
DUST
DUST
That were bloody marvelous, mate! We's chuffed to see Stubbs' own take Perfect Ron down so lovely-like!
We's chuffed, we is!
Who the hell are you two!
'E's Feckless Ted Cobb,
An' this one's Barry King!
This's Ted's first go at the American Fight,
And the organisers let Barry in 'cause his blog's so bleedin' hilarious!
Well, you're both gonna be bloggin' this Fight through a tube in your face if you don't go get me Sound and Motion.
Step to it!

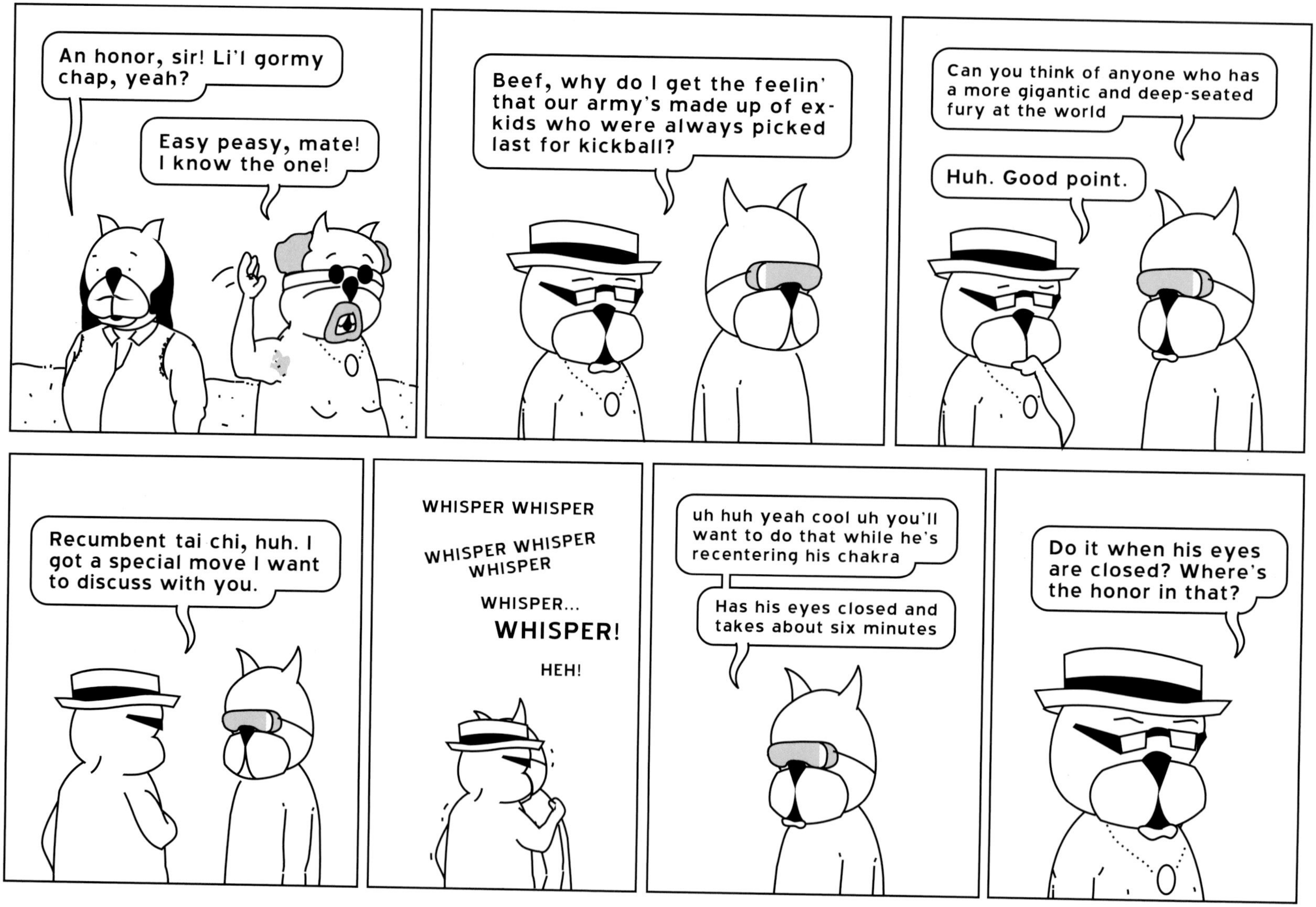
An honor, sir! Li'l gormy chap, yeah?
Easy peasy, mate! I know the one!
Beef, why do I get the feelin' that our army's made up of ex-kids who were always picked last for kickball?
Can you think of anyone who has a more gigantic and deep-seated fury at the world
Huh. Good point.
Recumbent tai chi, huh. I got a special move I want to discuss with you.
WHISPER WHISPER
WHISPER WHISPER WHISPER
WHISPER...
WHISPER!
HEH!
uh huh yeah cool uh you'll want to do that while he's recentering his chakra
Has his eyes closed and takes about six minutes
Do it when his eyes are closed? Where's the honor in that?

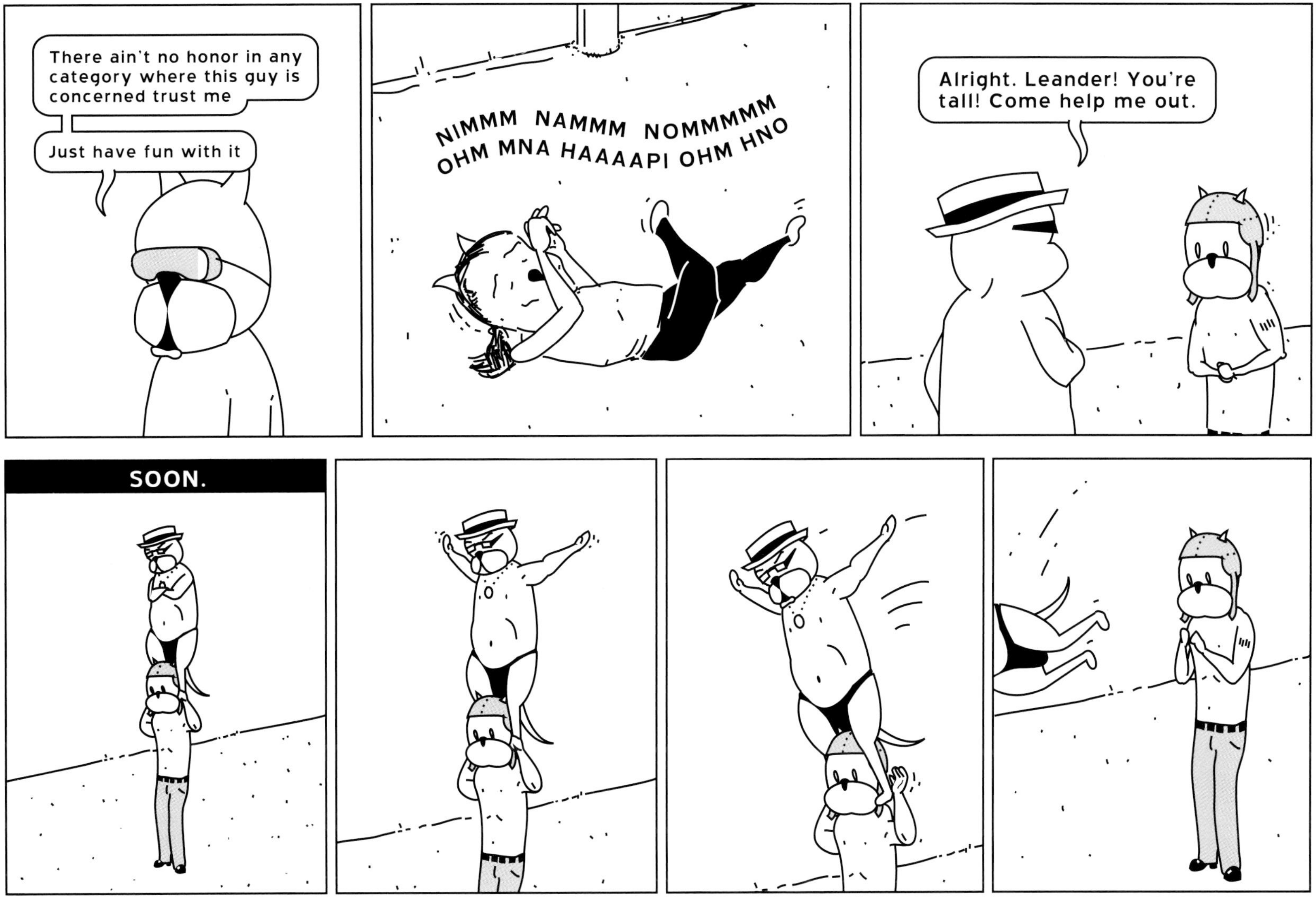
There ain't no honor in any category where this guy is concerned trust me
Just have fun with it
NIMMM NAMMM NOMMMMM
OHM MNA HAAAAPI OHM HNO
Alright. Leander! You're tall! Come help me out.
SOON.

I...AM...RUUUDE!
BEEEP
BEEEEP
BEEEEP
BEEEP
LATER THAT EVENING AROUND THE ACRES.
Some have said he was weaned on chicken milk and cocaine
He wakes up with Hennessy and oysters I know that much
Son of Rodney?
I heard he doesn't like music
I don't care what you ask me the boy's rude

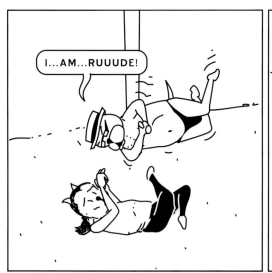

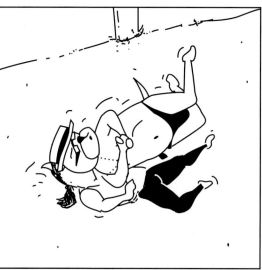

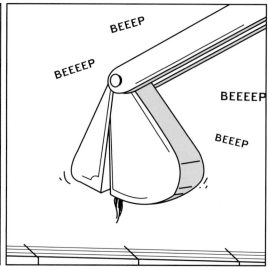

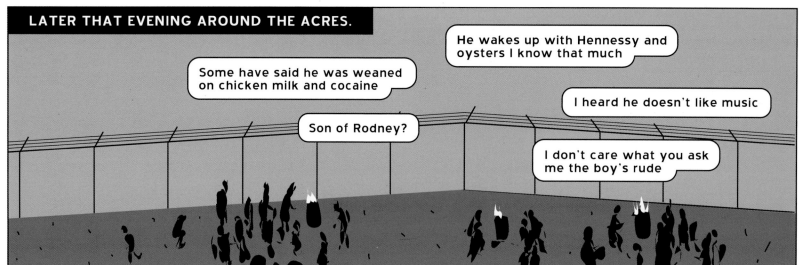

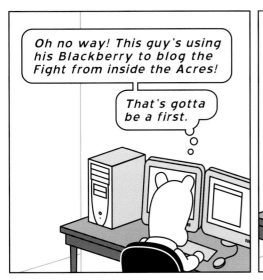

Oh no way! This guy's using his Blackberry to blog the Fight from inside the Acres!

That's gotta be a first.

Let's see if there's anything about Ray...

🎭 Gasps And Giggles 🎭
by Barry King **XML** **RSS**

Good news, Barryheads! I've made it through the first eight hours of Day One and have come under the wing of Son of Rodney, who by all accounts is the direct descendant of legendary champ **Rodney Leonard Stubbs**. A spitting image of the great RLS, he impressed us straightaway by taking down Perfect Ron Sipes with a single well-placed rabbit punch to the left shoulder mass.

He took Sipes?! Oh my god! GO RAY!

Things slowed considerably after that, as So-Rod and his best mate spent most of the rest of the afternoon strategising. At one point he gave us all a giggle by falling on a hippie chap, but then it was back to the X's and O's for him.

And what of England's own **Feckless Ted Cobb**? He's found a few blokes who'll gripe about **Arsenal** with him, and consequently So-Rod's ranks have swelled by about a dozen wankers!

Speaking of rank-swelling, Team Rodney's own **Leander**, a piscine local lad bent on the three-chord stuff, hooked up with a gaggle of mosh pit yobs and brought another twenty-odd souls into our mix.

Ray wouldn't roll with guys like that! What's going on? And what's with this "best mate" stuff?

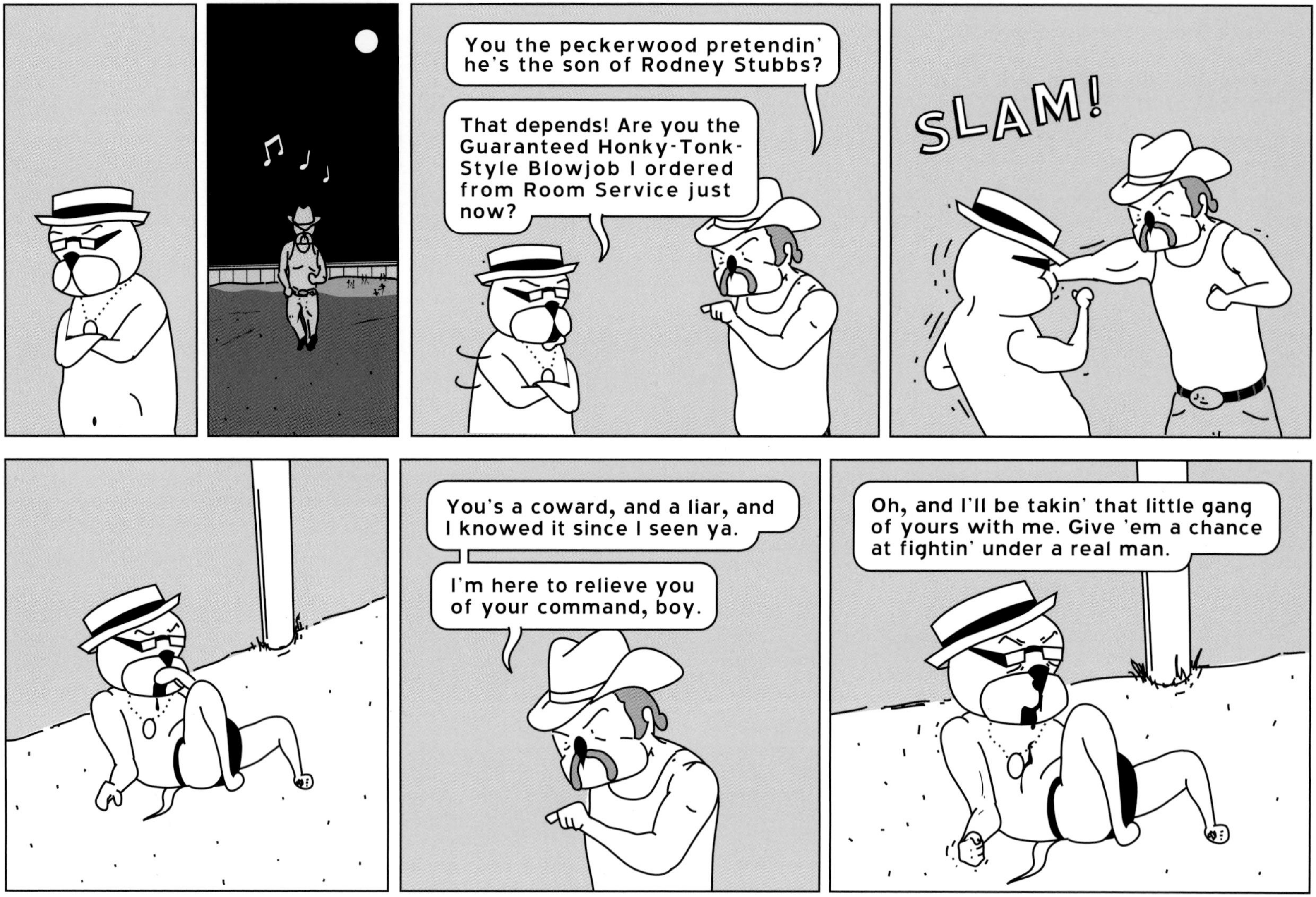
You the peckerwood pretendin' he's the son of Rodney Stubbs?
That depends! Are you the Guaranteed Honky-Tonk-Style Blowjob I ordered from Room Service just now?
SLAM!
You's a coward, and a liar, and I knowed it since I seen ya.
I'm here to relieve you of your command, boy.
Oh, and I'll be takin' that little gang of yours with me. Give 'em a chance at fightin' under a real man.

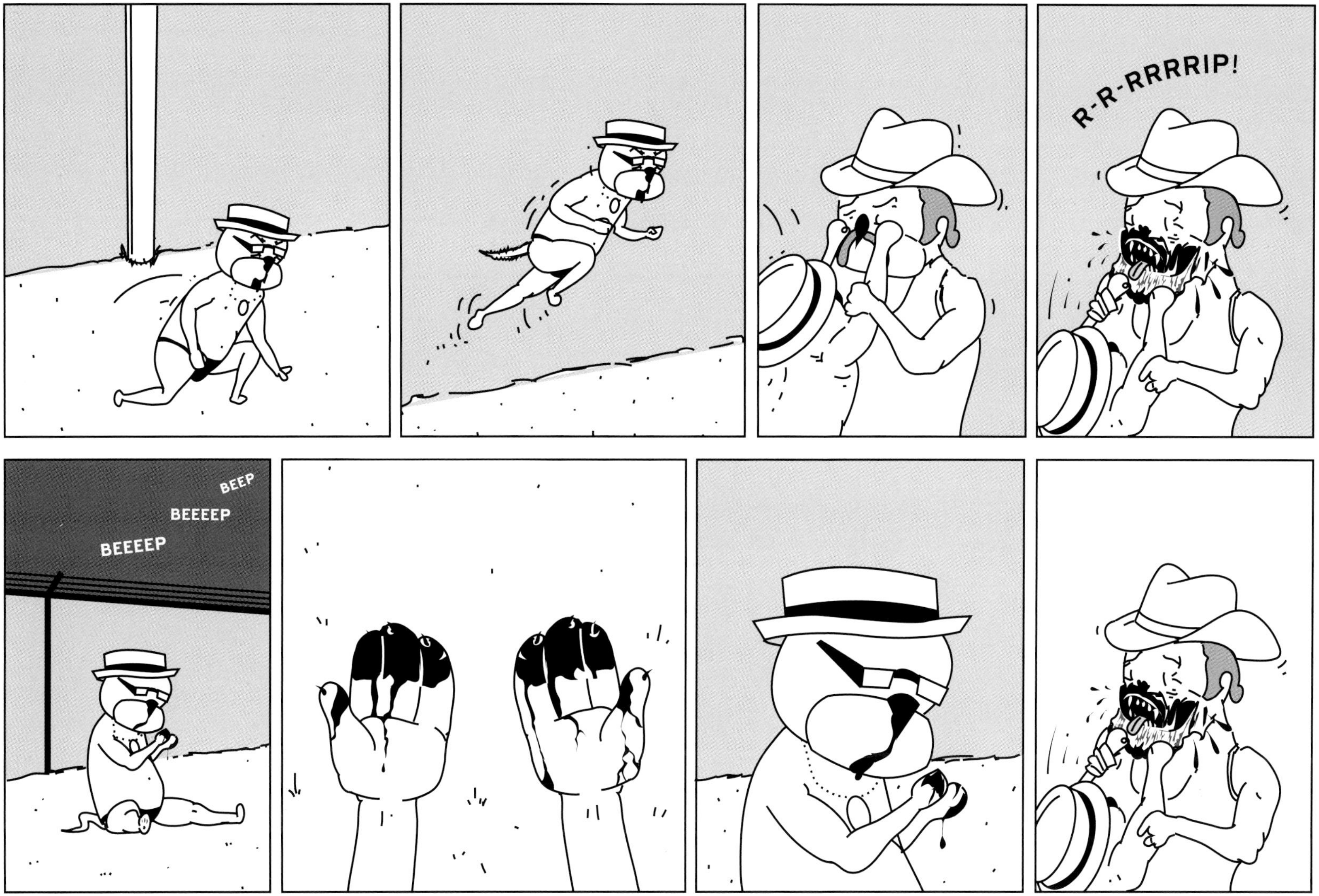
R-R-RRRRIP!
BEEEEP
BEEEEP
BEEP

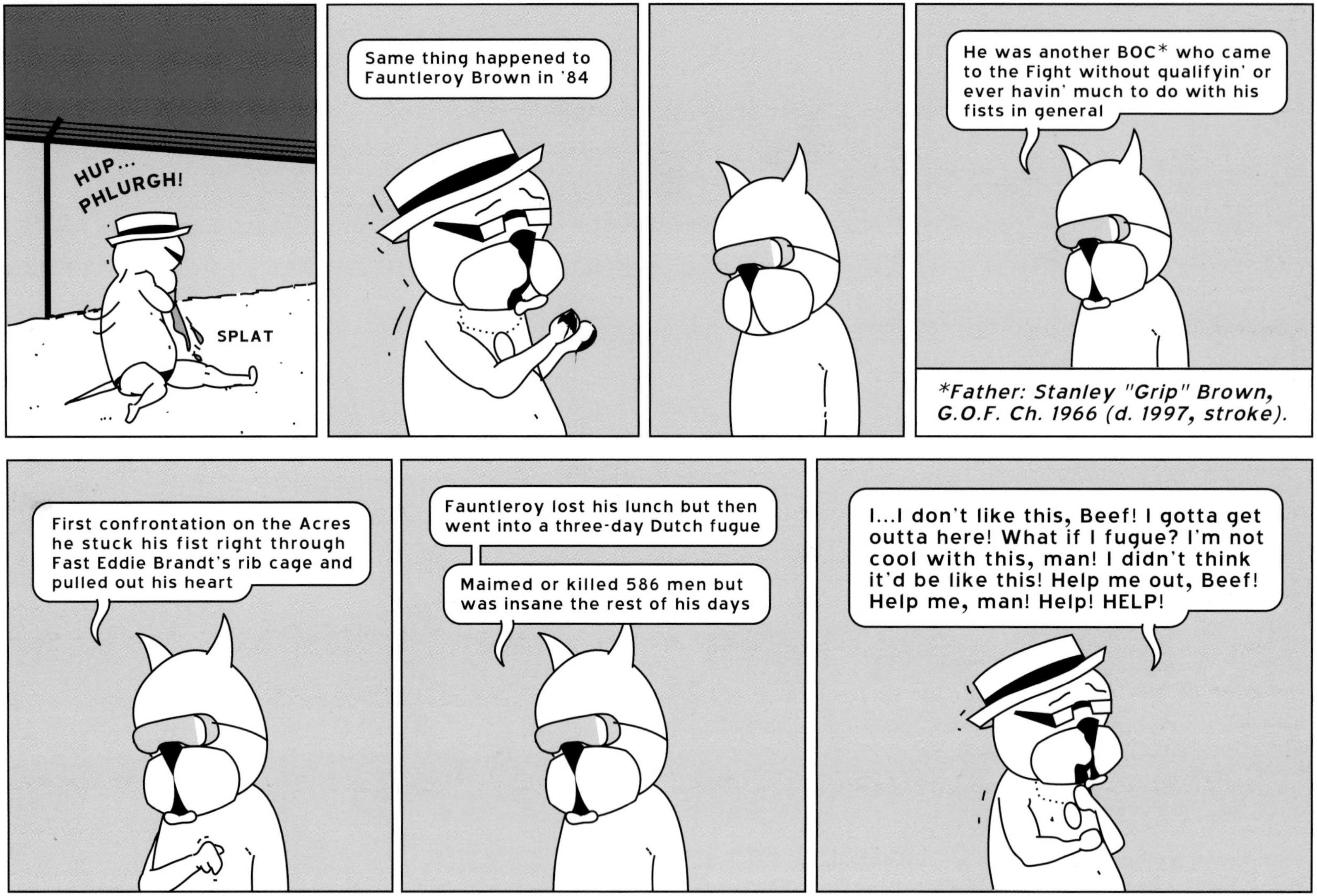
HUP...
PHLURGH!
SPLAT
Same thing happened to Fauntleroy Brown in '84
He was another BOC* who came to the Fight without qualifyin' or ever havin' much to do with his fists in general
*Father: Stanley "Grip" Brown, G.O.F. Ch. 1966 (d. 1997, stroke).
First confrontation on the Acres he stuck his fist right through Fast Eddie Brandt's rib cage and pulled out his heart
Fauntleroy lost his lunch but then went into a three-day Dutch fugue
Maimed or killed 586 men but was insane the rest of his days
I...I don't like this, Beef! I gotta get outta here! What if I fugue? I'm not cool with this, man! I didn't think it'd be like this! Help me out, Beef! Help me, man! Help! HELP!

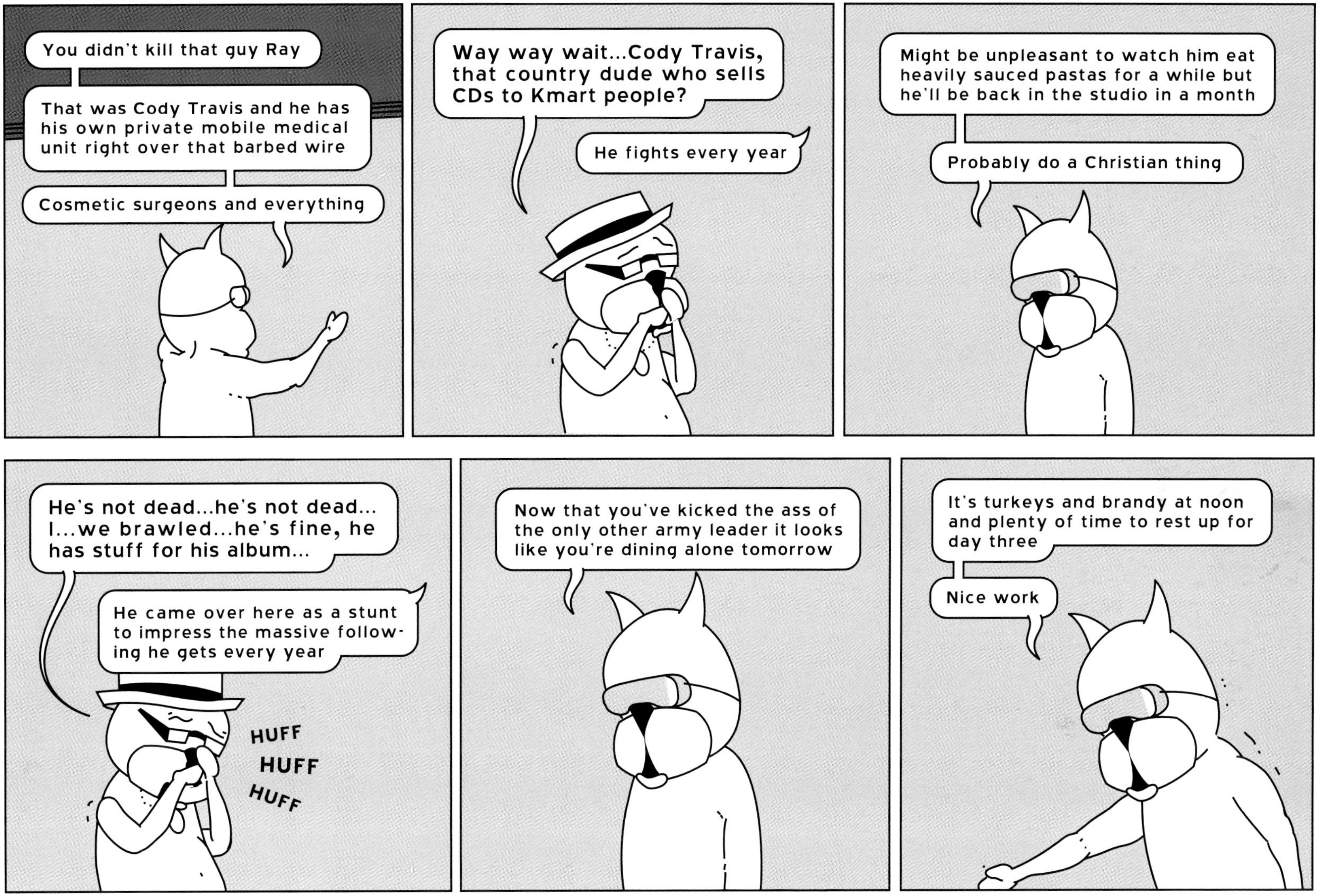
You didn't kill that guy Ray
That was Cody Travis and he has his own private mobile medical unit right over that barbed wire
Cosmetic surgeons and everything
Way way wait...Cody Travis, that country dude who sells CDs to Kmart people?
He fights every year
Might be unpleasant to watch him eat heavily sauced pastas for a while but he'll be back in the studio in a month
Probably do a Christian thing
He's not dead...he's not dead... I...we brawled...he's fine, he has stuff for his album...
He came over here as a stunt to impress the massive following he gets every year
HUFF
HUFF
HUFF
Now that you've kicked the ass of the only other army leader it looks like you're dining alone tomorrow
It's turkeys and brandy at noon and plenty of time to rest up for day three
Nice work

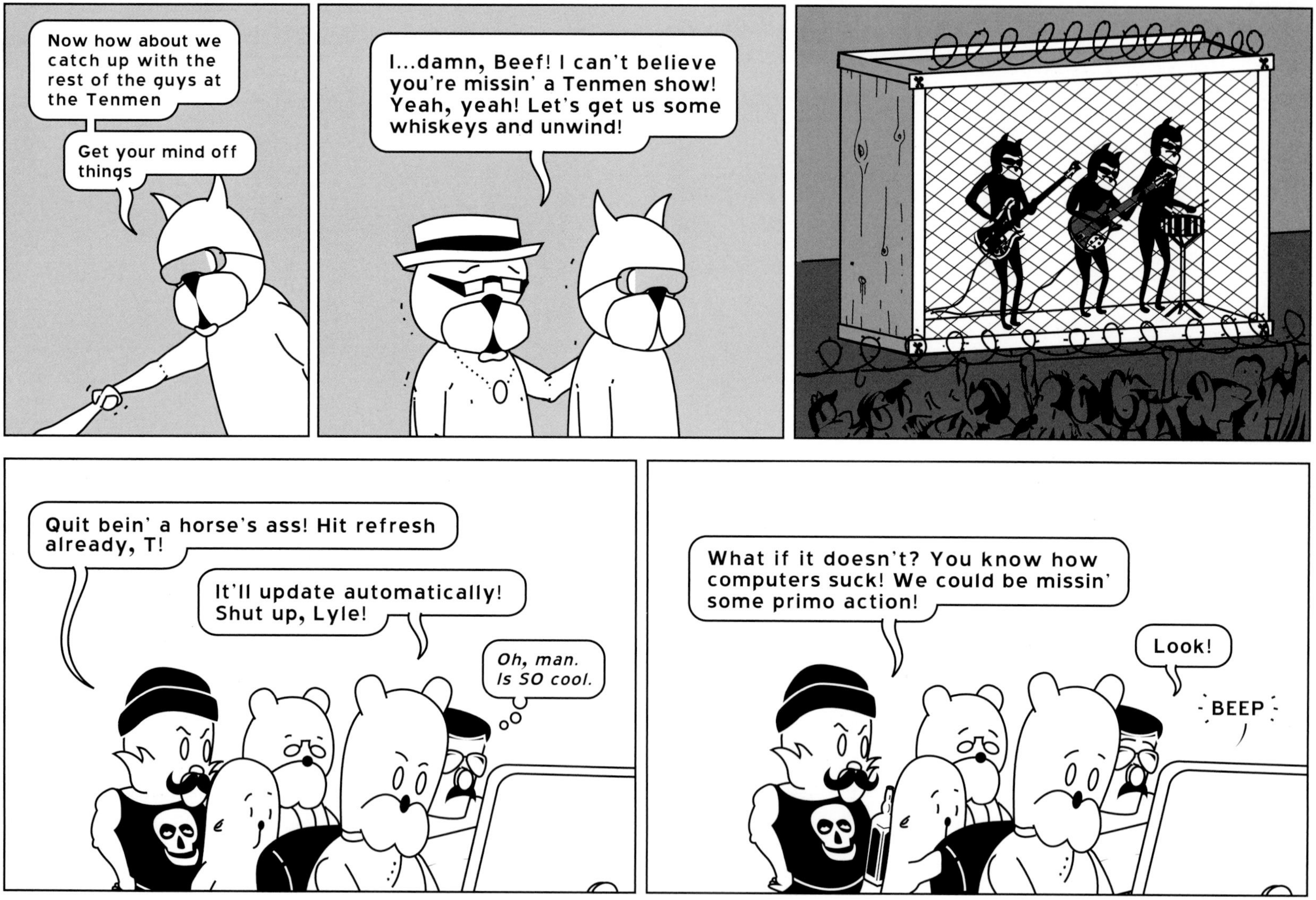
Now how about we catch up with the rest of the guys at the Tenmen
Get your mind off things
I...damn, Beef! I can't believe you're missin' a Tenmen show! Yeah, yeah! Let's get us some whiskeys and unwind!
Quit bein' a horse's ass! Hit refresh already, T!
It'll update automatically! Shut up, Lyle!
Oh, man. Is SO cool.
What if it doesn't? You know how computers suck! We could be missin' some primo action!
Look!
BEEP

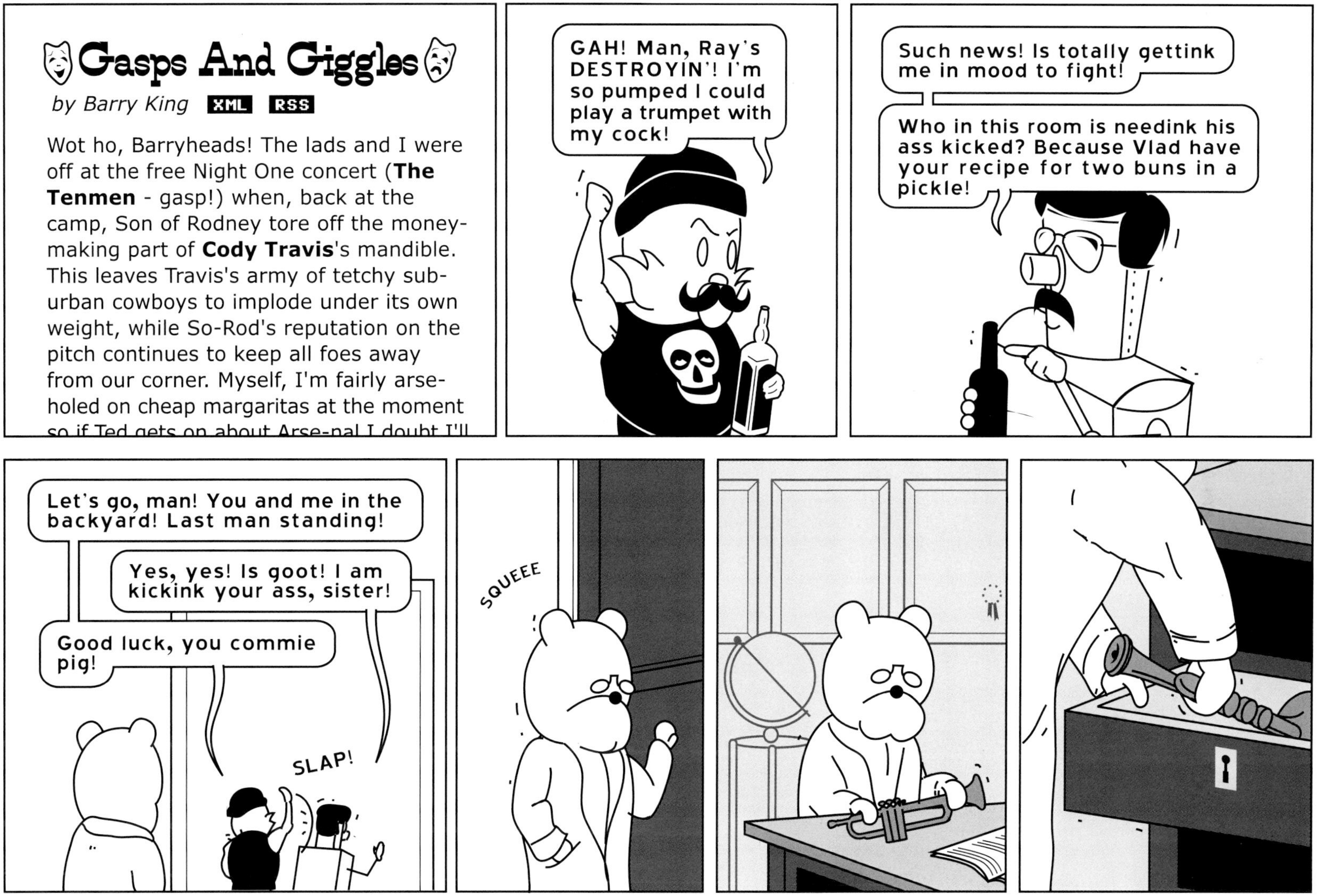
Gasps And Giggles
by Barry King XML RSS
Wot ho, Barryheads! The lads and I were off at the free Night One concert (**The Tenmen** - gasp!) when, back at the camp, Son of Rodney tore off the money-making part of **Cody Travis**'s mandible. This leaves Travis's army of tetchy sub-urban cowboys to implode under its own weight, while So-Rod's reputation on the pitch continues to keep all foes away from our corner. Myself, I'm fairly arse-holed on cheap margaritas at the moment
GAH! Man, Ray's DESTROYIN'! I'm so pumped I could play a trumpet with my cock!
Such news! Is totally gettink me in mood to fight!
Who in this room is needink his ass kicked? Because Vlad have your recipe for two buns in a pickle!
Let's go, man! You and me in the backyard! Last man standing!
Yes, yes! Is goot! I am kickink your ass, sister!
Good luck, you commie pig!
SLAP!
SQUEEE

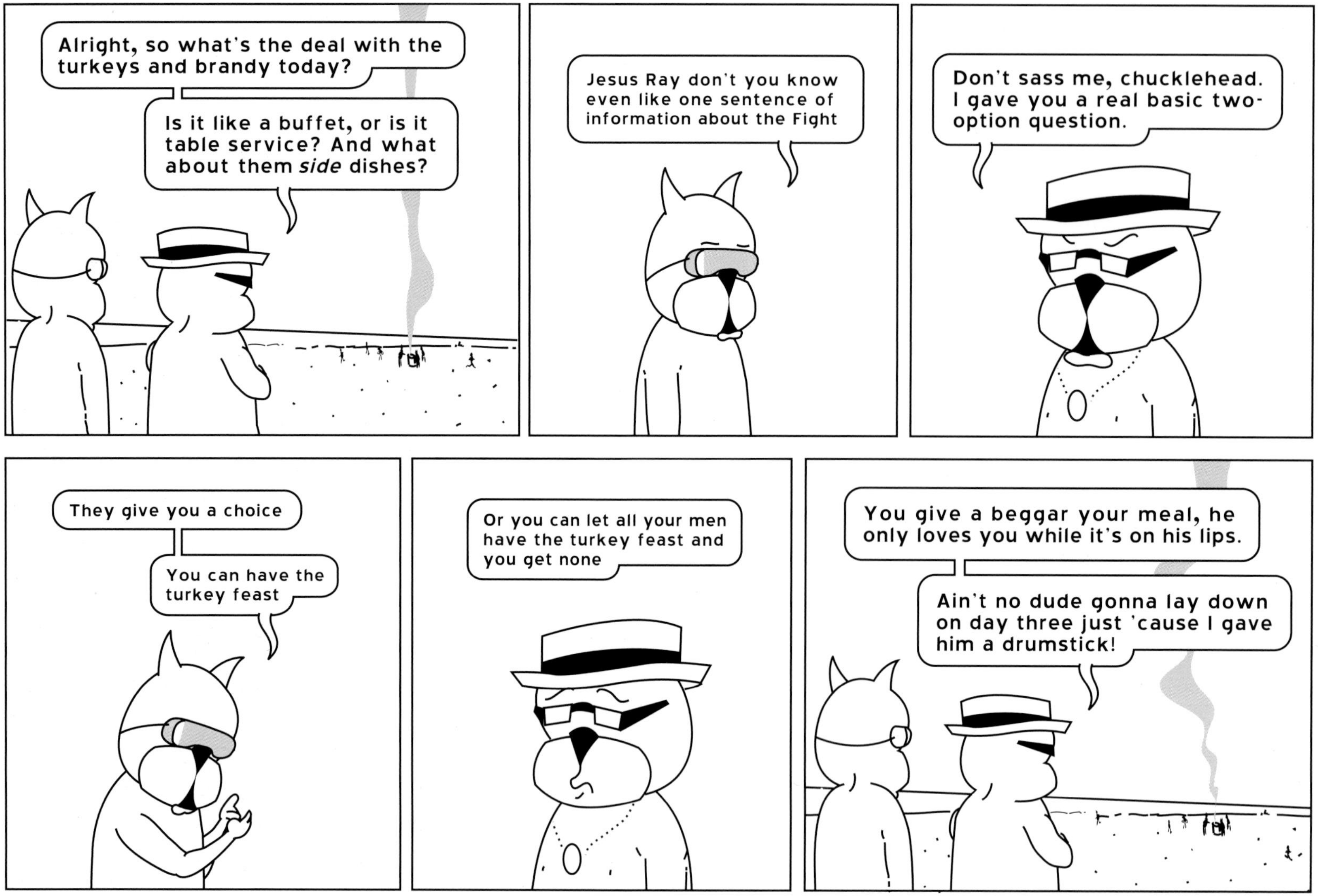
Alright, so what's the deal with the turkeys and brandy today?
Is it like a buffet, or is it table service? And what about them *side* dishes?
Jesus Ray don't you know even like one sentence of information about the Fight
Don't sass me, chucklehead. I gave you a real basic two-option question.
They give you a choice
You can have the turkey feast
Or you can let all your men have the turkey feast and you get none
You give a beggar your meal, he only loves you while it's on his lips.
Ain't no dude gonna lay down on day three just 'cause I gave him a drumstick!

Interesting

Very few men go that way

And NOW, these words of advice from Rodney Leonard Stubbs, Great Outdoor Fight champion 1973!

HISSSS

POP

SSSS

Ain't give no sucker your meal, it adds to nothin' and he is an animal all the while, no receipt on file, no loyalty no style.

WRRRRRR

SSSSSSS

TANDY

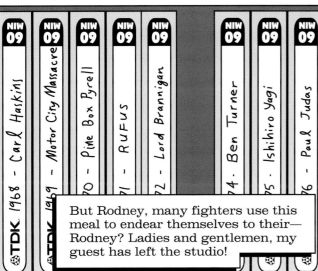

TDK 1968 - Carl Haskins

TDK 1969 - Motor City Massacre

NIW 09 - Pine Box Pyrell

NIW 09 - Rufus

NIW 09 - Lord Brannigan

NIW 09 - Ben Turner

NIW 09 - Ishihiro Yagi

NIW 09 - Paul Judas

But Rodney, many fighters use this meal to endear themselves to their— Rodney? Ladies and gentlemen, my guest has left the studio!

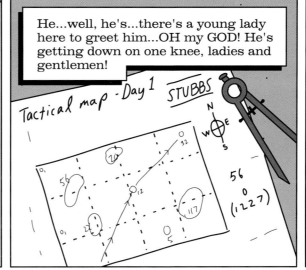

He...well, he's...there's a young lady here to greet him...OH my GOD! He's getting down on one knee, ladies and gentlemen!

Tactical map - Day 1   STUBBS

56
(1227)

It looks like...yes! Yes! Our champion is ASKING for this young woman's hand in marriage!

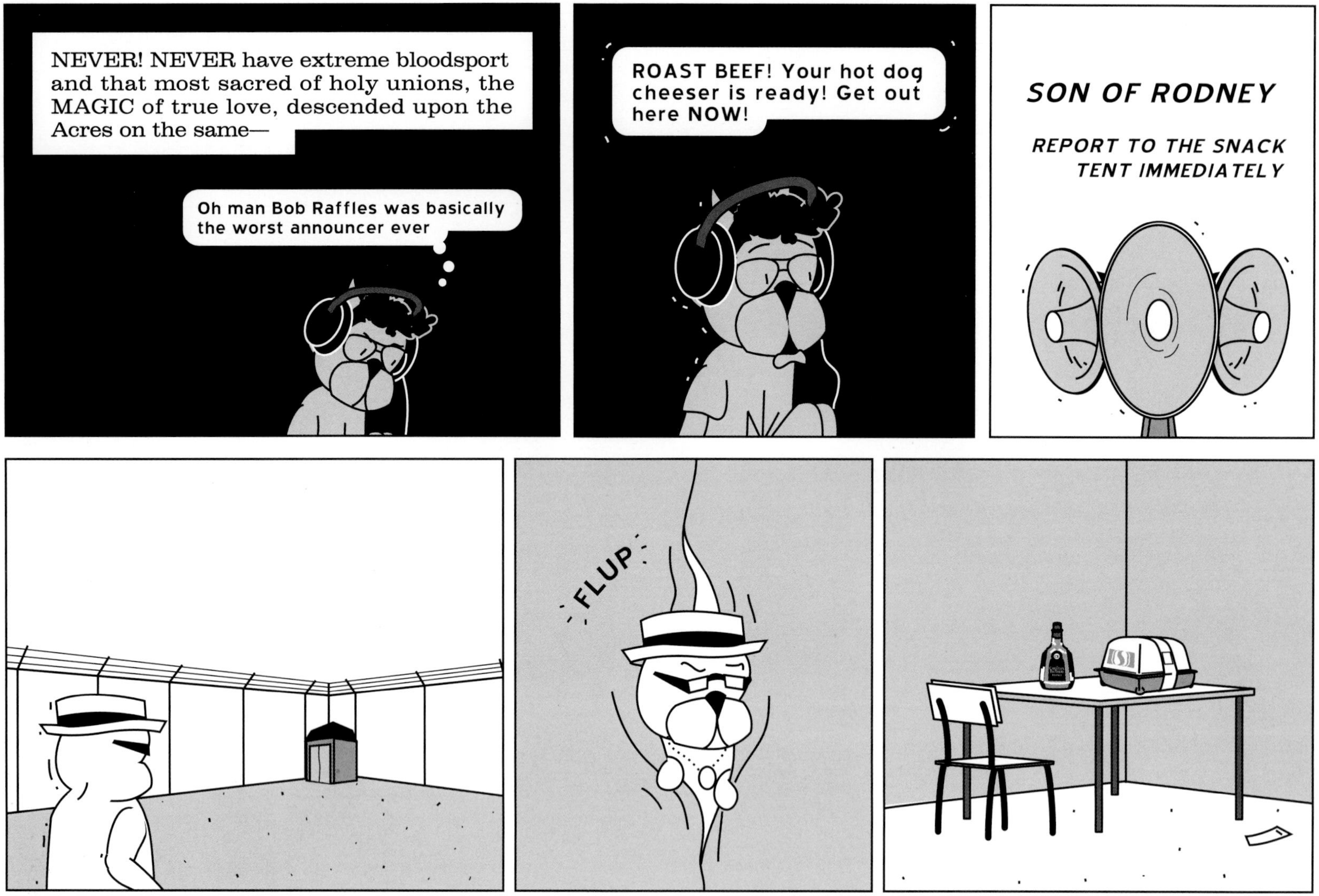
NEVER! NEVER have extreme bloodsport and that most sacred of holy unions, the MAGIC of true love, descended upon the Acres on the same—
Oh man Bob Raffles was basically the worst announcer ever
ROAST BEEF! Your hot dog cheeser is ready! Get out here NOW!
SON OF RODNEY
REPORT TO THE SNACK TENT IMMEDIATELY
FLUP

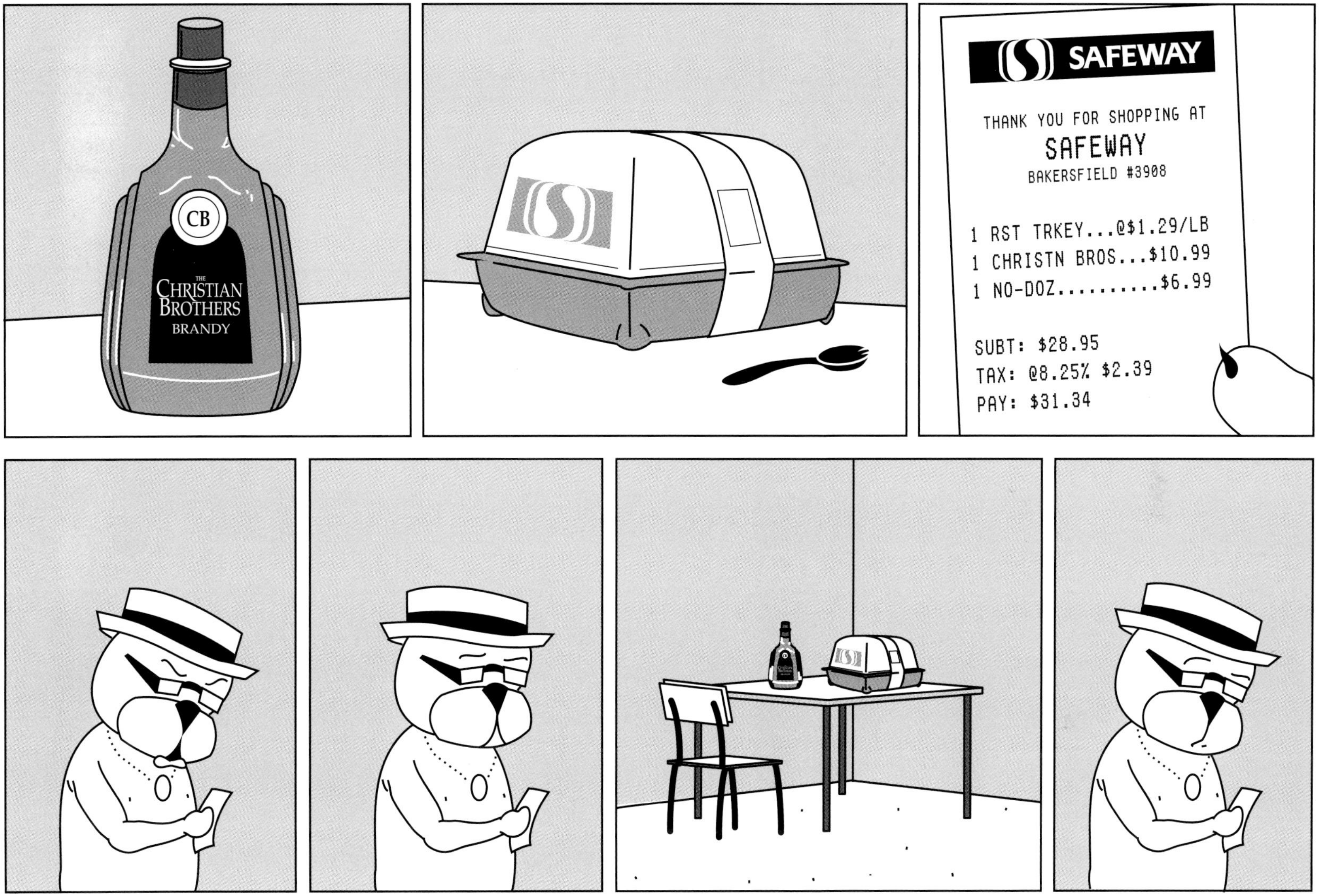
CB
THE CHRISTIAN BROTHERS
BRANDY
SAFEWAY
THANK YOU FOR SHOPPING AT
SAFEWAY
BAKERSFIELD #3908
1 RST TRKEY...@$1.29/LB
1 CHRISTN BROS...$10.99
1 NO-DOZ..........$6.99
SUBT: $28.95
TAX: @8.25% $2.39
PAY: $31.34

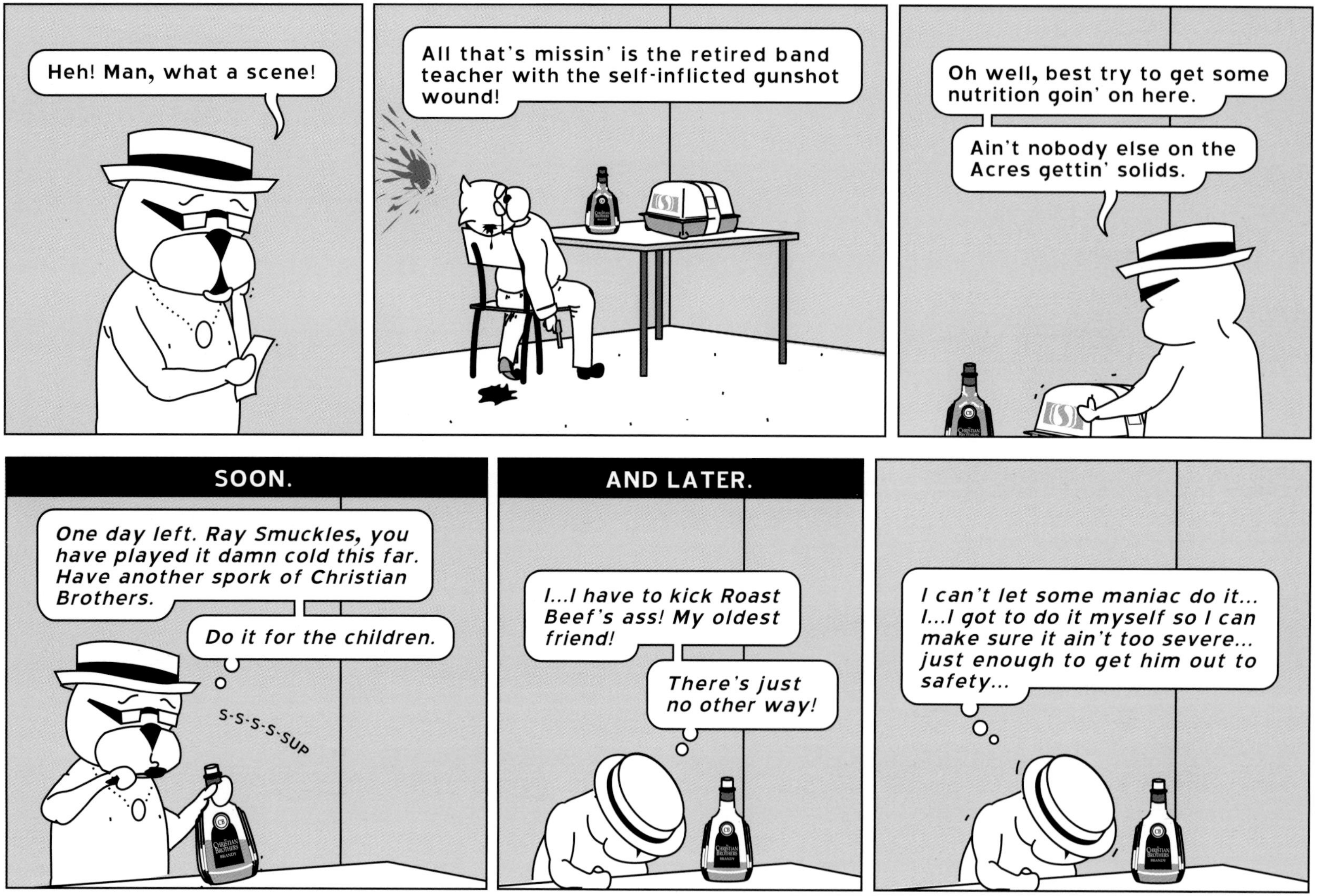
Heh! Man, what a scene!
All that's missin' is the retired band teacher with the self-inflicted gunshot wound!
Oh well, best try to get some nutrition goin' on here.
Ain't nobody else on the Acres gettin' solids.
SOON.
One day left. Ray Smuckles, you have played it damn cold this far. Have another spork of Christian Brothers.
Do it for the children.
S-S-S-S-SUP
AND LATER.
I...I have to kick Roast Beef's ass! My oldest friend!
There's just no other way!
I can't let some maniac do it... I...I got to do it myself so I can make sure it ain't too severe... just enough to get him out to safety...

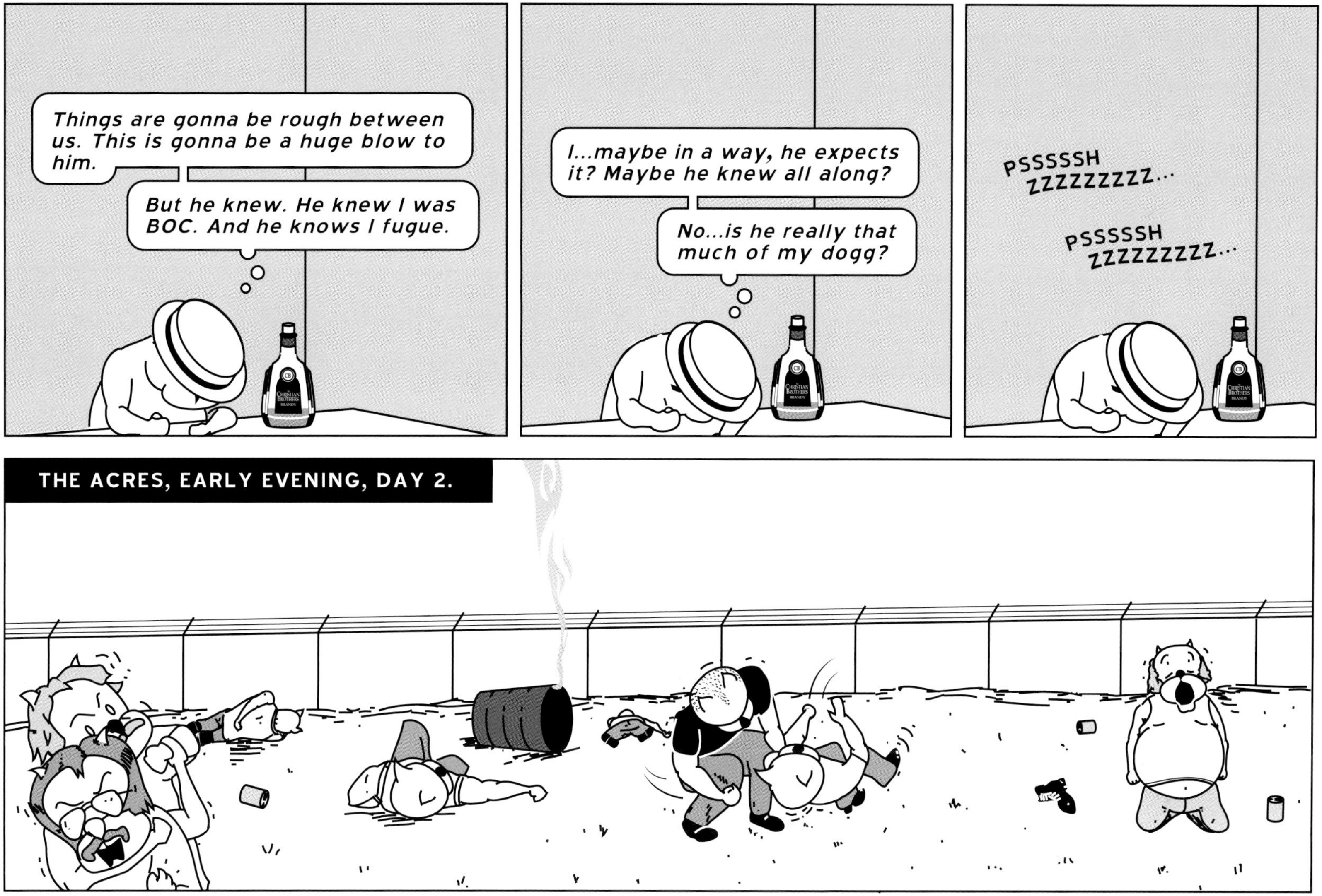
Things are gonna be rough between us. This is gonna be a huge blow to him.
But he knew. He knew I was BOC. And he knows I fugue.
I...maybe in a way, he expects it? Maybe he knew all along?
No...is he really that much of my dogg?
PSSSSSH ZZZZZZZZZ...
PSSSSSH ZZZZZZZZZ...
THE ACRES, EARLY EVENING, DAY 2.

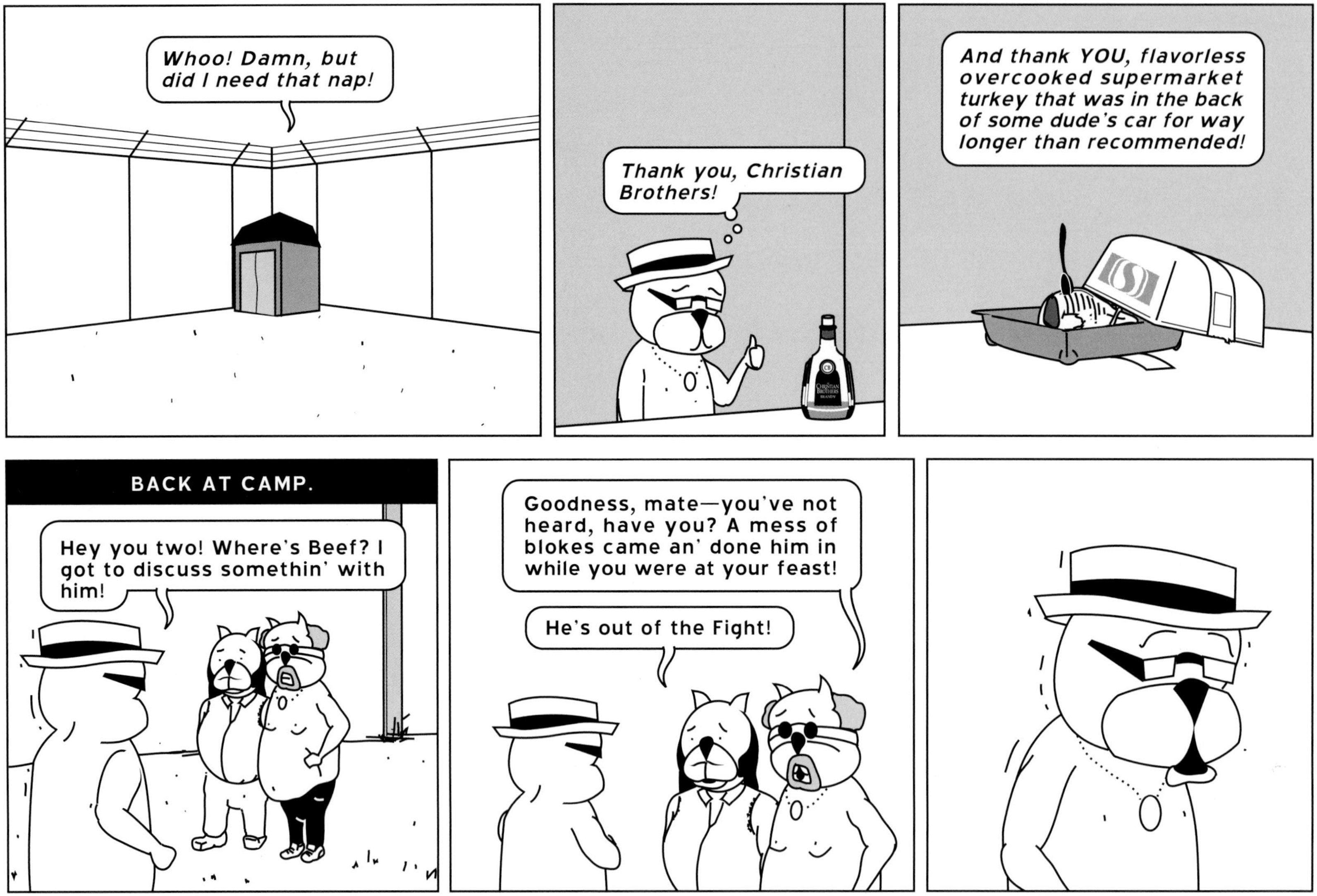
Whoo! Damn, but did I need that nap!
Thank you, Christian Brothers!
CHRISTIAN BROTHERS BRANDY
And thank YOU, flavorless overcooked supermarket turkey that was in the back of some dude's car for way longer than recommended!
BACK AT CAMP.
Hey you two! Where's Beef? I got to discuss somethin' with him!
Goodness, mate—you've not heard, have you? A mess of blokes came an' done him in while you were at your feast!
He's out of the Fight!

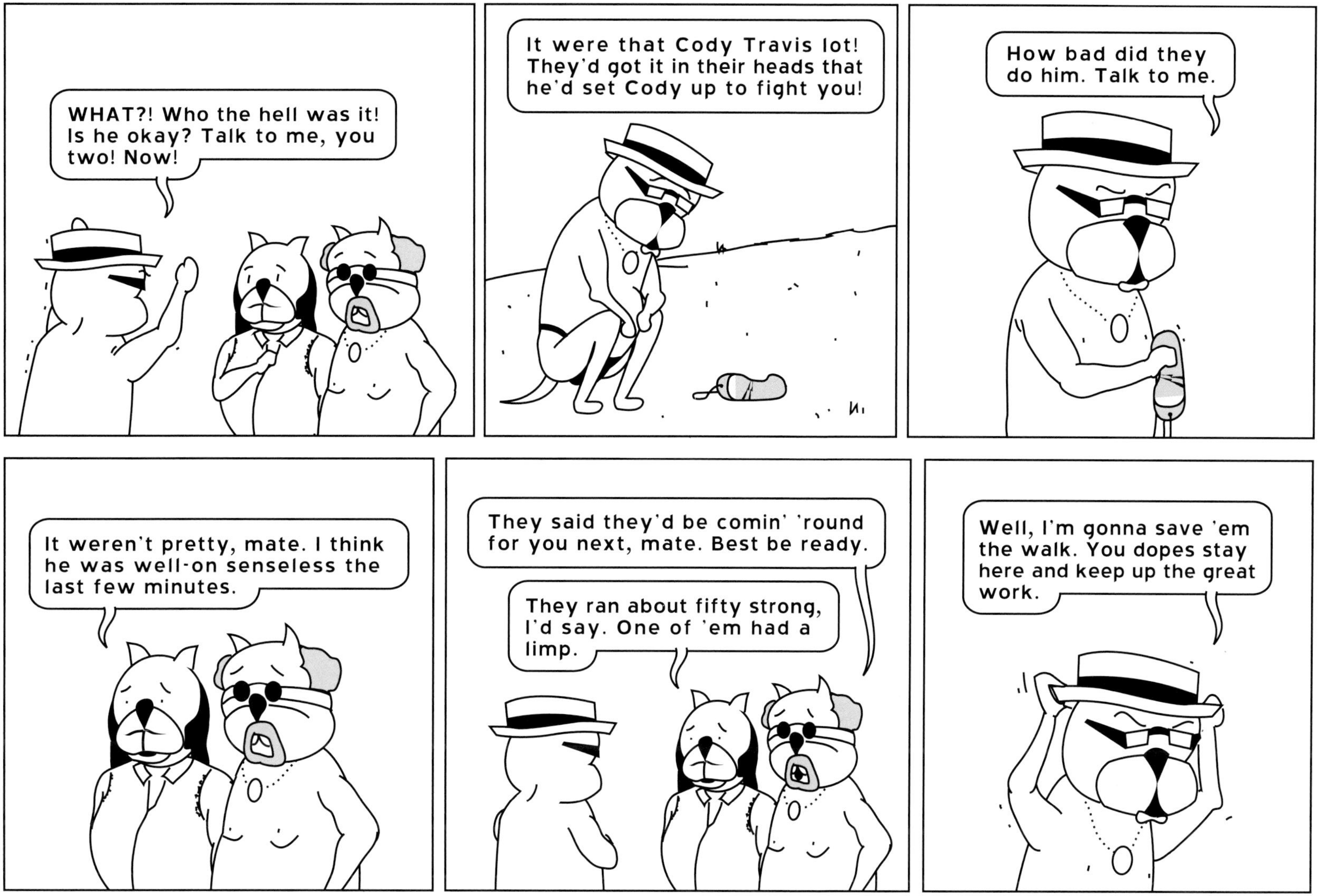
WHAT?! Who the hell was it! Is he okay? Talk to me, you two! Now!
It were that Cody Travis lot! They'd got it in their heads that he'd set Cody up to fight you!
How bad did they do him. Talk to me.
It weren't pretty, mate. I think he was well-on senseless the last few minutes.
They said they'd be comin' 'round for you next, mate. Best be ready.
They ran about fifty strong, I'd say. One of 'em had a limp.
Well, I'm gonna save 'em the walk. You dopes stay here and keep up the great work.

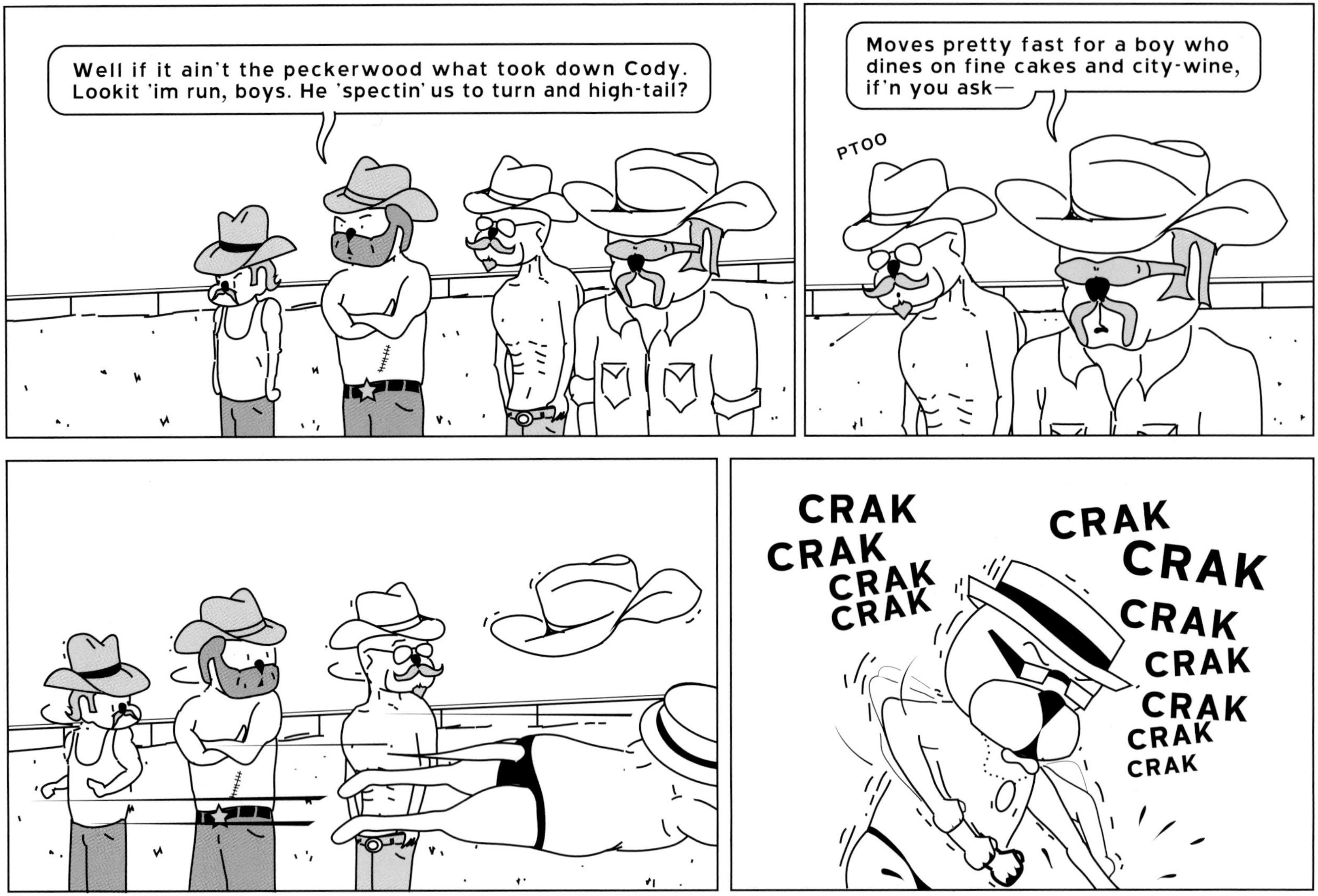
Well if it ain't the peckerwood what took down Cody. Lookit 'im run, boys. He 'spectin' us to turn and high-tail?
Moves pretty fast for a boy who dines on fine cakes and city-wine, if'n you ask—
PTOO
CRAK
CRAK
CRAK
CRAK
CRAK
CRAK
CRAK
CRAK
CRAK
CRAK
CRAK

ALRIGHT! Which one 'a you am I makin' into cowboy sauce next!

...and so on through the night did Son of Rodney turn Cody Travis' tick-pimps, boilbacks, and yard-sleepers into cowboy sauce.

The dawn of the third day saw a decimated field, with only a handful of weary, wary contenders left.

CHATTER CHATTER CHATTER CHATTER CHATTER CHATTER CHATTER

SHIVER

CHATTER CHATTER CHATTER CHATTER CHATTER CHATTER CHATTER JESUS H. CHRIST! CHATTER CHATTER CHATTER

Oh DAMN it! It's like six degrees out here! C'mon, stay lit!

POUF

SLIF

UGH nice work Ray

Beef! What in the hell?!

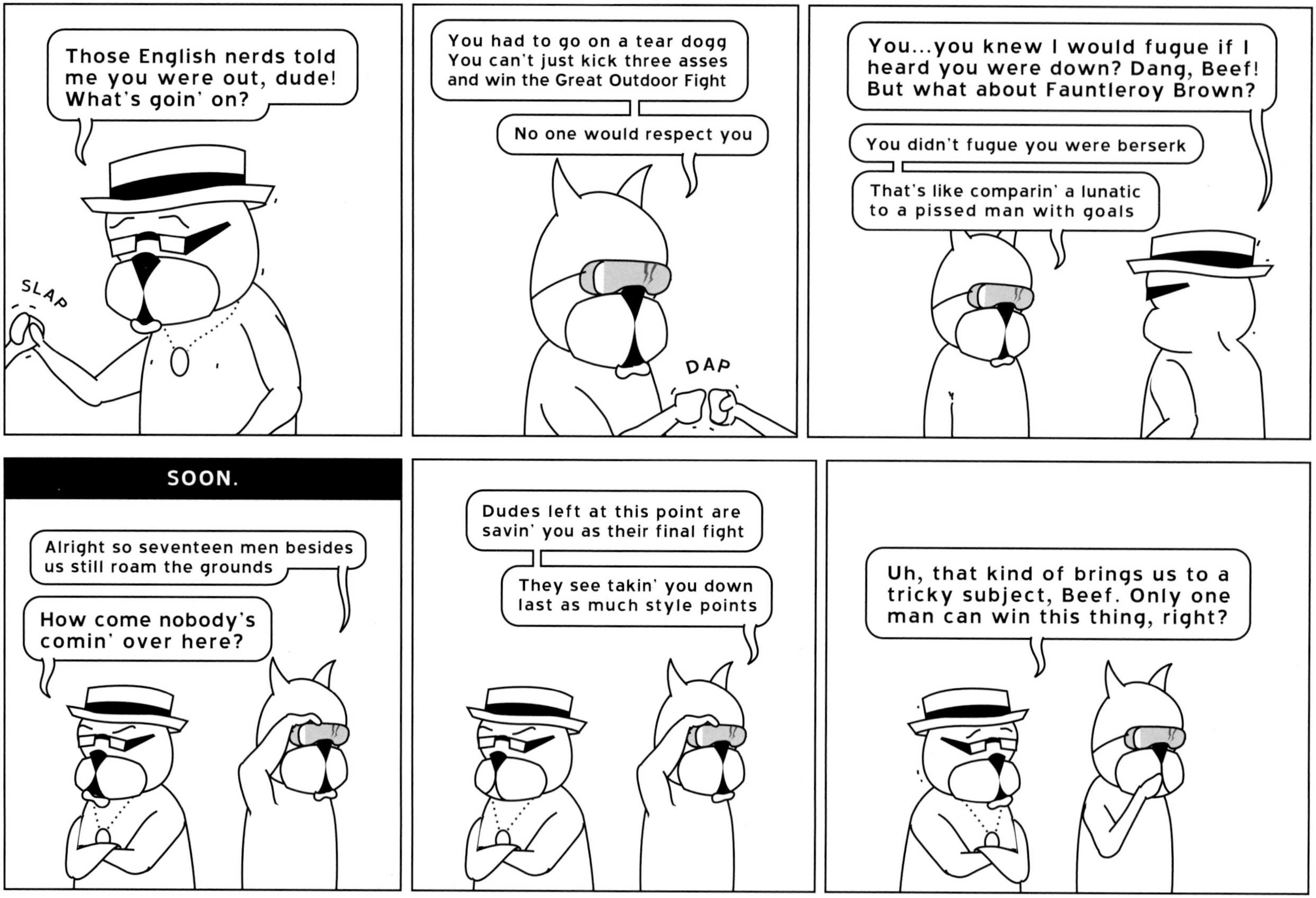
Those English nerds told me you were out, dude! What's goin' on?
SLAP
You had to go on a tear dogg You can't just kick three asses and win the Great Outdoor Fight
No one would respect you
DAP
You...you knew I would fugue if I heard you were down? Dang, Beef! But what about Fauntleroy Brown?
You didn't fugue you were berserk
That's like comparin' a lunatic to a pissed man with goals
SOON.
Alright so seventeen men besides us still roam the grounds
How come nobody's comin' over here?
Dudes left at this point are savin' you as their final fight
They see takin' you down last as much style points
Uh, that kind of brings us to a tricky subject, Beef. Only one man can win this thing, right?

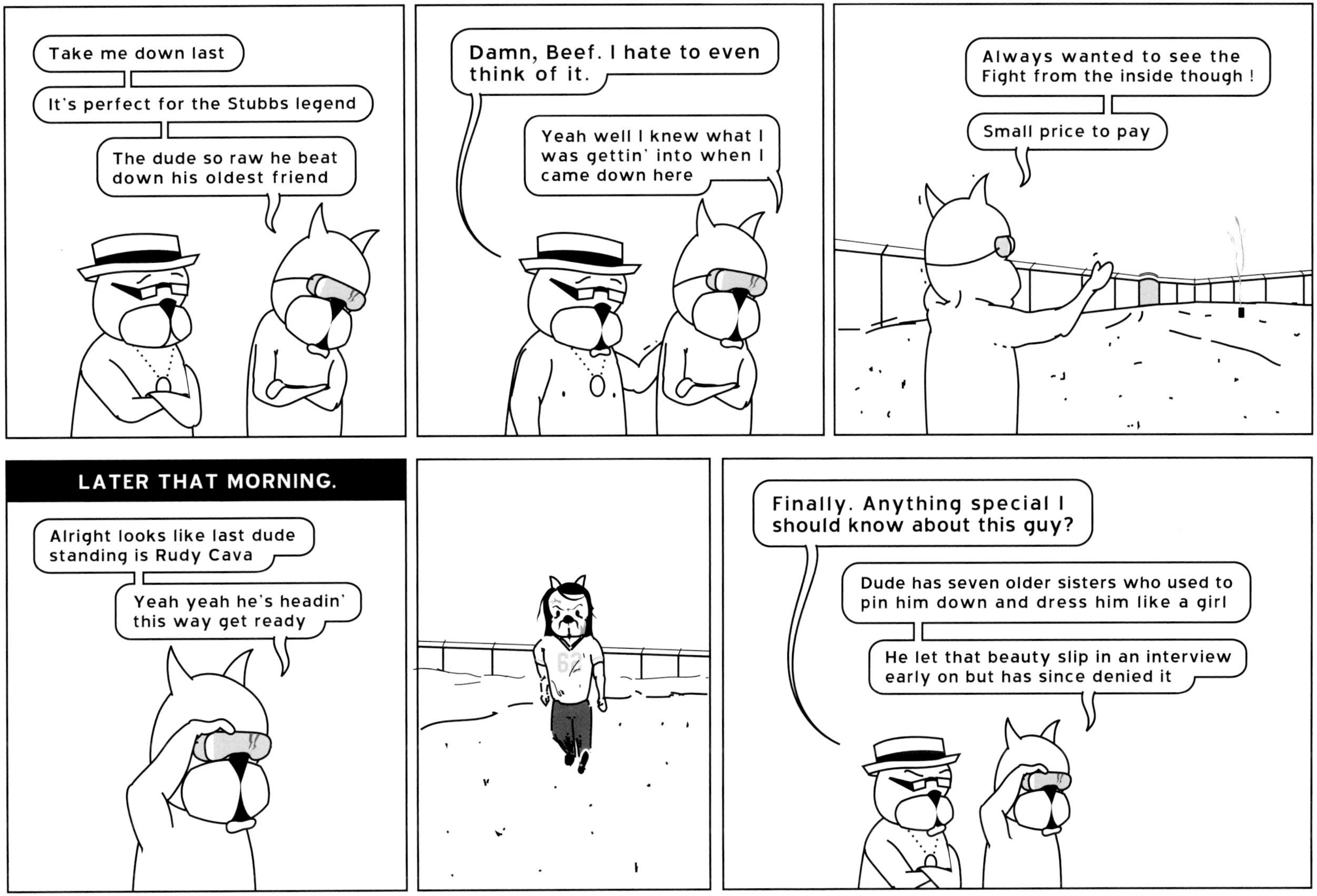
Take me down last
It's perfect for the Stubbs legend
The dude so raw he beat down his oldest friend
Damn, Beef. I hate to even think of it.
Yeah well I knew what I was gettin' into when I came down here
Always wanted to see the Fight from the inside though !
Small price to pay
LATER THAT MORNING.
Alright looks like last dude standing is Rudy Cava
Yeah yeah he's headin' this way get ready
Finally. Anything special I should know about this guy?
Dude has seven older sisters who used to pin him down and dress him like a girl
He let that beauty slip in an interview early on but has since denied it

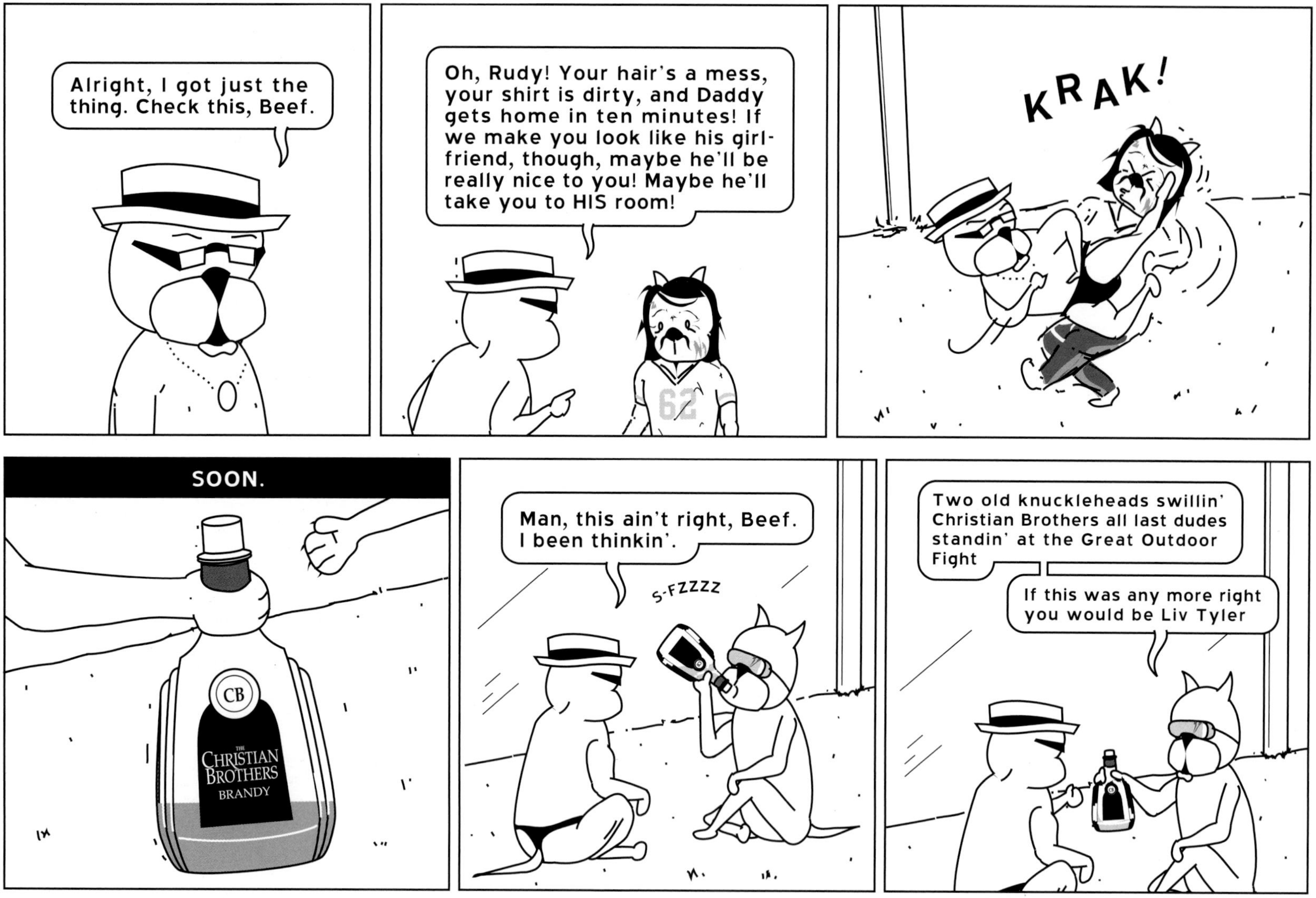

Alright, I got just the thing. Check this, Beef.
Oh, Rudy! Your hair's a mess, your shirt is dirty, and Daddy gets home in ten minutes! If we make you look like his girlfriend, though, maybe he'll be really nice to you! Maybe he'll take you to HIS room!
62
KRAK!
SOON.
CB
THE CHRISTIAN BROTHERS BRANDY
Man, this ain't right, Beef. I been thinkin'.
S-FZZZZ
Two old knuckleheads swillin' Christian Brothers all last dudes standin' at the Great Outdoor Fight
If this was any more right you would be Liv Tyler

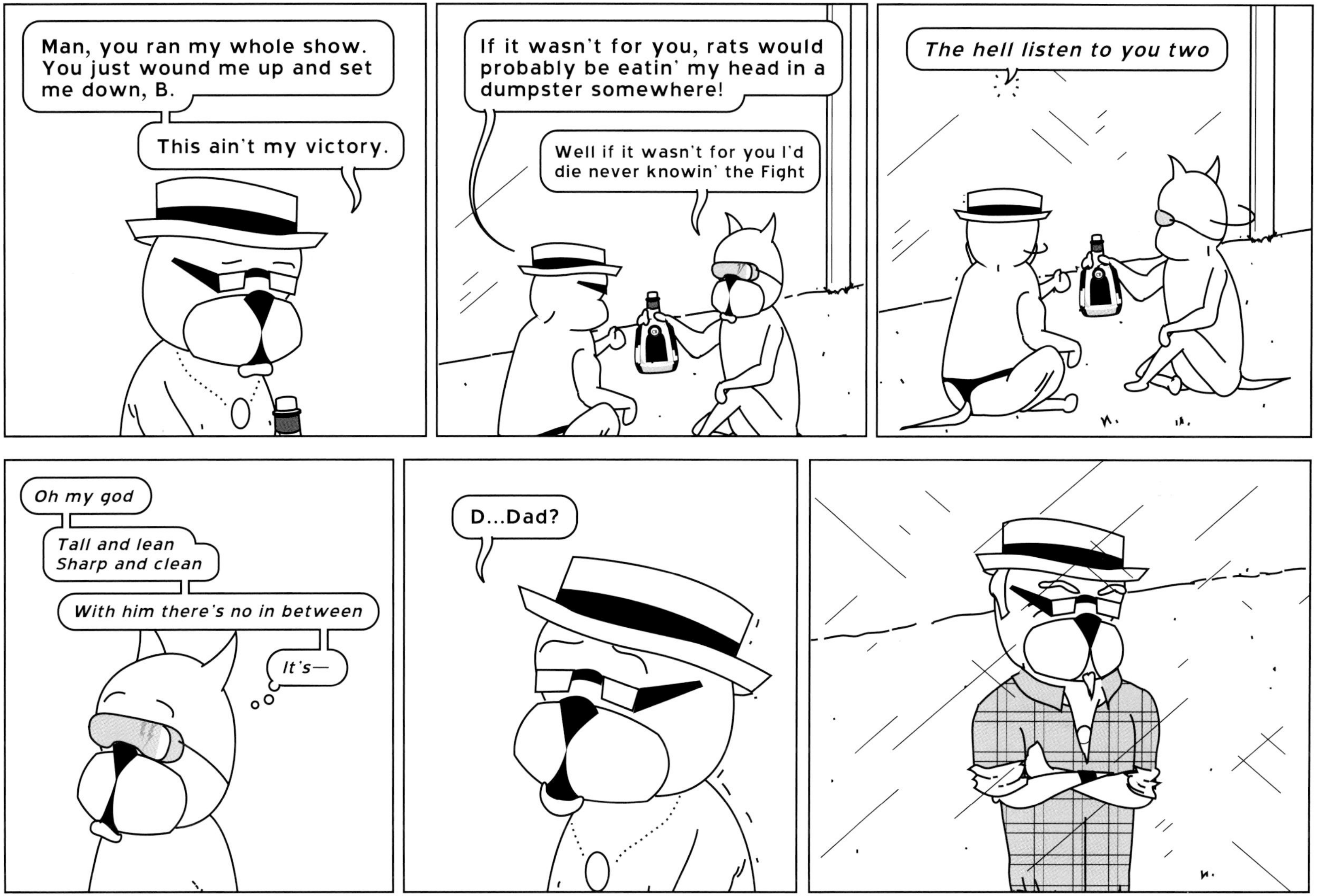
Man, you ran my whole show. You just wound me up and set me down, B.
This ain't my victory.
If it wasn't for you, rats would probably be eatin' my head in a dumpster somewhere!
Well if it wasn't for you I'd die never knowin' the Fight
The hell listen to you two
Oh my god
Tall and lean Sharp and clean
With him there's no in between
It's—
D...Dad?

Seriously, Ted! How come you stuff your pants?
You've not had my life. Don't judge me.
CLIK
CLIK
CLIK
TAP

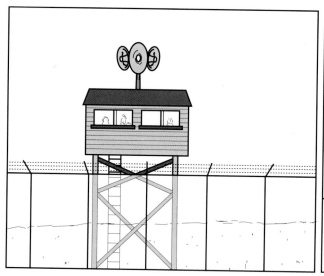

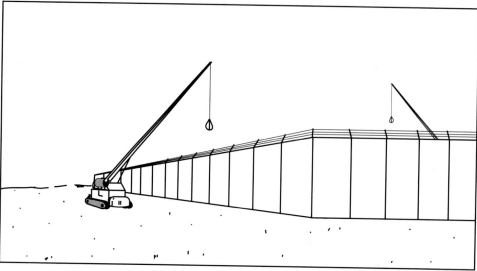

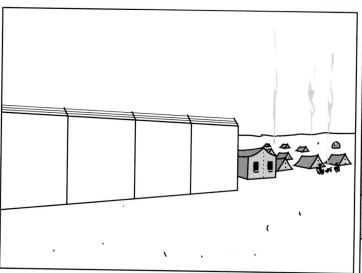

Who TeeVo Tomás di Tank Engine. I hate dees train.

CLIK

It's live! It's live! Barry just went live! Day Three!

zzzzzz

BEEP!

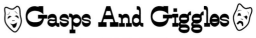

🎭 Gasps And Giggles 🎭

by Barry King **XML** **RSS**

The old **pyloric**'s gone wonky since I had me skull cracked in by **a quiet fellow in denim**...was a bit too busy catching up with **Fark** and missed his approach...not to worry, though, Barryheads! I've still got the best and freshest in Fight non-fiction!

Our lord and master **So-Rod** still stands in the Acres, but as I hinted previously, the rest of us were done up proper by the bigger and better sort.

Oh my god! Awesome! Awesome! Absolutely no way!

zz...zzz

The Latino Health Crisis joined us most recently, having lasted halfway through the second night before what I think he's describing as **an Italian ninja with drawings on his boobs** dispatched him. His English is a bit dodgy, so that's not the final word.

Prior to that fell **Leander**, the punk rock lad who was so engrossed in a contest to have neck veins like **Henry Rollins** that he passed out and dislocated his shoulder on a tyre rim. Now he's just hanging about bugging Ted about his "sub-Saharan comb-over."

Which brings us to **Ted**, who does indeed stuff with the best of 'em, but that's neither here nor there. I don't know why I mention it. Anyways, Ted had been ordered to guard the southern perimeter of our camp, but was fished in by a charming bloke who noted that the calluses on Ted's knuckles implied prior employment as a carpet fitter or floorer, and made pleasant trade talk before dishing up a full-service beating.

More on So-Rod as we see it!

- -

Up your arse, Fleet Street! The citizen blog shall destroy you! —BK

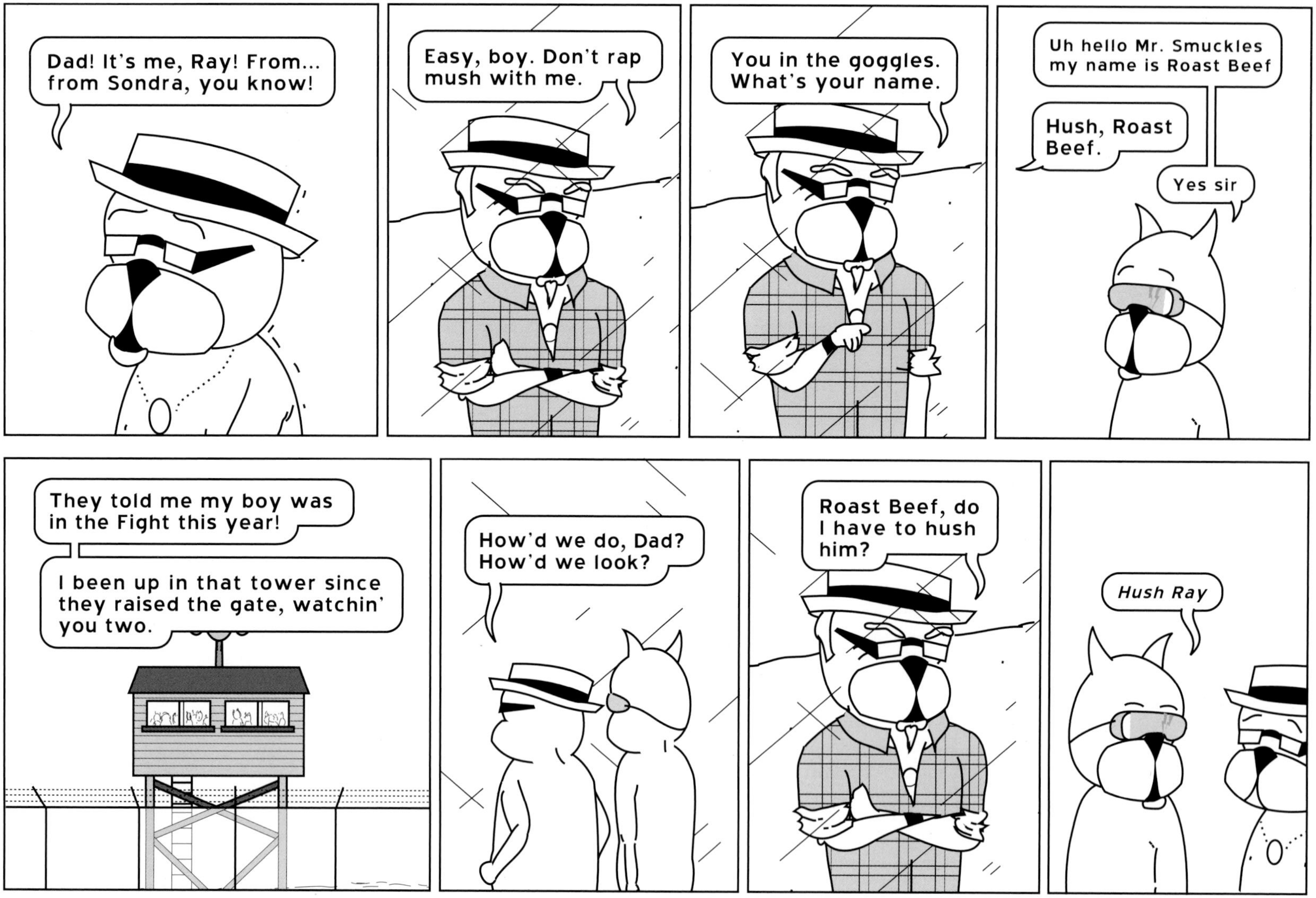
Dad! It's me, Ray! From... from Sondra, you know!
Easy, boy. Don't rap mush with me.
You in the goggles. What's your name.
Uh hello Mr. Smuckles my name is Roast Beef
Hush, Roast Beef.
Yes sir
They told me my boy was in the Fight this year!
I been up in that tower since they raised the gate, watchin' you two.
How'd we do, Dad? How'd we look?
Roast Beef, do I have to hush him?
Hush Ray

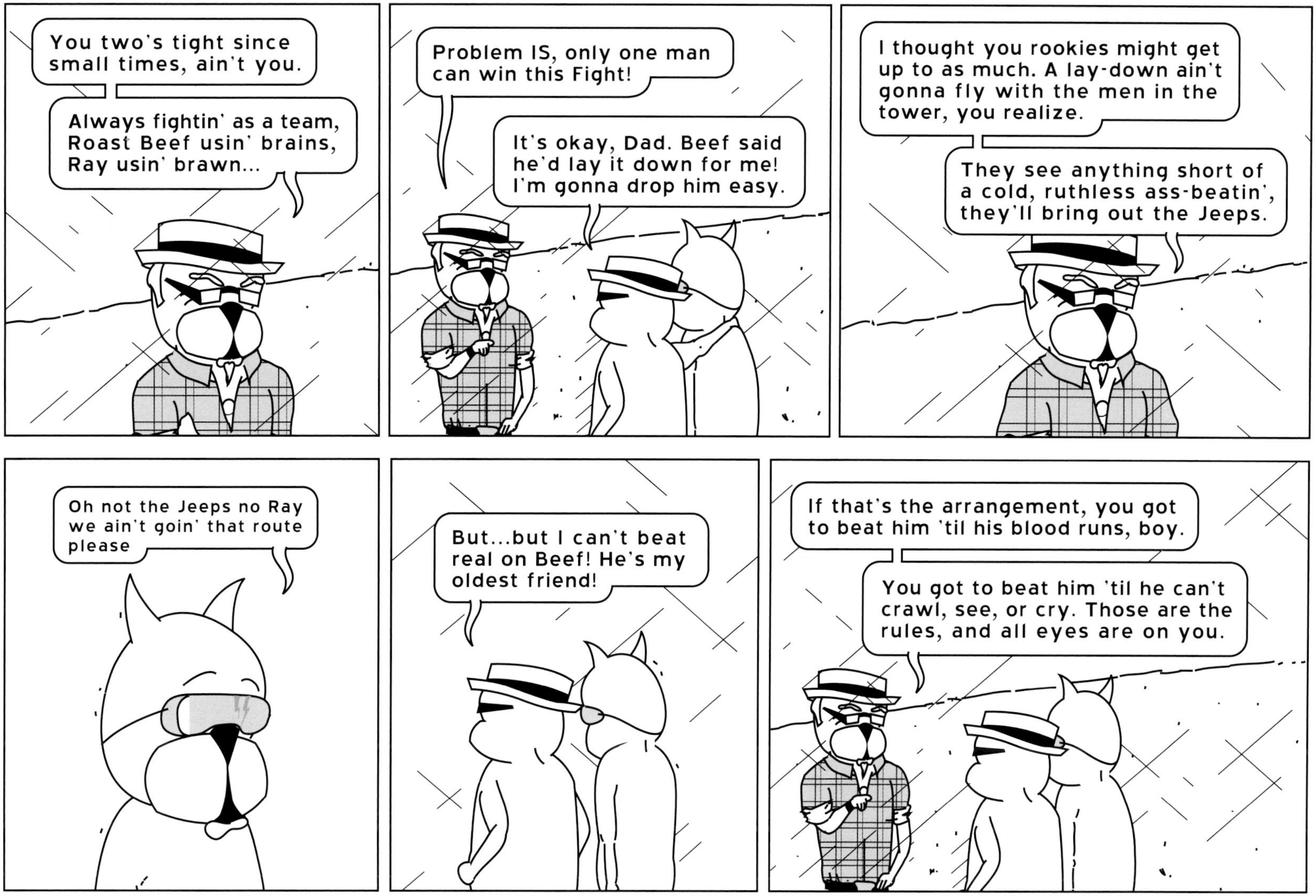
You two's tight since small times, ain't you.
Always fightin' as a team, Roast Beef usin' brains, Ray usin' brawn...
Problem IS, only one man can win this Fight!
It's okay, Dad. Beef said he'd lay it down for me! I'm gonna drop him easy.
I thought you rookies might get up to as much. A lay-down ain't gonna fly with the men in the tower, you realize.
They see anything short of a cold, ruthless ass-beatin', they'll bring out the Jeeps.
Oh not the Jeeps no Ray we ain't goin' that route please
But...but I can't beat real on Beef! He's my oldest friend!
If that's the arrangement, you got to beat him 'til his blood runs, boy.
You got to beat him 'til he can't crawl, see, or cry. Those are the rules, and all eyes are on you.

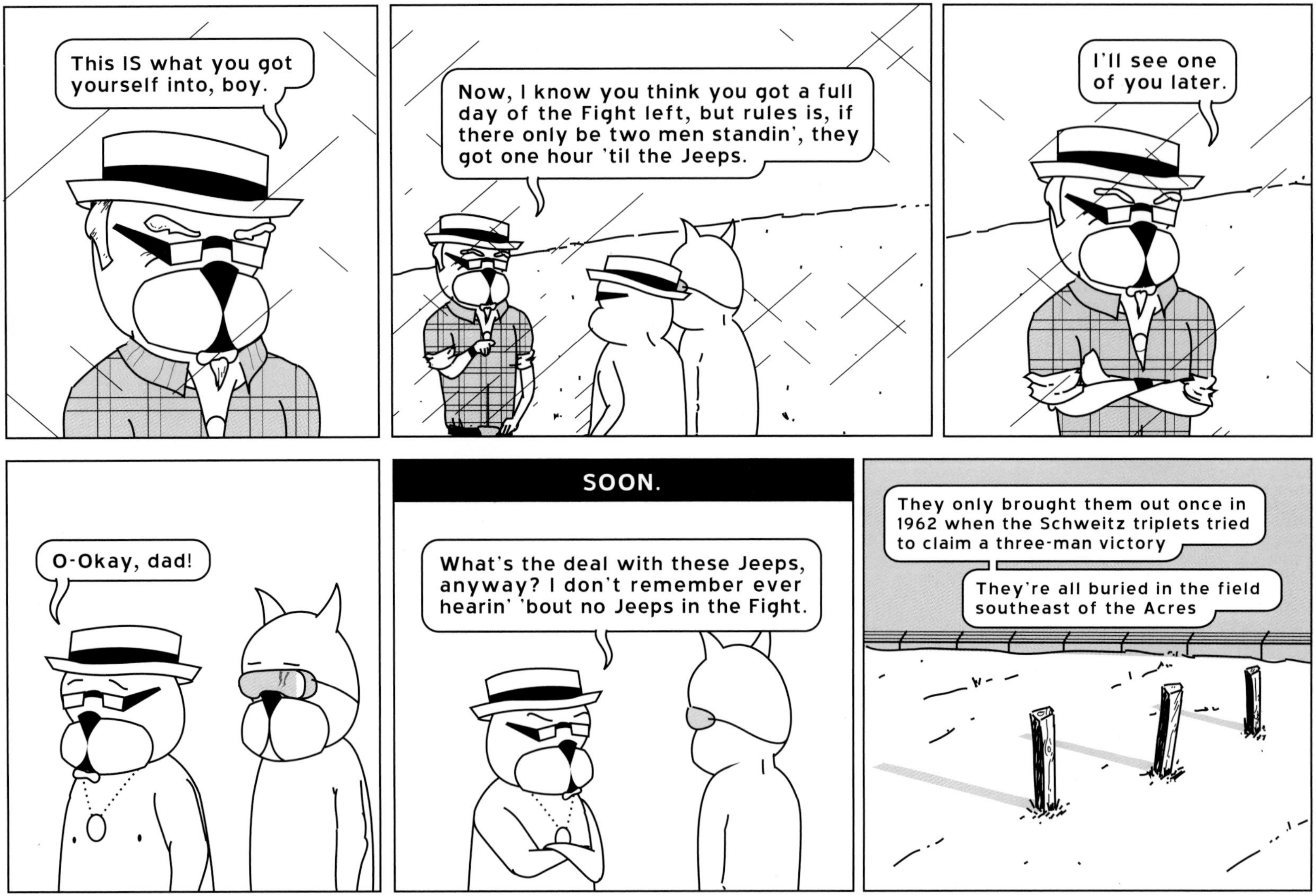
This IS what you got yourself into, boy.
Now, I know you think you got a full day of the Fight left, but rules is, if there only be two men standin', they got one hour 'til the Jeeps.
I'll see one of you later.
O-Okay, dad!
SOON.
What's the deal with these Jeeps, anyway? I don't remember ever hearin' 'bout no Jeeps in the Fight.
They only brought them out once in 1962 when the Schweitz triplets tried to claim a three-man victory
They're all buried in the field southeast of the Acres

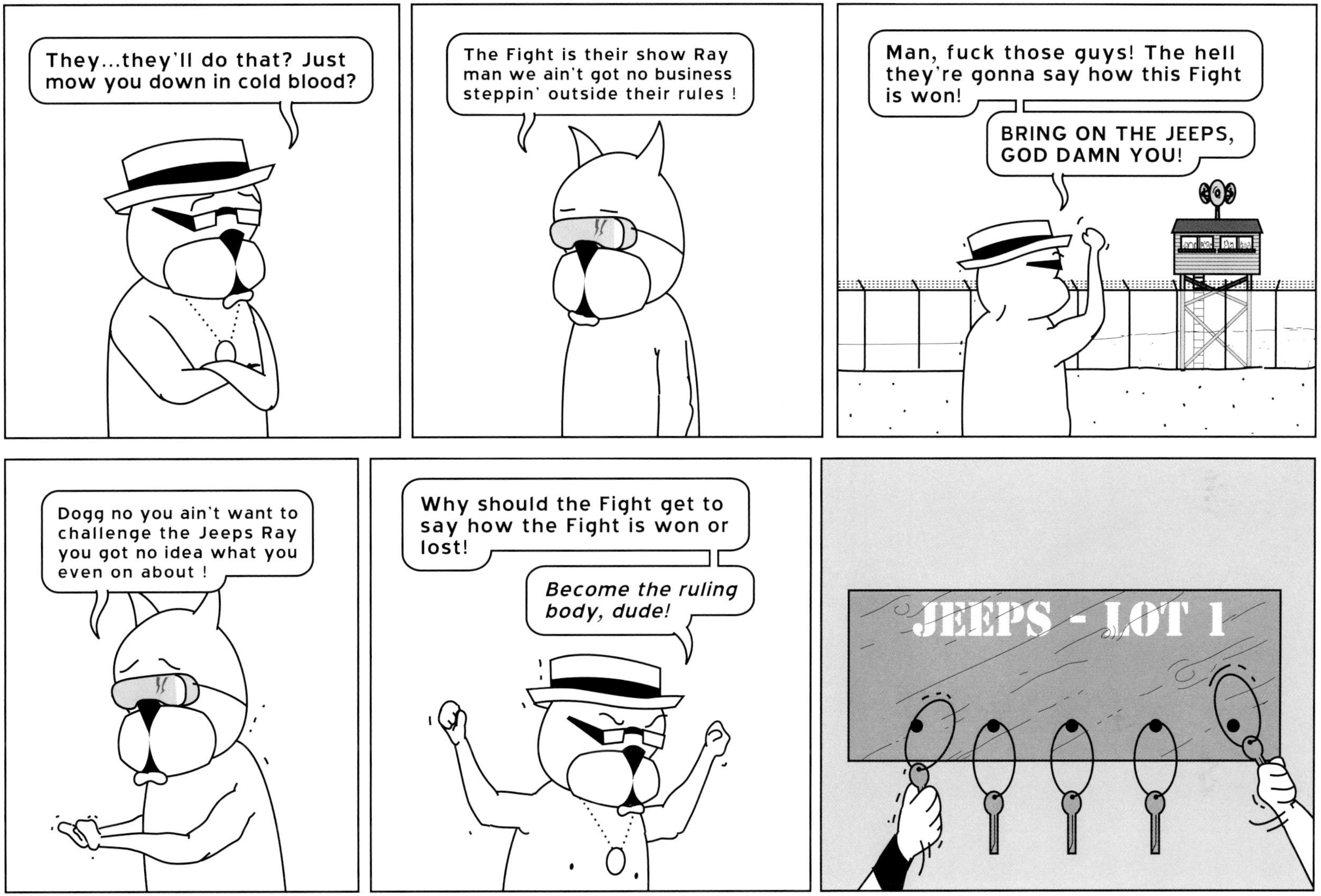

They...they'll do that? Just mow you down in cold blood?
The Fight is their show Ray man we ain't got no business steppin' outside their rules !
Man, fuck those guys! The hell they're gonna say how this Fight is won!
BRING ON THE JEEPS, GOD DAMN YOU!
Dogg no you ain't want to challenge the Jeeps Ray you got no idea what you even on about !
Why should the Fight get to say how the Fight is won or lost!
Become the ruling body, dude!
JEEPS - LOT 1

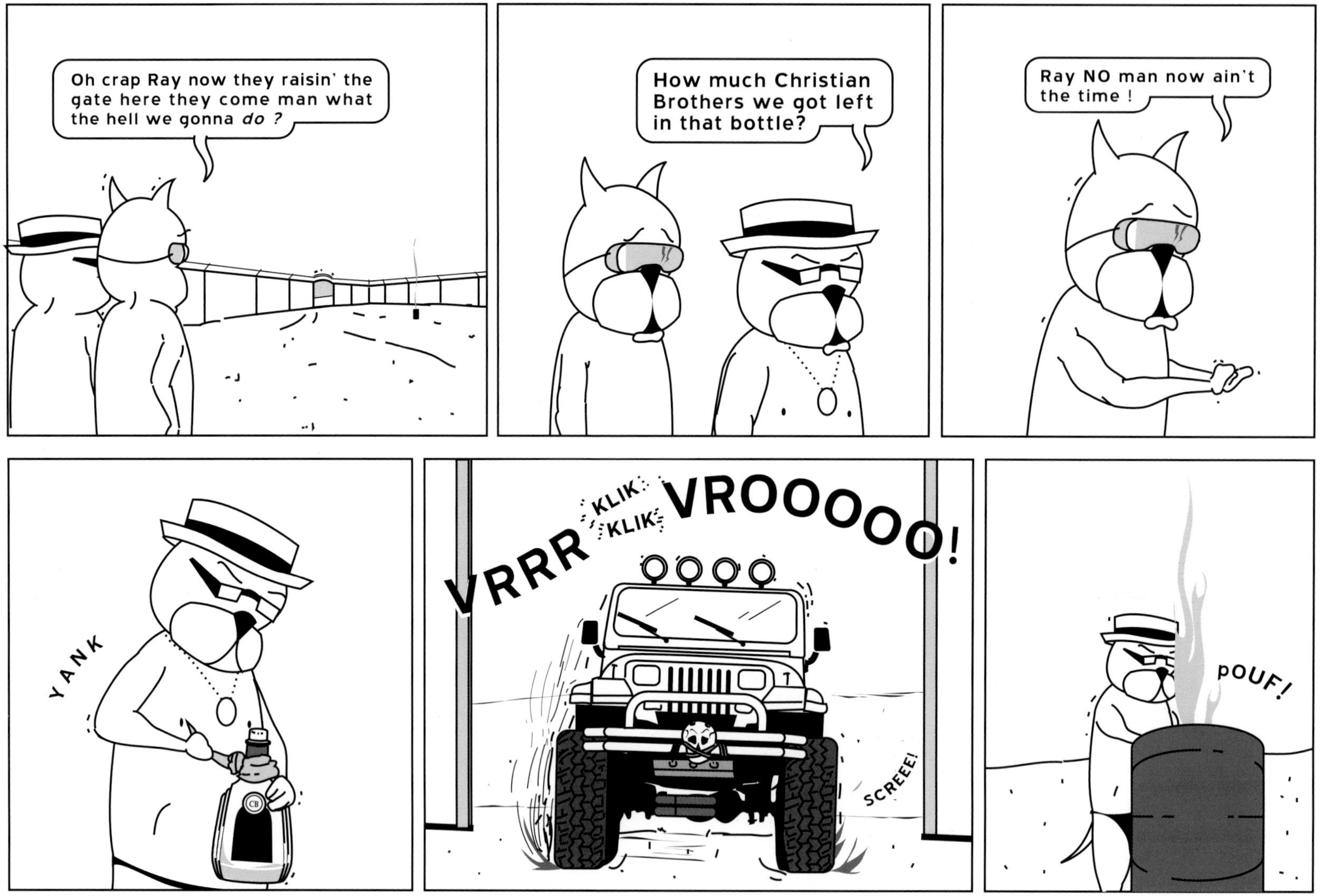
Oh crap Ray now they raisin' the gate here they come man what the hell we gonna *do* ?
How much Christian Brothers we got left in that bottle?
Ray NO man now ain't the time !
YANK
VRRR
KLIK
KLIK
VROOOOOO!
SCREEE!
POUF!

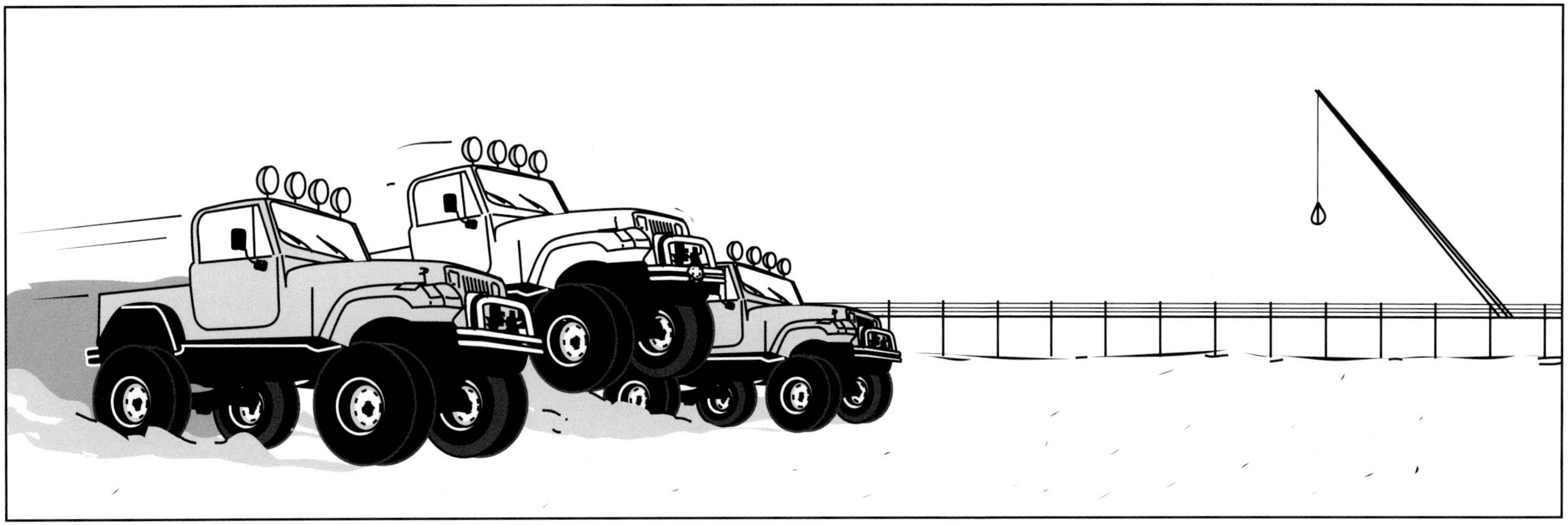

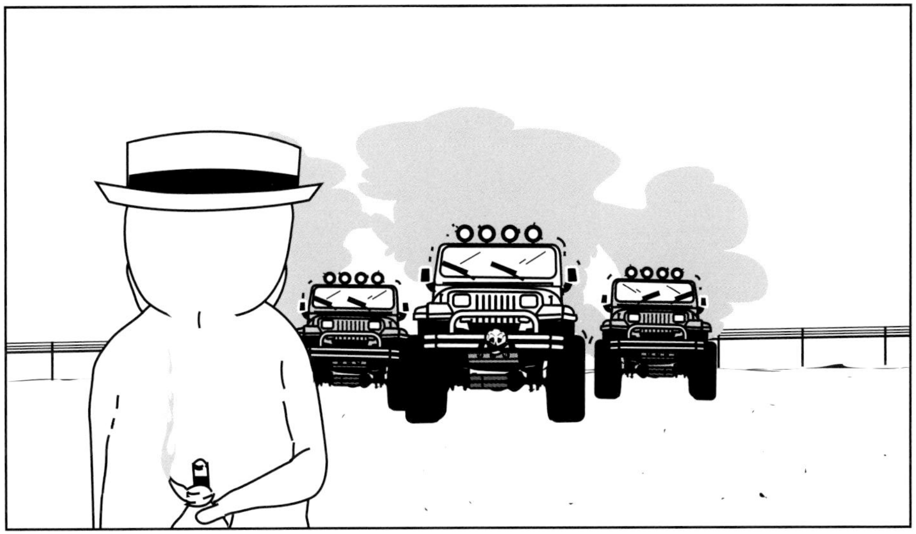

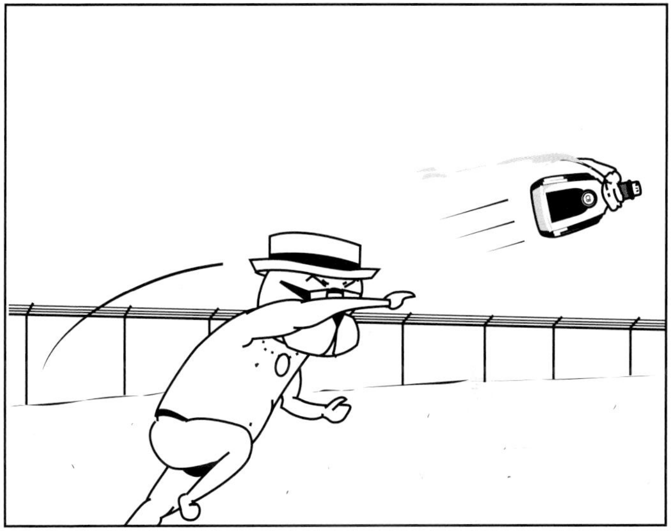

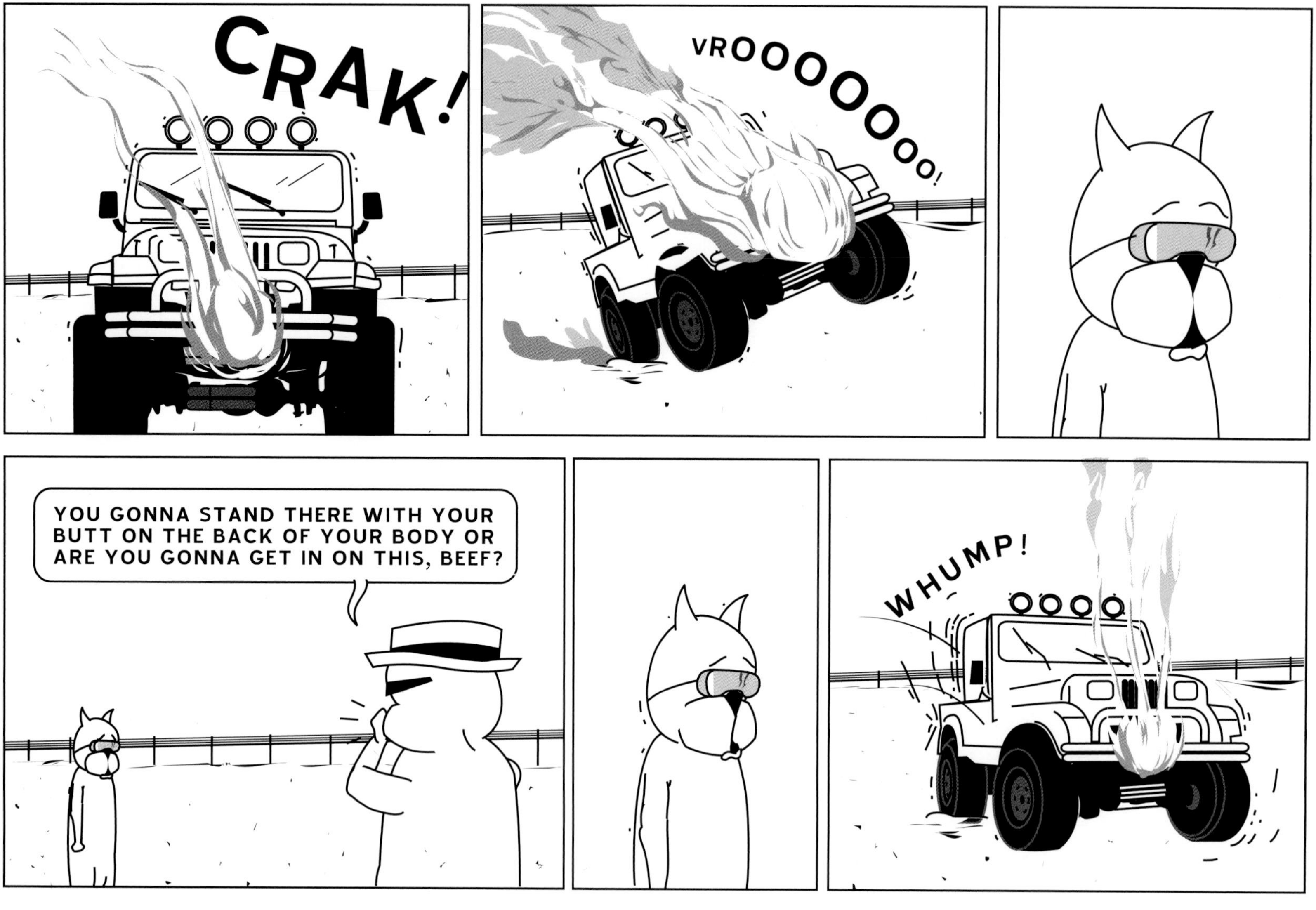
CRAK!
VROOOOOOOoo!
YOU GONNA STAND THERE WITH YOUR BUTT ON THE BACK OF YOUR BODY OR ARE YOU GONNA GET IN ON THIS, BEEF?
WHUMP!

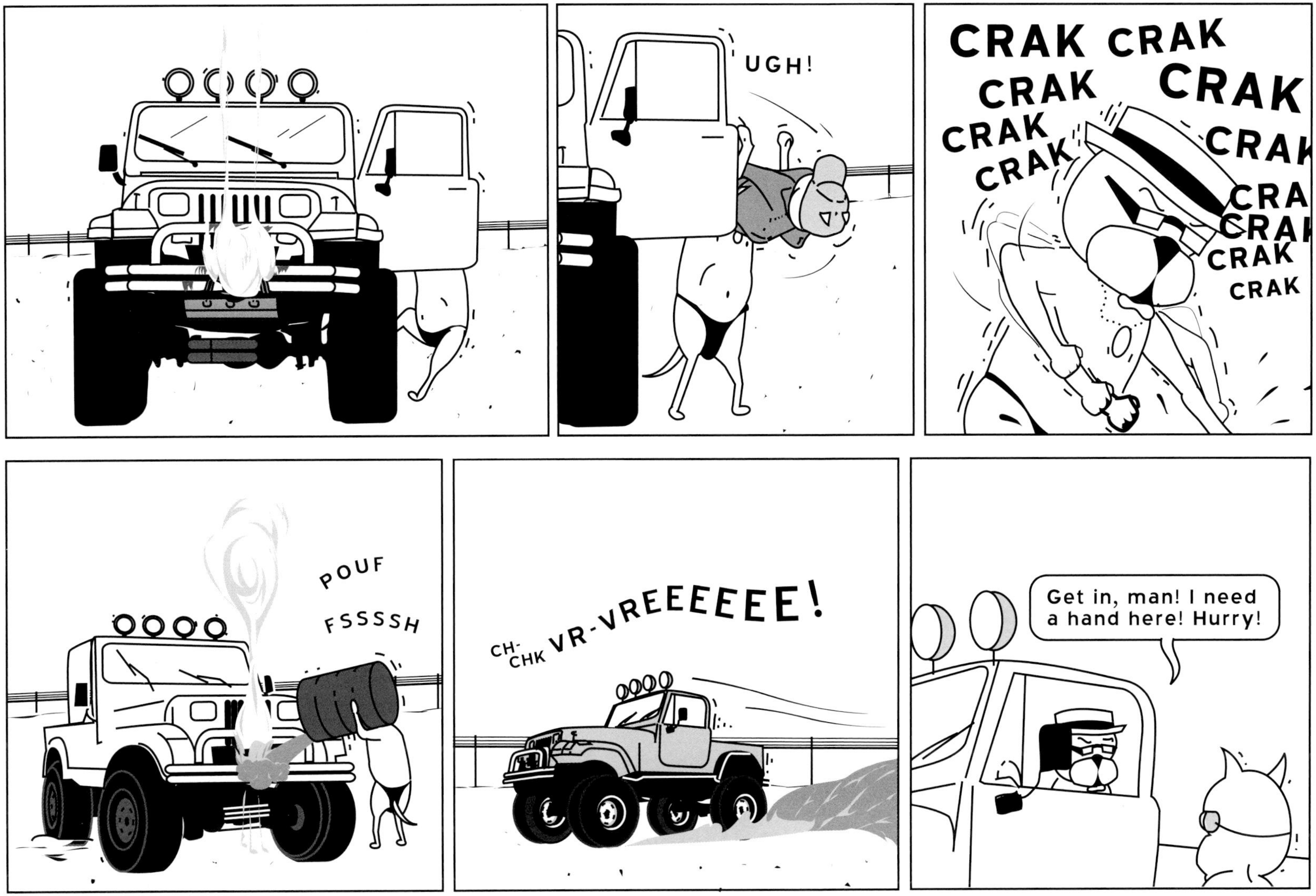
UGH!
CRAK CRAK
CRAK CRAK
CRAK
CRAK
CRAK
CRA
CRAK
CRAK
CRAK
POUF
FSSSSH
CH-CHK VR-VREEEEEE!
Get in, man! I need a hand here! Hurry!

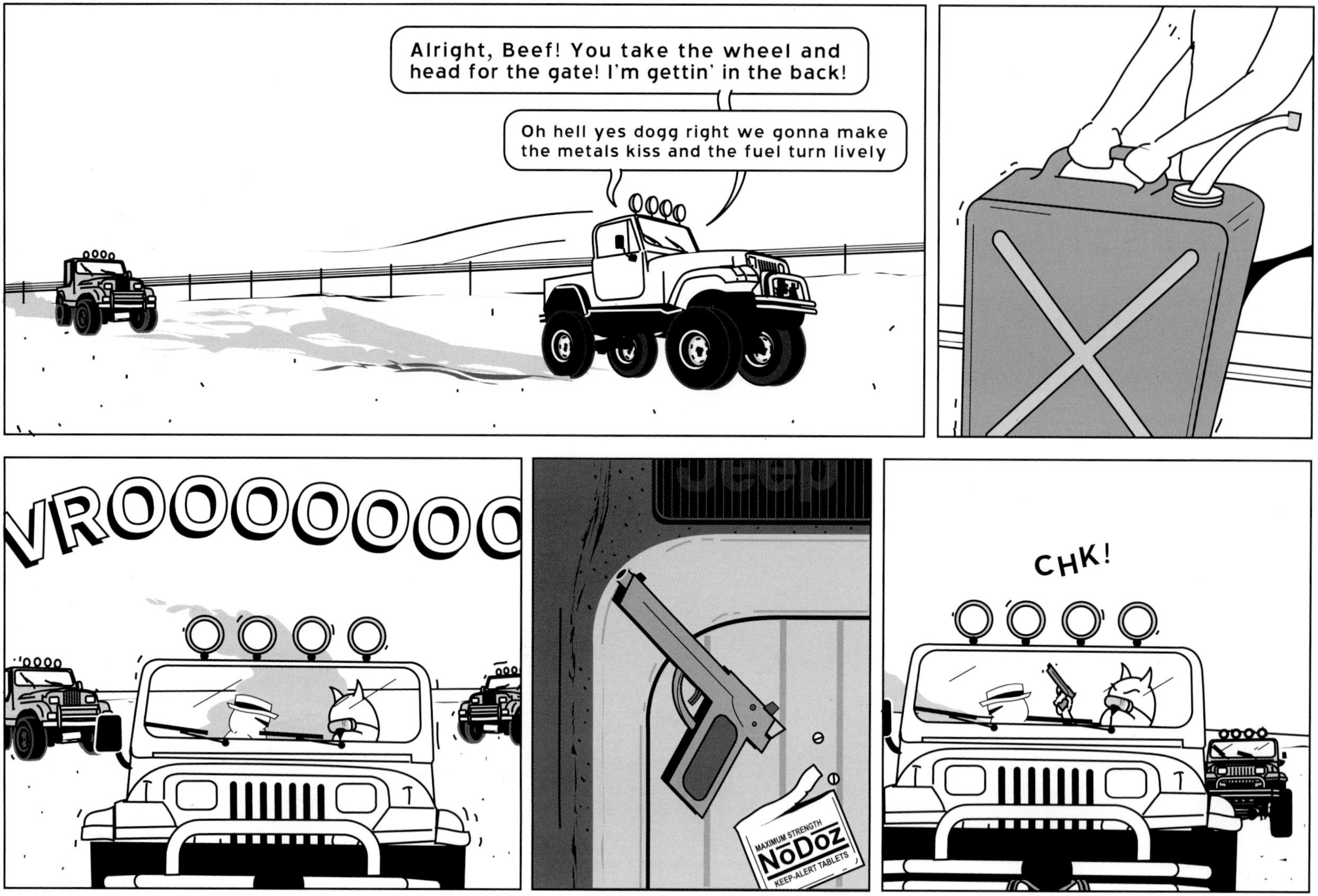
Alright, Beef! You take the wheel and head for the gate! I'm gettin' in the back!
Oh hell yes dogg right we gonna make the metals kiss and the fuel turn lively
VROOOOOOOO
MAXIMUM STRENGTH NoDoz KEEP-ALERT TABLETS
CHK!

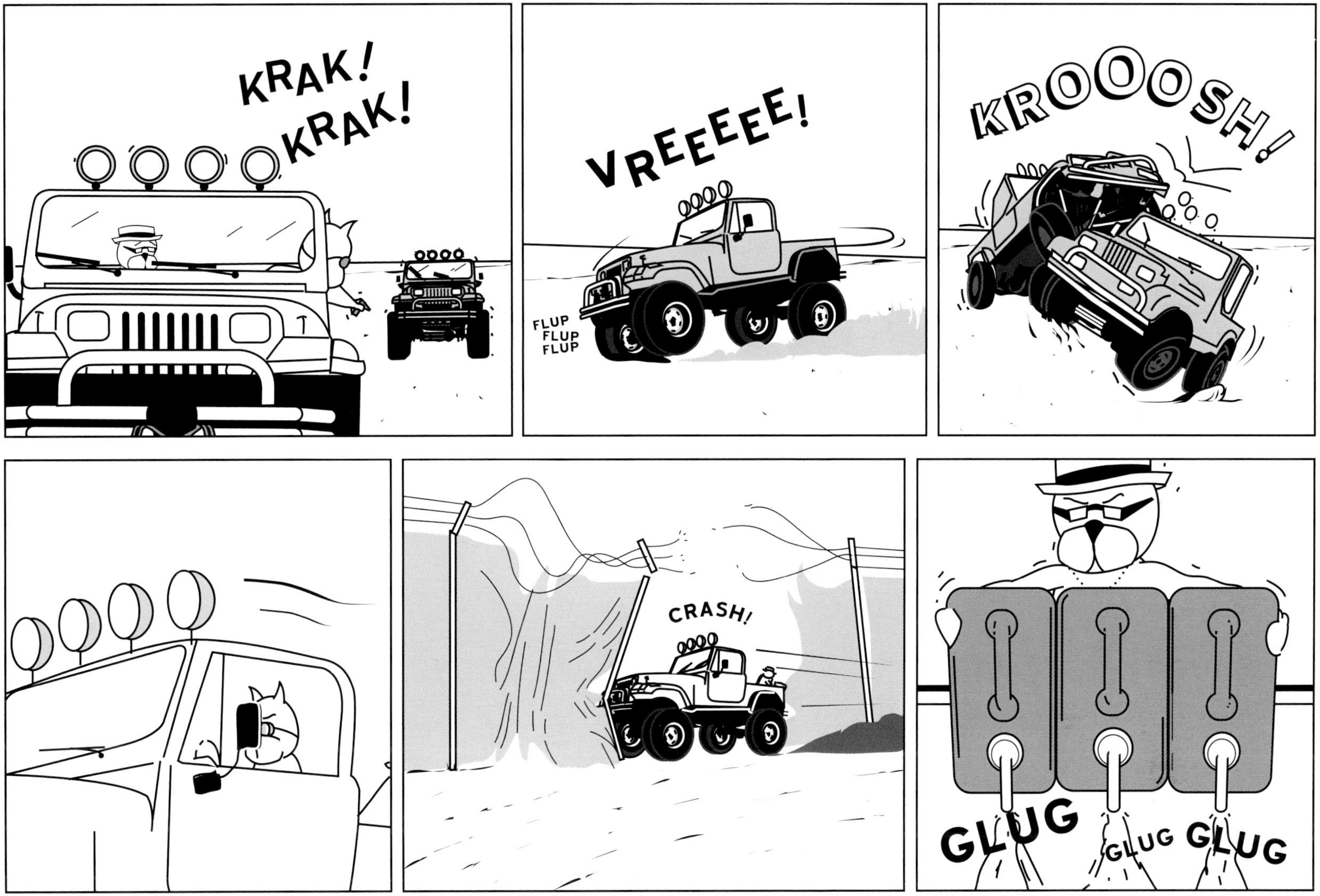
KRAK!
KRAK!
VREEEEEE!
FLUP
FLUP
FLUP
KROOOSH!
CRASH!
GLUG
GLUG
GLUG

KA-THUNK KA-THUNK KA-THUNK KA-
KRUNCH
Okay, shoot, man, shoot!
KRAK
POU F

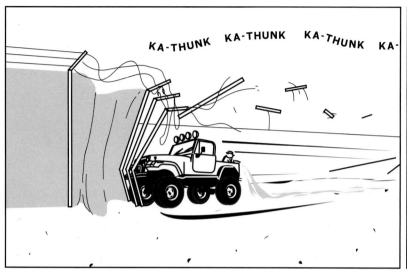

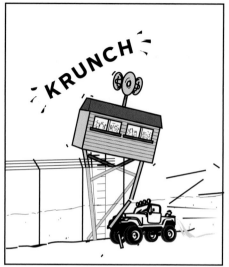

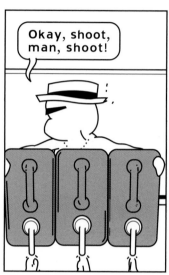

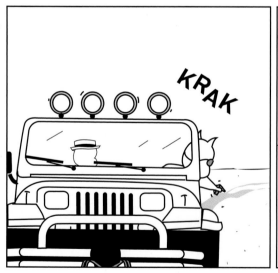

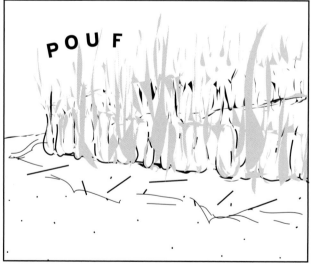

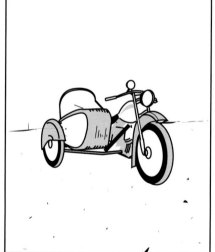

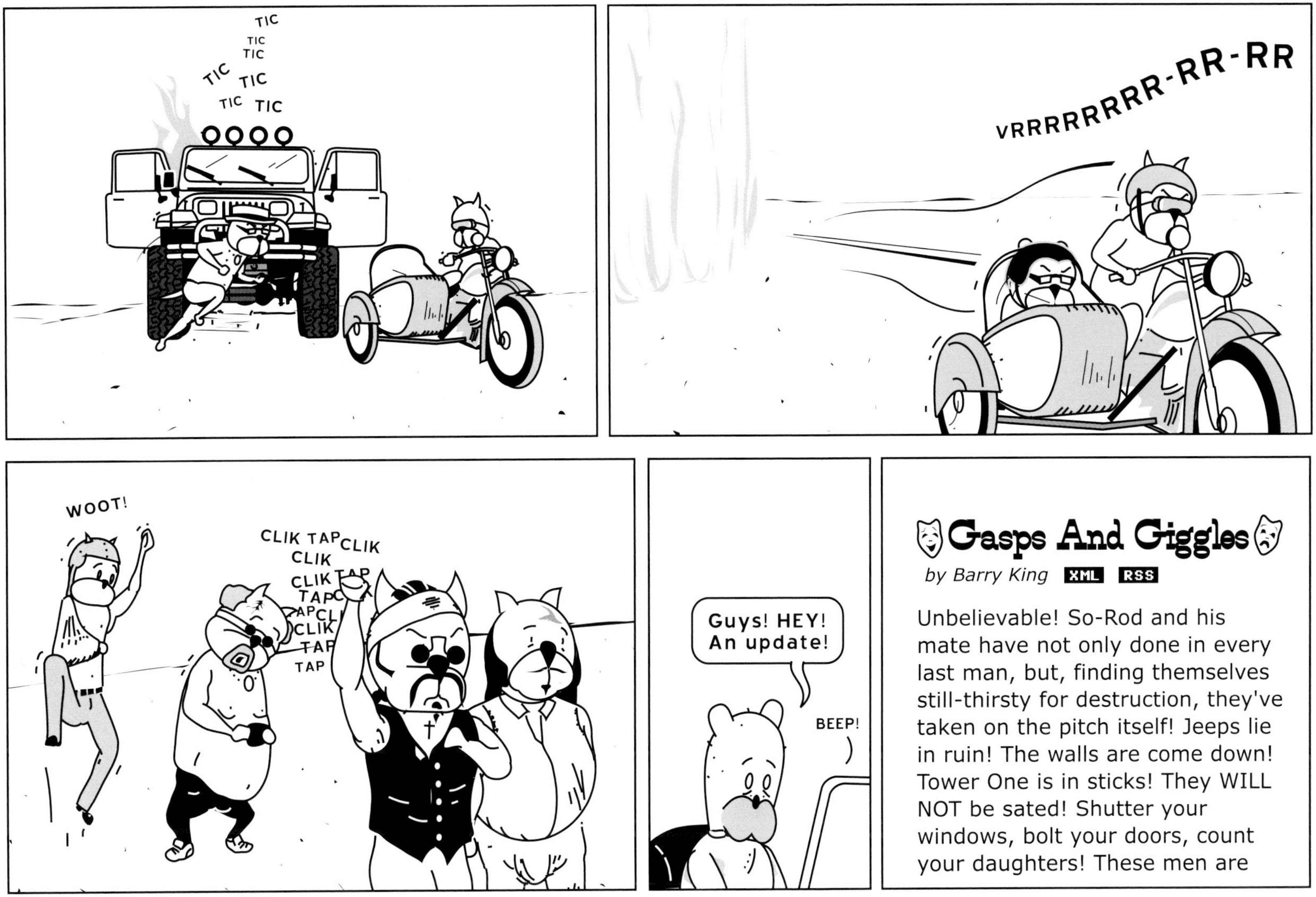

TIC
TIC
TIC
TIC
TIC
TIC
TIC
VRRRRRRRR-RR-RR
WOOT!
CLIK TAP CLIK
CLIK
CLIK
TAP
CLIK
TAP
Guys! HEY! An update!
BEEP!
Gasps And Giggles
by Barry King XML RSS
Unbelievable! So-Rod and his mate have not only done in every last man, but, finding themselves still-thirsty for destruction, they've taken on the pitch itself! Jeeps lie in ruin! The walls are come down! Tower One is in sticks! They WILL NOT be sated! Shutter your windows, bolt your doors, count your daughters! These men are

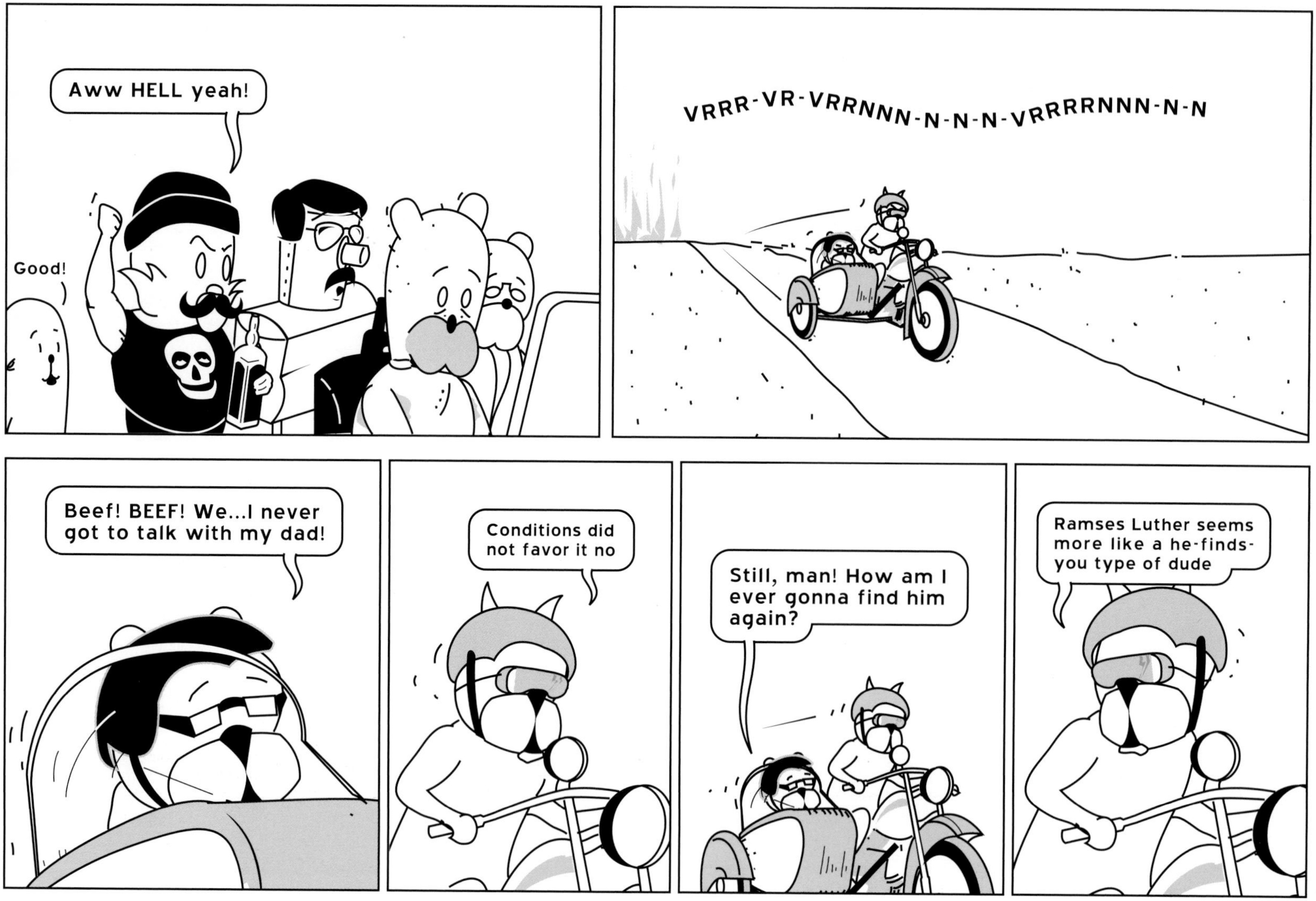
Aww HELL yeah!
Good!
VRRR-VR-VRRNNN-N-N-N-VRRRRNNN-N-N
Beef! BEEF! We...I never got to talk with my dad!
Conditions did not favor it no
Still, man! How am I ever gonna find him again?
Ramses Luther seems more like a he-finds-you type of dude

I...yeah. You think he's 'a be pissed at me for not doin' things his way?

Come on Ray the guy broke all the Fight rules his first time around

All standin' with no army and bustin' nontraditional moves

Now he sees his boy breakin' rules that ain't even written and makin' his own besides

Got to stir a familiar nerve in his old neck

Damn. This is a thing, isn't it?

This is completely a thing

Our every move is the new tradition

What should we do, man? This is the time!

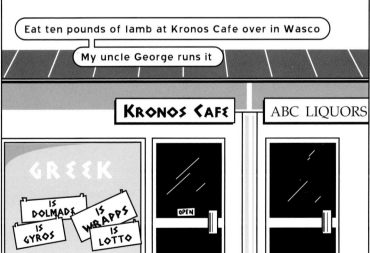

Eat ten pounds of lamb at Kronos Cafe over in Wasco

My uncle George runs it

KRONOS CAFE

ABC LIQUORS

GREEK

IS DOLMADE
IS GYROS
IS WRAPPS
IS LOTTO

OPEN

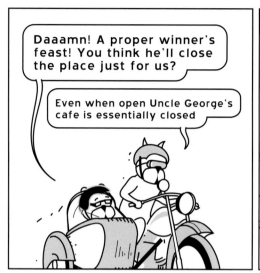

Daaamn! A proper winner's feast! You think he'll close the place just for us?

Even when open Uncle George's cafe is essentially closed

SOON.

Why, I no' believe it! Ar'rosto Beef! You come an' see me! An'a you bring some guy!

Hi Uncle George this is my friend Ray

Ray, Ray...you'a the rich boy, or you'a the jerk?

I'm the rich guy!

Good, good. I no like'a the jerks. When I am younger, sure, OK, but not so much now.

Maybe I change, maybe they change. Who knows?

We lookin' to do a bang-up feast Uncle George we ain't eaten well in some days

Good, good! I call, I get us a pizza. I know some guy. He have also this, "crazy sticks"? But they are bread.

We're getting food delivered to your restaurant ?

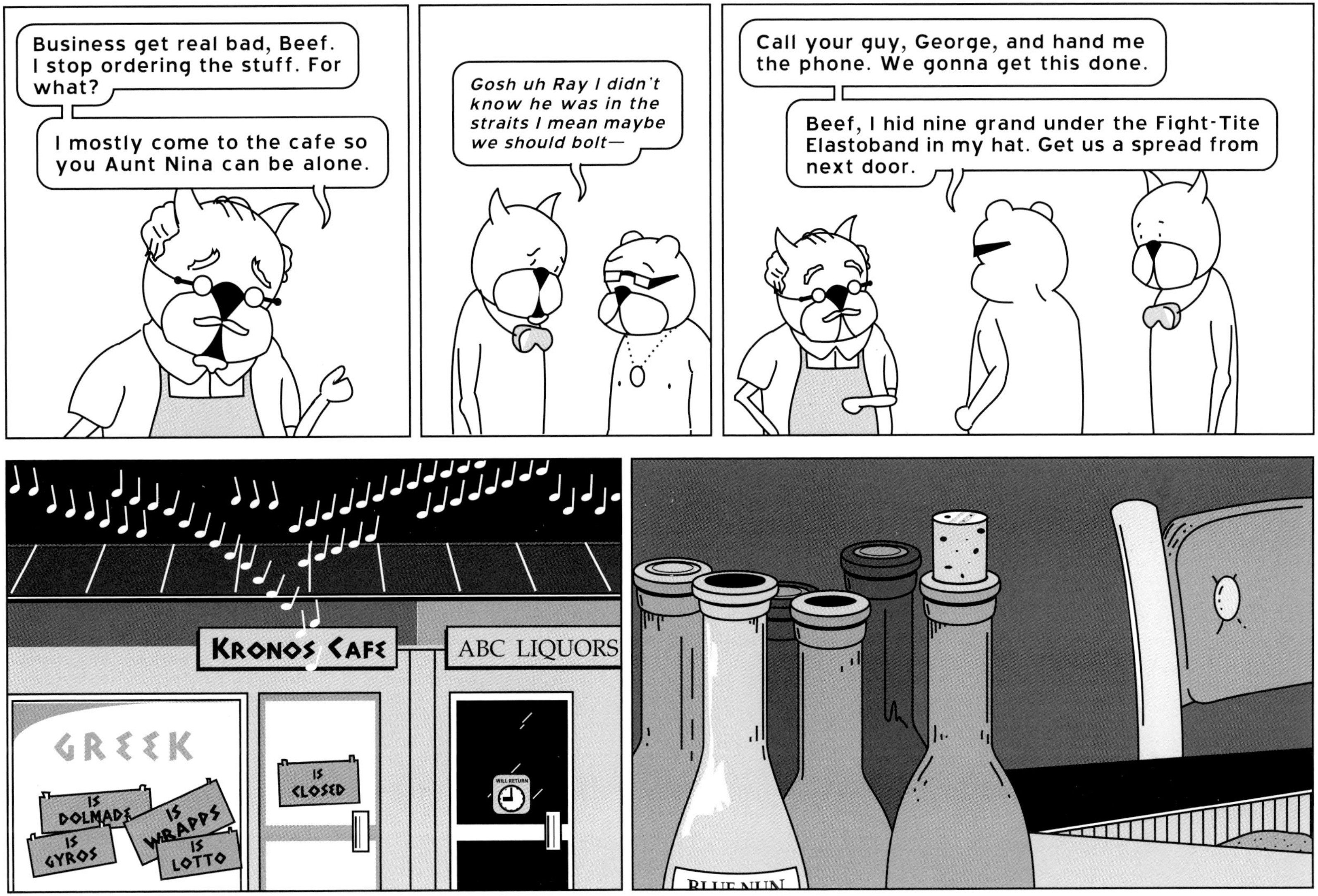
Business get real bad, Beef. I stop ordering the stuff. For what?
I mostly come to the cafe so you Aunt Nina can be alone.
Gosh uh Ray I didn't know he was in the straits I mean maybe we should bolt—
Call your guy, George, and hand me the phone. We gonna get this done.
Beef, I hid nine grand under the Fight-Tite Elastoband in my hat. Get us a spread from next door.
KRONOS CAFE
ABC LIQUORS
GREEK
IS CLOSED
IS DOLMADE
IS WRAPPS
IS GYROS
IS LOTTO
WILL RETURN

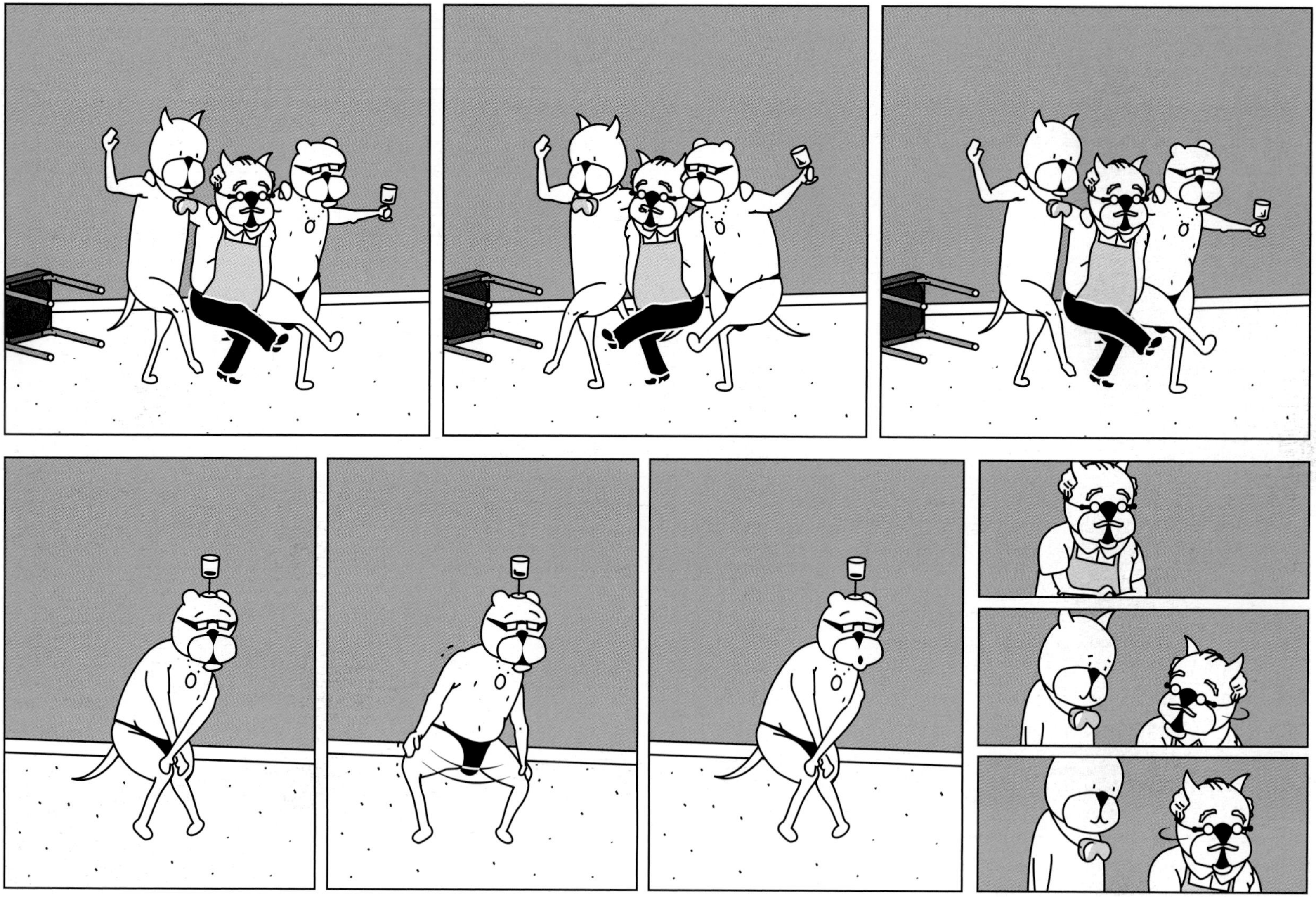

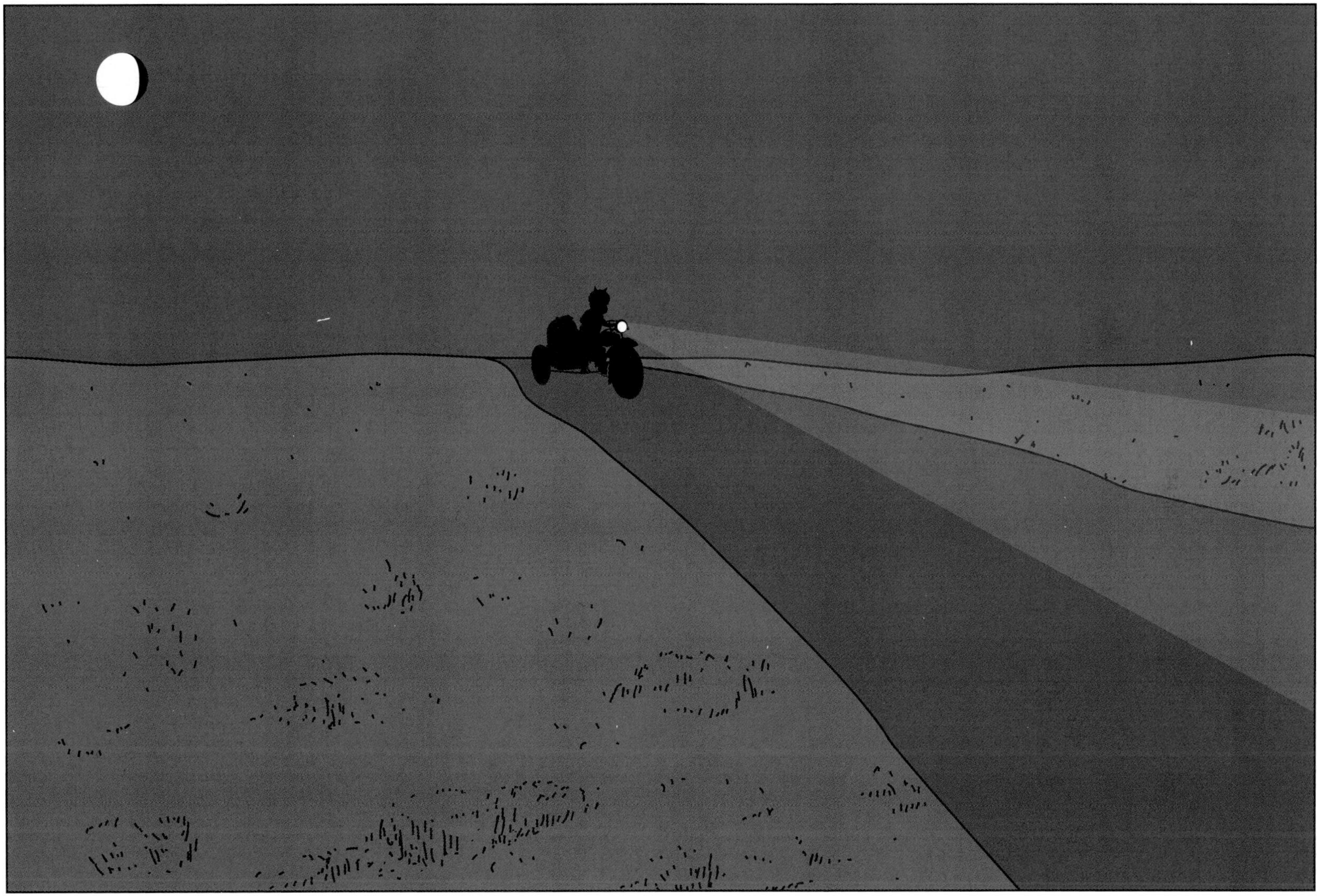

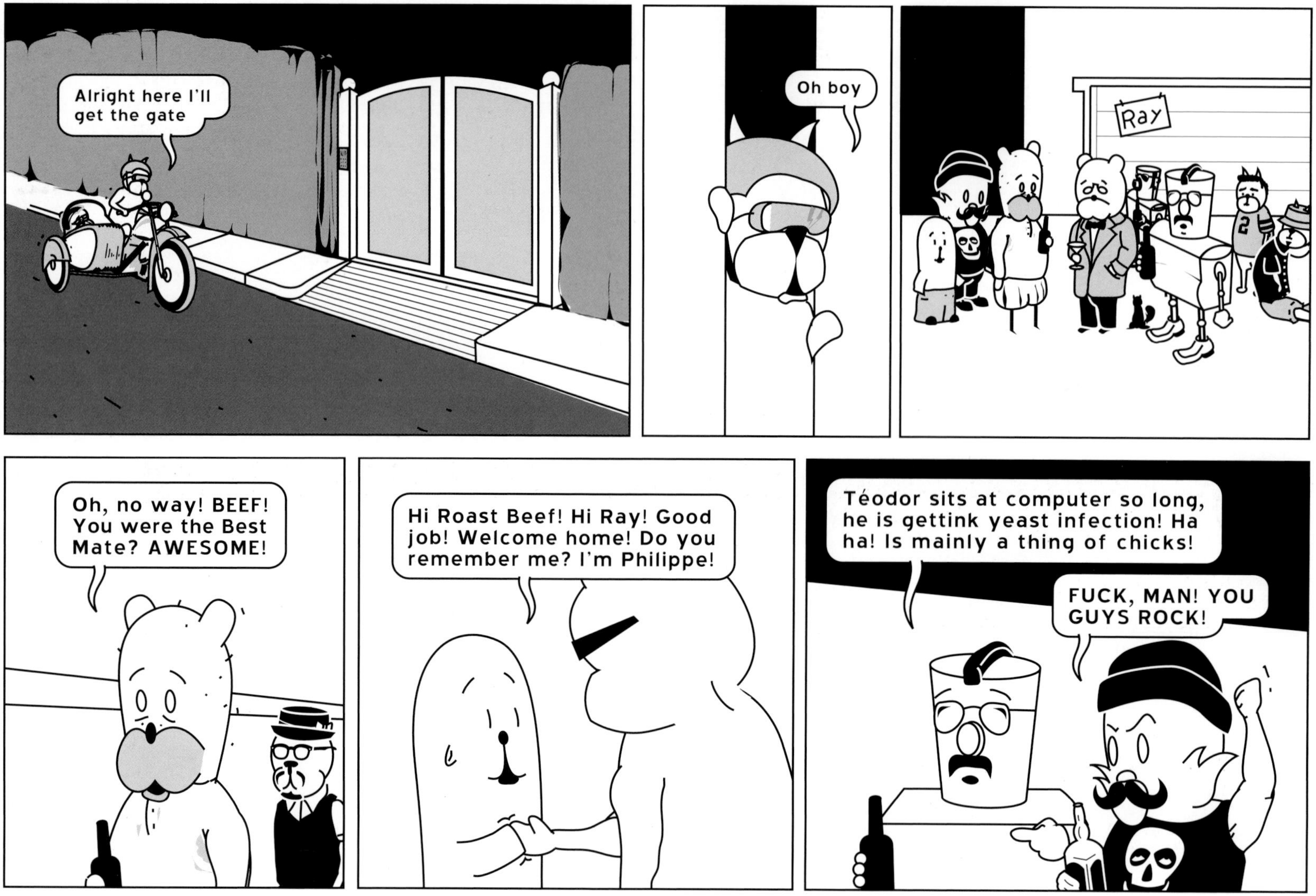
Alright here I'll get the gate
Oh boy
Ray
Oh, no way! BEEF! You were the Best Mate? AWESOME!
Hi Roast Beef! Hi Ray! Good job! Welcome home! Do you remember me? I'm Philippe!
Téodor sits at computer so long, he is gettink yeast infection! Ha ha! Is mainly a thing of chicks!
FUCK, MAN! YOU GUYS ROCK!

Where's most of your hair, Vlad?
Is in honor of you, dog! The Taxi Driver! Tough-est haircut possible!
Well it sounds real mild you might try Gyne-Lotrimin
What's next for Son of Rodney and his trusty sidekick? Talk shows? A line of vanity soups?
I wouldn't mind doin' a little signature panini press, but Beef would never sign off.
TINK
Of the many speculations I have encountered I favor those which would place you on the Ruling Body of the Great Outdoor Fight
Online and in the cafés you are regarded as the Fight's foremost thinker and perhaps the archi-tect of its future
Oh hell I ain't expect anything but if someone does come callin' I may hear them out
How were the Tenmen
FIN.

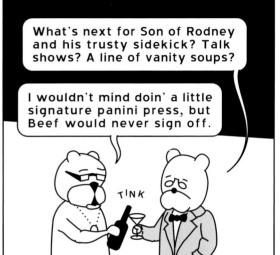

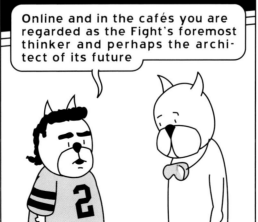

Recipes Original recipes from RECIPES OF THE GREAT OUTDOOR FIGHT: HEARTY FOOD FOR YOUR STRONG-HEARTED MAN

Editor's note: Consisting of slap-dash, wholly spurious, mainly irrelevant, untested, and often unusable recipes, this sloppy book is a shining example of the myriad attempts made to cash in on the Great Outdoor Fight craze that seized the nation in 1923–24. —JBS

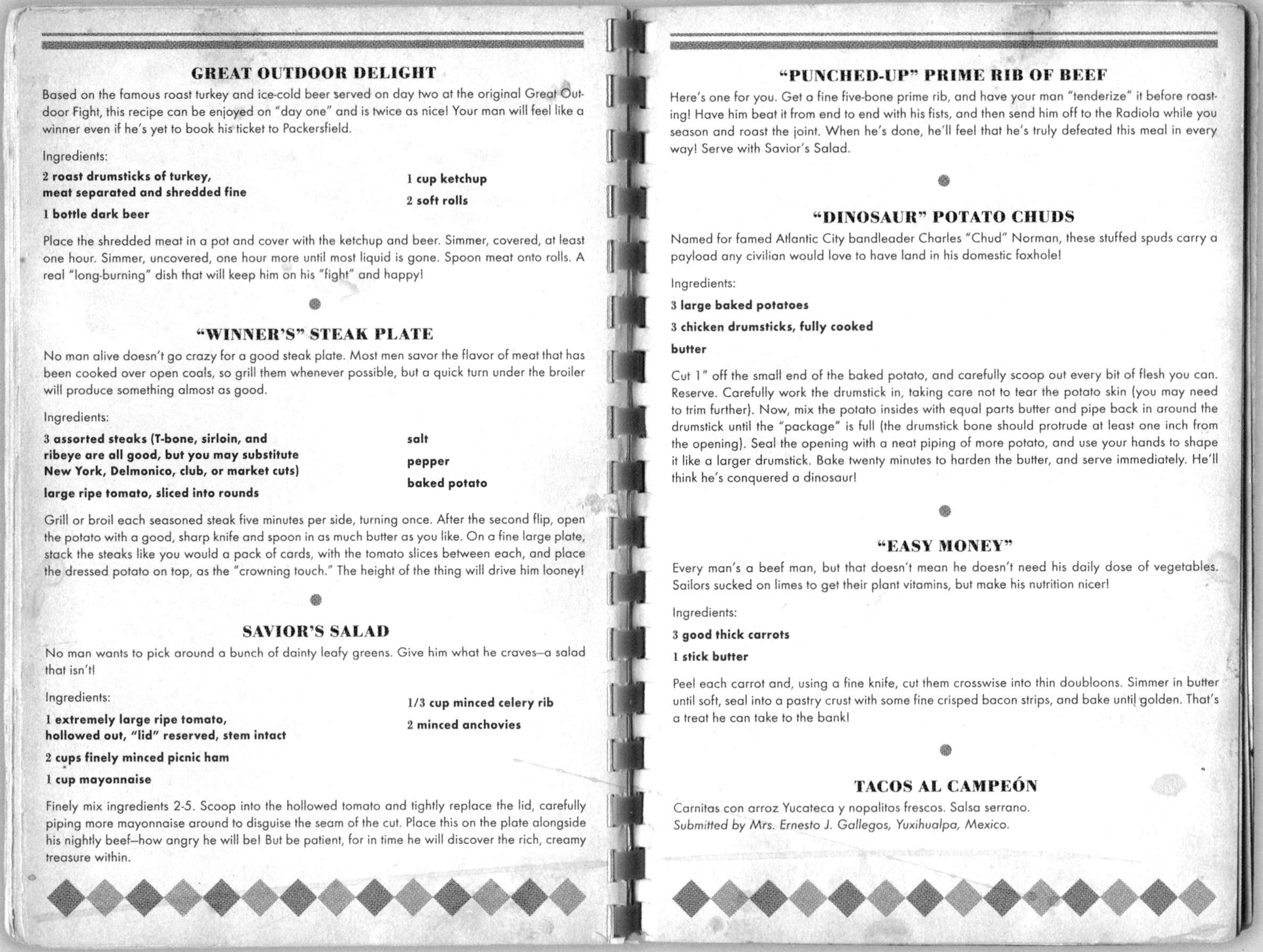

GREAT OUTDOOR DELIGHT
Based on the famous roast turkey and ice-cold beer served on day two at the original Great Outdoor Fight, this recipe can be enjoyed on "day one" and is twice as nice! Your man will feel like a winner even if he's yet to book his ticket to Packersfield.
Ingredients:
2 roast drumsticks of turkey, meat separated and shredded fine
1 bottle dark beer
1 cup ketchup
2 soft rolls
Place the shredded meat in a pot and cover with the ketchup and beer. Simmer, covered, at least one hour. Simmer, uncovered, one hour more until most liquid is gone. Spoon meat onto rolls. A real "long-burning" dish that will keep him on his "fight" and happy!
"WINNER'S" STEAK PLATE
No man alive doesn't go crazy for a good steak plate. Most men savor the flavor of meat that has been cooked over open coals, so grill them whenever possible, but a quick turn under the broiler will produce something almost as good.
Ingredients:
3 assorted steaks (T-bone, sirloin, and ribeye are all good, but you may substitute New York, Delmonico, club, or market cuts)
large ripe tomato, sliced into rounds
salt
pepper
baked potato
Grill or broil each seasoned steak five minutes per side, turning once. After the second flip, open the potato with a good, sharp knife and spoon in as much butter as you like. On a fine large plate, stack the steaks like you would a pack of cards, with the tomato slices between each, and place the dressed potato on top, as the "crowning touch." The height of the thing will drive him looney!
SAVIOR'S SALAD
No man wants to pick around a bunch of dainty leafy greens. Give him what he craves–a salad that isn't!
Ingredients:
1 extremely large ripe tomato, hollowed out, "lid" reserved, stem intact
2 cups finely minced picnic ham
1 cup mayonnaise
1/3 cup minced celery rib
2 minced anchovies
Finely mix ingredients 2-5. Scoop into the hollowed tomato and tightly replace the lid, carefully piping more mayonnaise around to disguise the seam of the cut. Place this on the plate alongside his nightly beef–how angry he will be! But be patient, for in time he will discover the rich, creamy treasure within.
"PUNCHED-UP" PRIME RIB OF BEEF
Here's one for you. Get a fine five-bone prime rib, and have your man "tenderize" it before roasting! Have him beat it from end to end with his fists, and then send him off to the Radiola while you season and roast the joint. When he's done, he'll feel that he's truly defeated this meal in every way! Serve with Savior's Salad.
"DINOSAUR" POTATO CHUDS
Named for famed Atlantic City bandleader Charles "Chud" Norman, these stuffed spuds carry a payload any civilian would love to have land in his domestic foxhole!
Ingredients:
3 large baked potatoes
3 chicken drumsticks, fully cooked
butter
Cut 1" off the small end of the baked potato, and carefully scoop out every bit of flesh you can. Reserve. Carefully work the drumstick in, taking care not to tear the potato skin (you may need to trim further). Now, mix the potato insides with equal parts butter and pipe back in around the drumstick until the "package" is full (the drumstick bone should protrude at least one inch from the opening). Seal the opening with a neat piping of more potato, and use your hands to shape it like a larger drumstick. Bake twenty minutes to harden the butter, and serve immediately. He'll think he's conquered a dinosaur!
"EASY MONEY"
Every man's a beef man, but that doesn't mean he doesn't need his daily dose of vegetables. Sailors sucked on limes to get their plant vitamins, but make his nutrition nicer!
Ingredients:
3 good thick carrots
1 stick butter
Peel each carrot and, using a fine knife, cut them crosswise into thin doubloons. Simmer in butter until soft, seal into a pastry crust with some fine crisped bacon strips, and bake until golden. That's a treat he can take to the bank!
TACOS AL CAMPEÓN
Carnitas con arroz Yucateca y nopalitos frescos. Salsa serrano.
Submitted by Mrs. Ernesto J. Gallegos, Yuxihualpa, Mexico.

Profiles in Strength

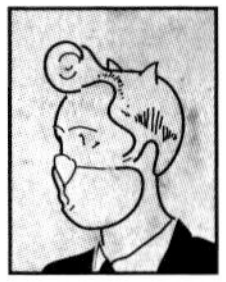

1933
"Poodle" Max Clay
(b. 1908)

Born Maxwell Kenneth Clay in Harlem, New York City, he made an early connection between the fighters' poses in the classically derived "Studied Glazes" of the Manhattan Second Subway decorative tiles, and the powerful stances he saw photographed in the sensational G.O.F. purple prose of the day. A withdrawn child, he filled book after book with accomplished sketches of these tiles, done completely from memory, and when he was old enough, he set up his easel on the platform to make charcoals.

When not scrutinizing his first loves, he often took to the library for a day's worth of study in its classics department. The reference librarians were proud of this young man who clearly wanted to train himself as a great artist; in truth, he was studying an art form few academics will ever recognize.

Too poor to attend college, he worked his way west as a tailor's assistant and eventually honed in on Bakersfield. Famous as not for the "pouf" of tightly curled hair he wore atop his forehead, Clay's fighting style was defined by the gracefulness of his takedowns, no doubt informed by his cherished Studied Glazes. Fight photographs always seem to catch him felling a man with a form and proportion fit for stone: never is he off kilter, everywhere he counterbalances the misdirected energy of his opponent. Some suggest that in his study of the Glazes he unlocked the ancient secrets of hand-to-hand combat. Many of the illustrations and reliefs on those tiles were copied directly from ancient Roman and Greek masters, artists of an age when people no doubt not only had to fight for survival rather than sport, but whose fighting drew on a much more recent tradition of barbaric survival, the world having barely been settled.

"Poodle" walked into the 1933 field a relative unknown, and quickly drew praise from commentators who could not take their eyes from the spare yet beautiful demolition he dealt out.

"Ever' time I look," said observer Col. George Gracechurch, "Theah war' anuthuh

>> HALL OF CHAMPIONS <<

1923 Szudor Pwalycsza
1924 "Red Rice" Laloux
1925 Gordon Mason
1926 Northcutt "Mike" Powell
1927 Sam Fenwick
1928 Carl Shoup
1929 Edwin J. Gorrigan
1930 Doug Irwin
1931 Oscar Fonseca
1932 Jake Lee
1933 "Poodle" Max Clay
1934 Marcus Gosney
1935 Mario Semprello
1936 Fred Carver
1937 Ephestus Brown
1938 Fish Lempinen
1939 Lutufyo Waseme
1940 Don Holmlund
1941 Elbenar Toxon
1942 Bill Cecily
1943 Abner J. Polhemus, Jr.
1944 Warren Davenport
1945 Simeon Cross
1946 Acamar L. Grove
1947 Hu Vo Nguyen
1948 James Kennedy

discus boy, anuthuh Michael-angelo, anuthuh moment o' life what should not but 'a been a bit o' stone. Such was Poodle's fightin' an' such did it em-press us so."

The years of study had paid off: a relatively unworn and unbruised Clay, his ancient lessons given a trial by fire, walked off the field the victor at 8:31 a.m. on Day Three. Shy with reporters, he said only this of his triumph:

There's a right way to do things. There's one right way. We've been thinking, fighting, for a long time. Hundreds of generations, since Achilles and Ajax. I didn't do something new here. I proved something old. Very old. I claim this victory for my father, Reuben Clay, and his father, Elam Clay.

With that, he shouldered his bindle and disappeared into the sea of departing cars. He would eventually work his way back east.

Decades later, in an interview with *Rolling Stone* magazine, a photograph shows an elderly, serene Clay in his study in Schenectady—on the shelves all around him are salvaged Glazes from the New York Second Subway platforms of his youth. In life, some beauty does not need to be bettered.

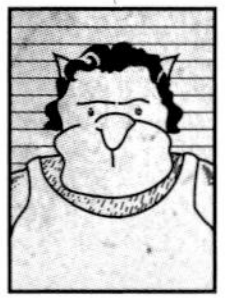

1949
Century Jim Nate
(b. 1925)

Century Jim Nate (b. Algoso Prebim Nugesão) is one of the Fight's greater curiosities. A soft-spoken boy from Belle Towers, Connecticut, he was the only son of two Portuguese restaurateurs, and by all accounts he looked to have an unremarkable future behind the stove ahead of him.

Noteworthy for his size (tall men came just to his sternum), and his weight (he was "two men," it is often written), he was a gentle giant. Reticent and peaceful, his kitchen breaks were often spent under an olive tree in the nearby public park, quietly perusing calm volumes of simple poetry (his headstone bears this doggerel: "I didn't last/But who hast"). A more unlikely champion there never was.

How did this man start down the path that led to The Acres? The genesis is in this anecdote, as related by his prep cook and lifelong friend Hal Randall:

Algo was real proud of his fish cakes, and they'd been something of a local specialty. Real fluffley [sic] *and moist, but real crisp on the outside. Well, this guy, Dread City Jake, was around at the time, and he was a bastard of a customer. Sent everything back, guaranteed. Wonder why he even dined. Anyhow, he ordered and sent back Algo's perfect fish cakes three times, and on the third time old Algo did something I never seen. He took his big old hands—he coulda' wrapped one clean around my head—and he took the pan the cakes fried in, still hot . . . quiet as a lamb, he bent it in half. He bent it down the damn middle. Red hot. No cook can do that. Few even try. And this is when it gets nasty. He goes out to the dining room, see, and he sits down with Jake. Jake gets real uncomfortable, 'cause he's a phony, all he does is send food back. Algo starts in on his whole philosophy of those fish cakes, and why they should be how they are, and he goes over every damn step of his process—and he cooks them all, don't you know, nobody cooks them but him. It's like havin' money made by George Washington. There's no way it's wrong. Anyhow, Algo got pretty worked* up while he was talkin', 'cause when he was done he wrapped his hand around Jake's collar and tie, picked him up with one arm, and carried him outside like a sack of laundry. He'd had enough, and he slapped Jake across the side of the head with his big open hand. Jake fell to the ground and shook like a bluegill . . . we all thought he'd had his neck snapped, but after Algo went back inside, he started to stir, and pretty soon he stood up.

God strike me dead, but Jake could only speak Chinese after that. No English. He was destroyed, just by that one slap. Did he know Chinese before that? No. He used to joke that "gracias" was his only French, and he'd say gracias wrong. Algo slapped the Chinese into him. Jake's brother had to fly in from Fort Worth and rename him China-Style Mike, just to create logic.

From there, Algo was prodded into entering qualifying rounds by Hal, a Fight fan, and the rest of the kitchen staff (two friendly dishwashers named Galvez). He impressed scouts with his massive, unyielding size,

and his utter unflappability. The steady blows of even the strongest locals were but slaps across his great shoulders, and none could reach his face.

His ultimate victory at The Acres was as quiet and steady as the man himself. Toward the final hours of day three, just like a good employee, he walked over to Franklin Mathis, the other last man standing, and slapped him so hard on the head that Mathis, too, forgot English (he did not, however, gain knowledge of Chinese, and simply remained mute for several years). The victor, he walked disinterestedly from the grounds, took a cheap train home, and supped on a fourteen-quart stockpot of kale and sausage soup.

The balance of his days were as peaceful as before: he returned to the family stove and continued turning out food. When pressed for interviews, he did not lift his head from the counter or his pans, and gave monosyllabic answers. Even as a man of sixty-three, the year of his passing, he could be seen on his breaks, reading and napping beneath the same old olive tree in the park.

· · ·

1949 Century Jim Nate
1950 *Chilanga*
1951 Daniel Neal
1952 Franky Tesmoreno
1953 Paul Augustus
1954 Tel Hpitlak
1955 Karl "Karosserie" von dem Bruch
1956 Yu Cha
1957 Desmond "Jake" Hollenfield
1958 Jimmy Diamond
1959 Jacques Gerard
1960 Grady Jackson
1961 Antonio Salvatierra, Jr.
1962 Bernd Ten Bakke (decision)
1963 Juno Quay
1964 Paul Clemson
1965 Andy "Clean" Wyatt
1966 Stanley "Grip" Brown
1967 Earl Morriss
1968 Carl Haskins
1969 Motor City Massacre
1970 "Pine Box" Pyrell
1971 RUFUS
1972 Lord Brannigan
1973 Rodney Leonard Stubbs
1974 Ben Turner
1975 Ishihiro Yagi
1976 Paul Judas
1977 Cole Freeman
1978 John Parnassus
1979 "Tricky" Ric Alba
1980 Sami Nikulainen
1981 Dylan Rochester

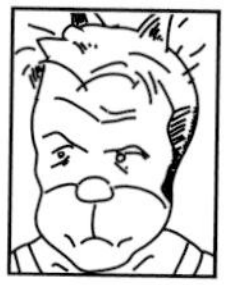

1965
Andy "Clean" Wyatt
(b. 1942)

The irony of English-born champion Andy Wyatt's nickname applies only to his mouth, not his fighting style, which was fist-forward, disciplined, and honest. A gratuitous employer of all things profane, however, his litany of R-rated put-downs and field-hectorings could be withering. R. Mithidge Sayers, who fought as a peer on the 1964 and 1965 fields, quotes verbatim this classic Wyatt prod:

> *You've fucking been tossing off. You don't give a damn about this fucking fight, you simpering shit. If you had half a diseased nut hanging from your body you'd come over here and give me the bollocks, but look at you, you pathetic pissing little girl—you're a little girl on a toilet, aren't you? You are, aren't you? You're a little fucking girl on a potty.*

Wyatt delivered this rant to Buck Tyler, and then immediately set about pummeling him so mercilessly that he had to be restrained from crushing Tyler's feet and ankles with a double-jackboot stomping, "so he'd never play footy again." (Buck Tyler, like most Americans, would never have played soccer again, regardless.)

Analysis suggests that these rants were Wyatt's way of working himself into a champion's lather, but many believe he came by his anger honestly, not as professional technique. Wyatt's childhood had been defined both by extreme poverty and the cruelty of his itinerant, alcoholic father, who often forced him to fight his brother for a can of Coke or a slice of bacon. When Wyatt's brother Randy turned to drugs early in life, he blamed himself, his natural physical advantage (Randy was a small boy), but most of all, his dad. If one observes the utter animal fury with which Wyatt destroyed his opponents, it's as though they were not even there, like he was looking through them. All foes—big or small, feared or anonymous—were the same to him, and the destruction of each brought him no closer to conquering his real demons.

Wyatt's father, penniless, died of a blood infection caused by a brawl in a London street shortly after the 1965 Fight, and his brother, by then a full-fledged junkie, died of a blood infection the next year. His own end does not give pleasant closure to this great competitor's life: he was shivved in the kidney by a common thug in Gracechurch street, and died of a blood infection three days later.

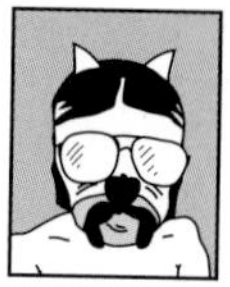

1967
Earl "The Big Turnaround" Morriss
(b. 1946)

Whiskey-fueled aggressor Earl Morriss fought the tremens as hard as he fought the men on The Acres, and after his ugly, foul-mouthed, self-soiling victory, he dumped himself into a pickup bed bound for Los Angeles. He hardly cared if he made it that far.

Once back in the basin, he bounced around the seedy dives of the dusty, arid, litter-strewn, single-story wasteland, living behind storage yards in a sleeping bag. Once he had grown too unkempt, too gin blossomed, his fingernails too blackened with soot and body filth to allow him entrance to the likes of the Maid Moxie, Attahasca Crest, or Silver Keys, he fell into a withdrawal- and starvation-induced hallucination that lasted for nearly a week. His condition gradually took the form of a Native American vision quest, in which he saw himself turn his life around, clean up, and enlist in the military, where he would save the lives of a dozen men in the marshlands of Vietnam. He also hazily recalled visions of a wife, a baby, and a responsible job repairing and delivering radiators.

Fortune smiled briefly on Morriss, for on the seventh day of his dry-out Hasius Recht, a young pupil from the Watts seminary, taking him for dead, knelt to perform rites over the cadaver, figuring it would be good practice. As he finished, the body croaked a weak, "thank . . . you . . . " Recht immediately fetched a glass of water and stack of buttered rye from a nearby diner. Soon, Morriss was sitting upright and telling Recht his wicked story; Recht sized him up as prime material for the lessons of Christ. After a few weeks at the Y.M.C.A., Morriss had regained the use of his mind and limbs; Recht, to the delight of his instructors, proudly marched him to the nearby U.S. Army recruitment office.

Morriss did indeed save a dozen ambushed men at Kien Hoa one afternoon in 1968 and, figuring he was headed home to a second chance at life, "found serenity." He said of that day:

The chopper lifted us out a few hours later, but the violent roar of the engine, the talk of the men around me, the firearms discharging here and there below us, it all went quiet beneath a warm blanket of calm. I knew I was invincible from there. Maybe it was Christ, who knows. They discharged me, so I took my pay and bought a '58 Chevy Apache. It was a real rattle-trap, probably a lemon from day one, but I knew how to keep it running well enough.

He began collecting discarded radiators, and had soon amassed enough makes and models to part out any piece his growing client base needed. He enjoyed his reputation as a "clean, reliable businessman," and even dated a few girls, although he never did find one that he thought was important enough to marry.

On the morning of April 6, 1978, Morriss walked down his front steps a little early to fix an exhaust manifold fastener before setting out on his first errand. Officers patrolling the area thought he was vandalizing the vehicle (the '58 Apache had a valuable bronze brake-line fitting on the

1982 Vince Salvo
1983 Gordon Heillot
1984 Fauntleroy Brown (B.O.C.)
1985 The Festival
1986 Wrong Man
1987 Pleasure
1988 Dean Mastis
1989 Angelo Parisi
1990 "Pug" Holden
1991 Dave Smith
1992 Carl Mohr
1993 "Scowlin'" Jake Speed
1994 Gruz "LTD" Shampis
1995 Kewishi Ndaba (ch. "Paul")
1996 Stephanov Stephanovich
1997 Envelópe Martinez
1998 "Curly" Yet Vo
1999 Mike Green
2000 "You've Got a Good Wiener, Friend"*
2001 Dallas Vannucci
2002 Mickey "Tex" Ahearn
2003 "San Antonio" Saunders
2004 Brad Austin
2005 Calvin Lubbock

* "You've Got a Good Wiener, Friend" is the only recorded instance of a commercial interest infiltrating the game. Dot-com startup Phrendz.com, a social networking website, gave fighter Ty Jessup $1,000 to legally change his name to this phrase, with a bonus of an additional 2,500,000 shares of their stock if he won. The

undercarriage, which was easily removed and sold for several dollars) and commanded him to crawl out from under the vehicle. The epaulet of Morriss's G.I. jacket caught on the manifold fastener and, while trying to wriggle himself free, the officers suspected that he was reaching for a weapon and opened fire. He was shot seventeen times and died under the truck. The officers were placed on paid administrative leave and eventually cleared of any wrongdoing.

Many older-generation fighters honor Morriss's memory and wrongful slaying by wearing black wristbands. Fighters of more recent decades, especially those born after Morriss's death, tend not to wear the band, as it is seen as "disrespectful posing" and "mere fashion" to them.

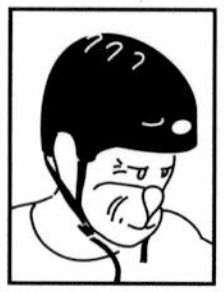

1988
Dean Mastis
(b. 1973)

Born Richard Dean Mastis in Fremont, California, one of dozens of indistinguishable working-class suburbs that ring the San Francisco Bay, Mastis first came to notoriety on the professional skateboarding circuit. The mid-1980s were the golden age of the half-pipe, the symmetrical wooden structure on which riders pushed ever harder for "high airs" and "shoebox grinds." Small, wiry, and possessed of a massive personal energy, Mastis literally ran laps between his competitive runs on the ramp. A natural acrobat, he invented such expert-level aerial maneuvers as the "Herkimer" (a 720-degree spin done upside down while bicycle-kicking at least three times), the "Click of the Sister Ribs" (a hard, finale landing where the rider catches the highest air possible, then lands on his feet on the deck of the ramp, subjecting his body to enormous G-force and, one might think, causing his ribs to compress together), and the "Cumshot," a misleadingly appellated aerial which actually involves urine.

Mastis came to the G.O.F. through the most haphazard of channels: he found himself skating in an oversized storm sewer near a secret-warehouse qualifying round, took interest, passed himself off as of qualifying age by using false identification, and proceeded to demolish the not-insubstantial field with his martial-arts-like nimbleness and inexhaustible well of strength.

Qualifying judges Mike Stonebluth and Hal Yarbrough remember:

Stonebluth: "The [bulkiest] physical fighter can always be taken by a David. We've always known that. But even in the Bible, David didn't slay two hundred fifty-seven Goliaths. He slew one. I mean, this kid didn't even have a rock, let alone a sling, but he wore that damn show out in two hours, and buzzed off on his skateboard like he was just warmin' up. I actually had to call after him and tell him what he'd done and where he was headed."

Yarbrough: "The kid was puny, and he talked too much, and his chest was thin as hell. He barely weighed nothin'. But I guess he didn't have to carry nothin' neither, 'cause he could flick around like a rat, you know, never see him between two places, but there he was wavin' at you when he stopped. He took down a lot of wannabe heroes that night. I never seen the like since or before, and I been on this ring thirty-eight years."

Mastis, all of fifteen, caught a ride to the 1988 G.O.F. and traded his skateboard for a half-dozen Polish sausages. On the strength of this protein, he ran hard all three days, scoffing when they offered him the day two feast of turkeys and brandy ("It ain't Thanksgiving," he is said to have yelled, "and I ain't wanna take no nap!"). In the final hour, he ran circles around favorite Grayson Hatcher before dispatching him with a clearly unpracticed, yet precisely landed, roundhouse kick to the temple. A natural at many things, Mastis glided to victory on his own physical merits perhaps more easily than any fighter "since or before."

Mastis returned to the professional skateboarding circuit, although his career path has also taken forays into juice shops and Internet technology start-ups. His chain of Malibu Juice Club franchises recently opened its 268th location (in Kløeppinga, Sweden), and, in 1999, he sold metamuse.com, an online diary platform he designed, to Amazon (Amazon used the technology platform to power its reader review sections).

This great fighter's complete lack of involvement in or communication with the G.O.F. organization since his victory has been widely regarded as a slight, and one prominent champion has referred to his win as "The one-night stand of a spastic kid with no sights on life, no care for the strife, just a jerked-up boy with nerves like a knife. I ain't like 'em that way." Other historians believe his victory is as valid as any other, and disparage the conservative faction for their "provincial" notion that champions owe anything to the event.

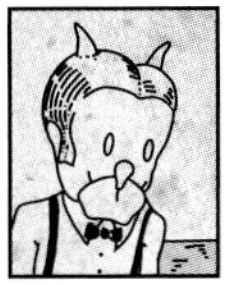

1927–73
Dewson Jesuvias Rell
(b. 1900)

Transcribed from an interview with Franklin H. Bellhew, grounds manager, 1948–79

Nawsuch, it's unlikely you'll come across the name of Dewson Jesuvias Rell in standard fight literature. That's because he wasn't a fighter. No sir, it takes a lot more than fighters to make the Great Outdoor Fight, and he was a concession man from 1927 right up until he went down sideways in seventy-three. He may have been the greatest of them all, outside the Gates.

Yeah, he was sellin' real basic stuff at first—lollipops, hard candy, some

idea behind the gimmick was simple: those who saw the unusual phrase in Fight coverage and future Fight literature would become curious, type it into an Internet search engine, and be redirected to the Phrendz website. Jessup fought like a man consumed, figuring that he could make his life's fortune in three days and retire.

The stunt backfired for Jessup when Phrendz ran out of venture capital and folded halfway through the Fight (obviously, he did not hear the news until it was over). Not only did his stock become worthless, but his $1,000 check, which he had honorably hidden in his motorcycle until after the event, bounced. For the next few years he dedicated himself to terrorizing the Silicon Valley estates of former Phrendz executives, often subjecting them to acts of arson and vehicular manslaughter. He remains at large, and while his ire seems to have abated in recent years, the men who crossed their promise to him still live in, what is considered among Fight scholars, a well-earned daily fear for their personal safety. Because he lives in hiding, Jessup cannot legally revert to his original name, and it is widely lamented that his gravestone will bear the terrible moniker, "You've Got a Good Wiener, Friend."

• • •

butterscotches. After a while, he expanded into chews and mints, and pretty soon he had loose bulk candy, chocolate half-dip pretzels, gums, you name it. Buy it by the bag, you could, all your favorites. By about 1938, they say, he had outfitted his legendary van—all done up in colors and drop-down counters, and it had these big white tires that he'd wipe down with Borax when the lines were quiet. They say he had them special-made, 'cause they didn't have no tread or anything, just perfect, white, round wheels with red glass hubcaps. The hubcaps were nice—they had a lily design in the middle, and he always parked so the lilies were straight up.

Himself, he never ate candy. I guess bein' around the stuff all day will do that to you. He sure could sell it though, and upsell it too. You'd go in there wantin' nothin' more than a bag of Jay-Bee and a couple feet of licorice, and before you knew it you'd have a little of his special honeycomb, or his latest imported melon jellies from Singapore. The man definitely was on top of things, candy-wise, and he could make every confection sound like it sang from the mountain of Aletha.

Oh, he wasn't without his failures, that's to be sure. There was the time he was convinced he could make a killing in pies and cake, but see, that just don't mentally fit around here. That's sharing food, and these men weren't that way while they were here. He ended up throwin' away five red velvet cakes that year, I recall, and he cursed up and down the whole time he was haulin' them to the dustbin. Oh, how it hurt to watch him put his shiny white boot down in the middle of his one Lady Baltimore cake. I don't think he knew that I saw that, but I was back doin' some rag buckets with cane bleach and there he went, all she wrote. He'd told some of us he was gonna get "five dollars, easy" for the thing. Well, damned if all he got was sugar on his foot.

By the end of his run there, he had somewhere in the vicinity of three hundred different treats, a freezer case, and a boy from the jail doin' Softee-Kones to order. It was a good move, havin' that boy from the jail, because it showed the men Dewson was also tryin' to help in the community. Makes no sense why, but they really liked that.

Dewson had a brain attack, or whatever they call it, durin' the 1973 Fight, on day two. It was actually pretty bad—he wasn't a clean one. Some guys know they're gonna go, they put a suit on and get in bed, leave the front door unlocked. Not Dewson. He was ringin' up some gummi Coke bottles for a fallen fighter, when all of a sudden he goes down on one elbow on the nice marble counter, and his nose starts gushin' blood. I was actually in line, gonna treat myself to some malt balls, and I saw it all. The blood didn't run out in that usual slow molasses way. It came outta one nostril, his right one, if you're facin' him, and it was like if you were holdin' a big trash bag full of grape juice, pretty big so that it had some pressure in it, and you stuck a Bowie knife in the very bottom. There were bubbles around the gush, which ain't typical. We had a guy on the Board back then, an old engineer, and he did some tests with chicken blood that showed Dewson's blood had to be at least, I think he said, 125 P.S.I. to bubble. Water pressure to your house is usually around 80 P.S.I., and you know what that looks like comin' out of the shower.

Anyhow, he drained out all at one go there, and that was pretty much it for him and the truck. There wasn't no savin' him. Don't get me wrong, we would have tried, but when you saw how much he was layin' in, you'd know too—the man was gone. They did what they could with the rest of his sweets, and used the money to set up some sort of fund for the boy from the jail. I think Dewson's daughter came down from Livingston and got the truck, but didn't like the way it drove and sold it in town here. Last I saw, it was under a tarp in some backyard along the railway. You can see it if you want—catch the 415 at Belway and watch on your left, it's about a half-mile down after some auto shops and gray apartments. Get off at Marcus Braeburn, catch the 229 comin' the other way, and you're done. Should cost you about three-fifty for the day pass.

• • •

A Select Glossary of Great Outdoor Fight Terms and Slang

• **ACRES, THE**
The three-acre fenced-in field where the Fight takes place each year. Located outside Bakersfield, California, on unincorporated farmland.

• **BLACK BANDS**
Champions from the late '60s and early '70s wear black wristbands in memoriam of fallen brother Earl Morriss. Morriss was slain by police officers in 1978 while changing his Chevy Apache's oil filter in Watts, a dangerous and racially volatile district of Los Angeles.

Officers, thinking Morriss was vandalizing the truck, ordered him to crawl out from beneath the vehicle. When he did not respond, they drew their weapons; after further entreaties, and observing nervous, quick actions by his body, they began to fear he was reaching for a firearm.

A cursory investigation revealed that an epaulet on Morriss's G.I. jacket (he had served in Vietnam after the G.O.F.) had caught on an exhaust-manifold fastener—Morriss had been desperately pulling himself free when the police opened fire.

To this day, Watts police are instructed to "mind the band" when confronting older gentlemen in brawls. The wrongful slaying has never been righted in the eyes of the G.O.F., and policemen are still considered accountable. A man with a black band is considered a triple threat, and officers are advised to fire their weapons only as a matter of last resort—a significant departure from department code.

• **BRILLANTINE DAN**
A fighter who is too handsome, and causes rumors.

101

• CALAMARI

Calamari, a deep-fried squid appetizer, is a dish not typically encountered by the sort of man who fights in the G.O.F.—at best, his low haunts feature fried catfish or bluegill. Such as it is, calamari has become a rite of passage which older fighters introduce to younger fighters, regardless of placement or status, once the Fight has ceased. Several fry houses around The Acres carry this item specifically for this purpose, although the batter and dipping sauce at Bobcat's Fish Shack is held in the highest regard. Typically, the higher strata of fighters self-select to gather here, and the lesser known pair off either to Butcher's, Cal Dabra's, Xitjo Mes, or the numerous, nameless shacks that lie down Arundale Mile Road out of town.

• CHIDIOCK, A

A fighter who admits to an interest in poetry. So named for Chidiock Tichborne, author of "Tichborne's Elegy," the favorite poem of 1941 champion Elbenar Toxon. Toxon recited the piece verbatim upon his victory before falling where he stood, the victim of fatal internal injuries.

• GATES, THE

The first Gates were, of course, Ken Crandall's barn doors—more serious gates would follow. In the 1950s, two multi-ton steel blasting shields on sliding tracks served as Gates, pulled open and shut by great anchor chains welded to decommissioned U.S. military tanks. In the 1970s, the Gates were large panels of corrugated steel welded to the sides of opposing 18-wheel Freightliner tractors, and heated with propane backburners to prevent meddling.

These complicated, high-maintenance systems, despite their dramatic appeal, eventually frustrated the organization. Today, the "gates" are essentially a glorified automatic garage door. It is remotely controlled via the tower, and its half-inch aluminum panels are essentially inviolable.

• JEEPS, THE

Since the beginning, the threat of automotive violence has been a central enforcement strategy against contestant misbehavior. Ken Crandall vowed to run over the first group of dilly-dallying fighters in 1923, at which point the men wisely decided to settle things with their fists. From that year forward, a large vehicle was always kept at the ready, "to help break any ties."

In postwar years, the G.O.F. amassed a collection of former military Jeeps, and this became the enforcement arm's symbolic marque. Fight historians note a dark period in the event's history when, due to an ill-advised and largely unapproved endorsement deal, the Jeeps of the 1989 G.O.F. were replaced with new, red Mazda Miatas. Fortunately, the "Jeeps" were not needed that year, which came as a relief to veteran Jeep driver Ken Sheffelt, who said that driving around in the Miatas during pre-fight maneuvers "made us all feel like a bunch of dickheads."

• "MADE IN THE MILLING"

A fighter who is "Made in the Milling" comes by his victories naturally, without strength or combat training, study, nutritional supplements, the development of personal philosophies, or use of alcohol or drugs (unless he has used drugs and alcohol since very early in life).

• PANCAKE MATTERS

Important issues which are to be discussed the following morning, once hot tempers have cooled and some temporal perspective is possible. Usage: "Sure, he done up Dollar Dorset with rocks in his fists, but Dollar was turned on Benzedrine, so them's pancake matters."

• PAPER TARGETS

As much of the field is anonymous, some fighters are often propped up as, or rumored to be, men who they are not, typically to draw attention away from an army leader. This is often done without their knowing, although in 1963, when Steve Cimino's men conspired to use Juno Quay as Cimino's decoy, or "paper target," this strategy backfired. Quay, energized by his sudden celebrity, swelled out his chest, bested the field, and eventually drove Cimino and his crew into a corner. Thus trapped, one by one they came forward to claim to be the "real" Steve Cimino. This misapplication of the paper target strategy confused Quay, who had never heard of Cimino. All he knew was that in order to win he had to beat them all senseless, which he did.

• SACUMEÑO

A Spanish-language Catholic mass held on the morning of the third day. Historically all are welcome, though non-Chicano fighters tend to shy away. The liturgy begins with an invocation of the Deeds of Jarrod, followed by a double reading of the Lord's Prayer, and concludes with a blessing on all men who wish to sire sons. There is a brief pause after the second prayer so that fighters wishing to receive the blessing may tuck a pumpkin seed into their cheek.

• SLAP-DOWN GAME, THE

A game of skill that the fighters use to pass the time in the parking lot and camps before the opening of the Gates. One man holds his palms out, facing upward, and the other man places his palms facing down over them. The first man tries to slap the tops of the other man's hands before the other man can draw them away.

• TAMP A SWEETIE

To collect discarded cigarettes, crumble the unsmoked tobacco into a chew tin, sprinkle with a packet of sugar and a few drops of water, and seal. The resulting mixture, when aged half a day, rolls a cigarette which burns with a slight caramel taste that masks the acrid flavor of secondhand tobacco.

• TICK

A fighter who roams the grounds preoccupied with finding water. Typically Hungarian.

• WENDEL

A fighter, killed on the field, whose corpse crawls out of the Acres of its own accord. The Gates are lifted solemnly, and all in attendance stand and salute this miracle. Even though it only occurs about once every twenty years, a brass musician is always on hand to perform the "Siegfried Horn Call" (Wagner) while the deceased makes his exit. So named for Ernst Kelmhaas Wendel (1934), the first fighter to exhibit this phenomenon.

· · ·

Originally posted at http://raysmuckles.blogspot.com/

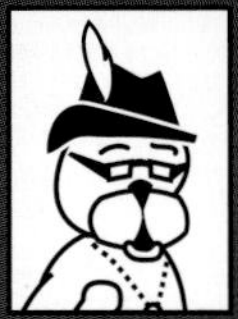

■ damn fine evening.

Hey, Chochachos.

It is maybe not even twice in every five years a man has a feeling like this. All our spent dudes who came out to congratulate us on the Great Outdoor Fight finally wobbled they' asses home, some like T havin' actually slept less than us, and all kinds of a mess. Me and Beef stayed at the low-key festivities 'til the end, both knowin' we kind of had to wrap up and rap on it before we hit the hay. Once Lyle had done his thing with the cops, and old Cornelius made fishin' plans with somebody, we sat real calm at that boss Smith & Hawken teak I got by the pool and lit up a few quiet ones. He took off his busted-up woodshop goggles and set them on the table. It was cold Epilogue.

Thing was, we neither could say the big-ass things you got to say at times like this. Ain't no eloquent-assed Ralph Fiennes gonna be playin' my part as I go, "dogg, that was a stone fuck." And ain't no war-weary Laurence Fishburne gonna be pullin' off some dusty goggles as he replies, "I ain't pooped in five days. Excuse a man."

But the thing is, we stuck out and dapped and he walked kind of shaky to the pool house, which is unusual 'cause he is always so steady, and I made my way upstairs for a real hot and thorough shower. Old dust flowed down the drain in long dark streams, and I the hell felt much rejuvenated. That kind of rejuvenated where you immediately want to fall into crisp white sheets, though. I just wanted to tap this down before the moment escapes me. Tomorrow I fully expect a well-rested us will hold court a little more fully. For now, no man in the world has earned his bedtime like I have, and I am going to SLEEP.

posted by Ray @ 6:44 AM

Originally posted at http://orezscu.blogspot.com/

Beef = new G.O.F. think tanker?

Man, I've never seen so much online discussion about the G.O.F. I guess I've never looked for it, but this year, with Ray and Beef calculating a huge B.O.C. surprise overthrow, everybody's on home row at full tilt. I read thousands of threads while the action was unfolding, most of which were based on Barry King's offshore blog, and a handful of which actually made decent points.

I loved the full-level razing of the grounds, and as a fan I'd like to see the concept of the Fight rise up from the ashes in a new format. In fact, I'm surprised it took this long for the contestants to try to overthrow the grounds themselves. Anyhow, for my money, the guys at alt.gof.new have a lot of it figured out: for grandeur and drama, they have to take Beef on in an executive-level advisory role. He clearly knows more about the Fight than any of them, and, as many software security companies have demonstrated, you need to hire your most dangerous adversaries. Why do you think you see so many sixteen-year-old Ukrainian kids driving around in Maybachs?

I don't want to be too nosy or anything this year, but I'm sure they're going to call him and I'm pretty hopelessly interested in seeing how it all plays out. You stick around a place long enough, you see things like this happen.

Posted by Téodor at 11:40 PM

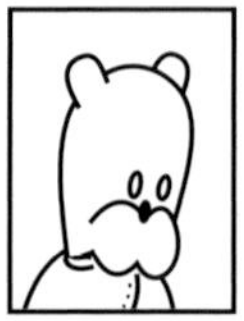